LIBERAL LEGALITY

In his new book, Lewis D. Sargentich shows how two different kinds of legal argument – rule-based reasoning and reasoning based on principles and policies – share a surprising kinship and serve the same aspiration. He starts with the study of the rule of law in life, a condition of law that serves liberty – here called liberal legality. In the pursuit of liberal legality, courts work to uphold people's legal entitlements and to confer evenhanded legal justice. Judges try to achieve the control of reason in law, which is manifest in law's coherence, and to avoid the peril of arbitrariness, such as personal moral judgment. Sargentich offers a unified theory of the diverse ways of doing law, and shows that they all arise from the same root, which is a commitment to liberal legality.

Lewis D. Sargentich is Professor of Law at Harvard Law School. He has taught jurisprudence and legal theory courses there for four decades, including seminars on subjects ranging from natural law to legal skepticism.

Liberal Legality

A UNIFIED THEORY OF OUR LAW

LEWIS D. SARGENTICH
Harvard Law School

CAMBRIDGE UNIVERSITY PRESS

CAMBRIDGE
UNIVERSITY PRESS

University Printing House, Cambridge CB2 8BS, United Kingdom

One Liberty Plaza, 20th Floor, New York, NY 10006, USA

477 Williamstown Road, Port Melbourne, VIC 3207, Australia

314-321, 3rd Floor, Plot 3, Splendor Forum, Jasola District Centre, New Delhi - 110025, India

79 Anson Road, #06-04/06, Singapore 079906

Cambridge University Press is part of the University of Cambridge.

It furthers the University's mission by disseminating knowledge in the pursuit of education, learning and research at the highest international levels of excellence.

www.cambridge.org
Information on this title: www.cambridge.org/9781108442367
DOI: 10.1017/9781108673860

First published 2018
First paperback edition 2019

A catalogue record for this publication is available from the British Library

Library of Congress Cataloging in Publication data
NAMES: Sargentich, Lewis D., author.
TITLE: Liberal legality : a unified theory of our law / Lewis D. Sargentich, Harvard Law School, Massachusetts.
DESCRIPTION: Cambridge : United Kingdom ; New York, NY, USA : Cambridge University Press, 2018.
IDENTIFIERS: LCCN 2017050594 | ISBN 9781108425452 (hardback)
SUBJECTS: LCSH: Law – Philosophy. | Rule of law. | Liberalism. | BISAC: LAW / Jurisprudence.
CLASSIFICATION: LCC K230.S2549 A35 2018 | DDC 340/.11–dc23
LC record available at https://lccn.loc.gov/2017050594

ISBN 978-1-108-42545-2 Hardback
ISBN 978-1-108-44236-7 Paperback

For Valerie

Contents

Preface: Law's Quest

Legality is our topic. According to the vocabulary I use in this book, legality is law's aspiration. It is law's excellence, a sought condition of law.

When legality is realized, a regime of law exists in social life. What I am calling liberal legality, in particular, is a regime of law that helps to secure liberty. In this book, liberal law is so called because it aspires to achieve a condition of lawfulness that is prized by a political position that prizes equal liberty.

Liberal legal practice aspires to achieve the control of reason in law and the governance of law in life. Our law, on account of its aspiration, is liberal law.

This slender volume focuses, as its title indicates, on the commitment – the project – of liberal law. In its pages, we will examine the conception of reason-controlled law in control of society, its constituents, and implications. My objective is to identify and explore the high ambition of liberal legal practice. The aspiration of liberal practice is to bring about and sustain a condition of legality in law and life. This aspiration is a ramifying commitment. We will identify the components of the commitment, and draw out its main implications for the conduct of legal argument.

Argument conducted by reason is our way of doing law. The undertaking to secure law's governance in the world is a project that law in our society tries to carry out. So, in studying the content and implication of the aspiration of liberal legal enterprise, we learn about the formative commitment of our legal practice, and we see how that commitment gives rise to basic features of our manner of legal striving.

But our law has many aspects. Its quest to realize a certain conception of legality, here called liberal, while a prominent aspect, rich in consequence, is not the only one. Why should we focus just on this aspect? Here at the outset, by way of apologia for the present project, I offer two reasons for focusing on the aspiration to realize liberal legality, entrenched in our law, and on how it unfolds. The two main reasons for looking at the foundational commitment of liberal law are, I think, first, intrinsic interest, and second, that we care.

A very good reason for making something the focus of study is intrinsic interest. The liberal kind of law is, I would think, of considerable intrinsic interest for anyone interested in thinking about law.

Liberal law undertakes a rather pure quest. Its high aspiration is to achieve a sort of apex of lawfulness – law-fullness. Liberal practice of law aims to formulate the laws as precepts that, in their statement and in operation, exemplify essential law-like qualities. Law-like laws are general, impersonal, regular, coherent, rationally realizable prescription. Law-like law, at work securing liberal legality, is the quintessence of law. Legal study, trying to figure out how law works, has got to pay attention to this kind of legal striving. For someone interested in law as such, inquiry into the idea of law-fullness that inspires liberal law's quest is a pretty inevitable project. The present study conducts such an inquiry.

A second reason for focusing attention on liberal legality has to do with the importance – the value – of the commitment of liberal law. This commitment is of great value, or so I believe. And I would think that this belief is widely shared.

Liberal law is great in ambition. It is controlled by an aspiration of enormous practical significance. It works to bring about a situation of legality, the regnancy of law in social life, lawfulness – not arbitrariness – in exercise of collective power. The quest to realize law-like qualities in law for the sake of the governance of law in life is not just familiar; it is inspiring. It is an undertaking we care about. So, for many – maybe most – students of law in our society, the project of studying liberal law, the better to understand the content of its commitment and the trajectory of its pursuit, may be thought to be worth doing.

Introduction

Toward Unification

Slogans and mottoes in praise of law are a central fixture of our legal culture. A number of stirring law-affirming expressions are encountered again and again in the contexts of law in our society – in its law schools and legal forums, courts and legislatures.

Words chiseled in the courthouse wall proclaim "equal justice under law." Historic documents teach readers today that theirs is "a government of laws, not men," meaning by "men" arbitrary officials. Judges remind lawyers, and lawyers remind judges, that "like cases should be judged alike." Much-repeated Latin maxims epitomize law's place in life. "No offense without a law," declares a tutelary slogan – *nulla crimen sine lege*. A ringing denial meant to chasten the king long ago, carried forward to our law-formed world, promises: "not under man but under God and the laws" – *non sub homine sed sub Deo et lege*.

The familiar law-affirming expressions, taken together, set up a fundamental opposition between a regime of lawfulness and absence of law. They call for control of life by law, not by the will of the authorities: government of laws not men, *non sub homine*. They require treatment according to law, not law-less judgment: justice under law, like cases decided alike, *nulla crimen*. Together they picture impersonal law, accessible to reason, regularly operating in life.

Behind the various proclamations in praise of law is, I believe, a fundamental conception of what law ought to be. This is a conception of legality. Legality is a sought situation in which lawfulness is realized.

The several expressions noted above, and many kindred slogans, contain ideas about essential conditions of lawfulness. When these ideas are studied in relation to one another, with a view to defining sought properties for our law today, they may be seen to fit together. They constitute a unified conception of legality. According to the unified conception, law's excellence lies in the confluence of law-like qualities of generality, impersonality, coherence, regularity, and rational application.

In the vocabulary of this book, the conception of legality that underlies and unifies the grand phrases of law-affirmation is the idea of law-like law. This terminology – law-like law, law-like legality – will turn out to be very helpful, but at first glance it seems puzzling. Isn't law, by definition, law-like?

In this book, the idea of law-like law is not at all a definition. It is a prescriptive conception, and a demanding one. It focuses on certain qualities of well-developed laws: generality, impersonality, coherence, and the like. It prescribes that these qualities – law-like qualities – should be realized throughout the realm of law.

The idea of law-like legality says how law's precepts should be formed, and what law ought to bring about in the world. According to its preachment, law should take the form of general, impersonal, coherent prescription that operates to sustain rational resolution. Law should be law-like in form and operation, in order to uphold people's legal entitlements and confer even-handed legal justice. Law should be a body of rationally connected reasons that serve as grounds of rationally determinable dispositions.

Law-like law, according to the lexicon of this book, is liberal law. Another name for the idea of law-like law is the liberal conception of legality. The idea that laws should be law-like is a liberal conception because of the connection between law-like law – general, impersonal, coherent – and equal liberty. This kind of law serves liberty. Of course, the law-like form of law, by itself, doesn't confer liberties. But when people in society resolve to establish freedoms in life, and to secure equal freedom by law, the law-like form of law is the best way to secure it. More on this a little later.

Our law, in virtue of its aspiration, is liberal law. That is, our legal practice works to develop law-like laws – general, consistent, and so on. It does so in order to realize the sought ends of liberal legality – securing entitlements under law, conferring justice under law. The defining objectives of liberal legal striving – entitlement, justice, law-likeness, rationality – are, when described in down-to-earth terms, readily recognizable as aims of our law. These aims, entrenched as workaday aspiration in our legal practice, are familiar to its practitioners and observers. By studying liberal legality, we learn about the way we do law in our own society.

The thesis of the book is that the liberal conception of legality is the controlling commitment of our law. It states the high ambition that directs ongoing legal activity. It forms the practice of legal argument in our society.

In the terminology of the present study, a practice of legal argument is a discourse of law, instituted in society, in which participants put forward legal reasons as grounds of judgment. At the center of the practice are society's judges rendering decisions in the courts. Our practice of law, on account of its controlling commitment, is liberal legal practice – the practice of liberal legality.

To say that liberal commitment controls our legal practice is to make two claims. First is the claim that the liberal conception can control – it is the sort of thing that might, when embraced, control law. Second is the claim that the liberal aspiration does control – it is indeed in control of our law. It is the reason why we do law the way we do, not another way.

First, my claim is that the liberal conception of legality is a substantial intellectual construct. It has sufficient integrity and power that it may serve as the source of effective instruction in the doing of law.

The liberal conception is formed at the intersection of convergent lines of thought about law. It integrates multiple interrelated elements. The conception of liberal legality contains assumptions about what it means to depend on law, and only law, not the will of another; what it means for law to be impersonal; what happens when law is in abeyance. The complex conception brings together ideas about kinds of capacities exercised, and not exercised, in grasping law's meaning; the kind of rationality needed in judging of situations; the nature of arbitrariness.

The commitment formed by the coming together of these elements – the conception of law-like legality – is a highly general allegiance. It speaks to all the performances of legal practice. It supplies the prescriptive content that underlies and unifies the grand law-celebrating messages rife in the rhetoric of our legal practice. It is a demanding conception of what law and legal decision ought to be.

Second, I want to show that salient features of our practice of legal argument are generated by commitment to realize liberal legality. The liberal conception of law-like legality controls the practice.

The salient features of our legal practice are characteristic projects and assumptions. Characteristic projects are particular ways of arguing legally. Characteristic assumptions are cautionary guidelines about what can go wrong. My claim is that law's general commitment gives rise to the specific projects and assumptions of our law.

Liberal conception defines a general situation in which legality is realized. Legality is sustained when the laws exhibit law-like qualities in form and operation. It turns out that legal argument might bring about law-like legality two different ways. One way is to hammer out legal rules, and use the rules as grounds of law-like judgment. The other way is to formulate practical moral principles and policies which are law-like in nature, and use these ideal aims as legal grounds. Since legality might be realized by two kinds of argument, a dual impulse to undertake both kinds arises within legal practice.

The liberal conception also defines in general terms how legal argument might fail to achieve legality. Brought to bear on the specific projects of liberal law, this general understanding gives rise to specific assumptions about what can go wrong in law. And corresponding to the concrete ways in which the two kinds of legal argument might fail are specific admonitions about how to avoid failure. Liberal law goes forward on the assumption that law-like precepts of both kinds – rules on the one hand, principles and policies on the other hand – are the artefacts of intent construction.

In short, characteristic projects and characteristic assumptions arise within legal practice controlled by liberal commitment. That is the thesis advanced by the analysis which commences after this introduction ends. The projects and related assumptions constitute a framework of elements of legal endeavor. The framework defines the distinctive pattern of pursuit of our law. Thus, foundational commitment to realize liberal legality underlies development of the fundamental features of our law.

By our law I mean American law in particular, and, by extension, law of kindred legal systems. Many other legal systems today share the same aims in virtue of which American law may be said to be liberal law. Our kind of law – that is, law of the kind done in the United States, defined in terms of its characteristic workaday aspiration – comprises doing of law in a number of other legal orders as well, but by no means all on earth today, much less all that have existed in the whole sweep of legal history.

0.1 FORMATIVE COMMITMENT

Liberal law's aspiration may be stated – briefly – two different ways. One is to focus on the sought properties of the laws themselves – how law's precepts ought to be formed. The other is to emphasize legality in life – what law ought to bring about in the world. Both ways formulate aspiration in line with the liberal conception of legality.

In its most general statement, the liberal conception of legality says that the laws should be law-like. The liberal conception is, in a word, the idea of law-likeness. Liberal law's aspiration is to develop laws that display, to a high degree, law-like qualities of generality, consistency, impersonality, regularity, accessibility to reason.

The idea of law-like law is an austere conception. It identifies proper legal grounds with a specially qualified set of practical reasons. Still it encompasses much more than just hard and fast rules, or rule-like generalizations. Principles, policies, and purposes underlying rules are admissible grounds of judgment, provided they are law-like in nature.

In more elaborate statement, the liberal conception of legality says that the law should be law-like for a purpose. The purpose is to uphold two law-formed conditions in the world: entitlement and justice. Liberal law aims to honor people's legal entitlements, which are valued positions of persons that depend just on the meaning of the standing laws, grasped by exercise of reason. It aims to achieve legal justice, which is conferred upon persons brought to judgment when like cases are judged alike, according to general laws. Law-like legality is a perfected condition of law in which legal entitlement and legal justice are sustained through rational legal resolution.

The idea of law-like legality is liberal in that the condition of law it prescribes is intimately related to human liberty. Law-like law is liberty-serving law, the kind of law needed in order to secure individual liberty in society – the kind required by political commitment that prizes equal freedom of individuals. Of course, the law-like form of the laws doesn't guarantee that the content of the laws affirms this or that liberty. But when laws recognizing particular liberties do exist, the laws of liberty ought to be law-like in form and operation – general, impersonal, consistent, rationally determinable. All the laws ought to be law-like, in order for liberty to be well instituted.

Equal freedom is disserved if judgments of the courts are the product not of law-like argument leading to rational resolution, but of arbitrary decision. Arbitrary resolution is judgment based on sheer power or moral predisposition. Liberty in the polity diminishes if legal judgments about people's options and facilities are the upshot of the manipulative power or the personal morals of disposing legal authorities, rather than a regime of law-like law.

We should note that judgment seen from the standpoint of the liberal conception of legality to be arbitrary may be thought to be quite proper when viewed from the standpoint of a contrary conception of law's excellence. Many contrary conceptions are known to legal history. The antithesis of a regime of law-like law is a legal order which rejects liberal commitment to law-likeness altogether.

Consider, for example, a non-liberal conception of law's aspiration which praises context-dependent judgment by specially wise judges. According to that conception, decision of a case in the courts is well justified when it is responsive to a rich narrative of a unique past state of affairs, or when it has in mind the unique set of future consequences the decision might bring about. In deciding, wise judges exercise special insight into the nature of humans and the needs of society, wisdom which they uniquely are understood to possess.

It is worth remembering that, in many legal orders of the past, and some of the present, judging of cases in their incomparable contexts is thought to be proper, and specially wise judges are thought to preside – the elders, a priesthood, agents of a political party specially in tune with the demands of social development.

By contrast, seen from the standpoint of the liberal commitment to law-like legality, contextual judgment springing from uncommon wisdom is arbitrary disposition. Decision that restricts its view to a unique state of affairs or unique consequences is denial of legal justice – the opposite of deciding like cases alike. Decision by judges exercising special insight is denial of legal entitlement – the opposite of judgment based on the meaning of the standing law, accessible to reason, not the will of the authorities. And absent a regime of legal entitlement and legal justice, the liberty-securing service of law-like law is absent.

The condition of legality in life here under discussion, identified as a compound of entitlement and justice, is also – frequently – called by another name. Another name for the governance of law in life is the rule of law. Liberal political commitment, eager to secure liberty by a regime of rational law, prescribes that the laws should rule. However, in this book, for the most part I use a different terminology. I speak of liberal legality, or law-like legality. For the most part, I don't speak of the rule of law.

The reason for my usage is this. The idea of the rule of law, much discussed, is sometimes taken to refer to rather specific institutional formations. Then the idea's meaning comes to be freighted with rather considerable detail about the operation of government in relation to society. By contrast, as I wish to present it, the idea of liberal – or law-like – legality is a highly general conception. It is fairly abstract, and far-reaching, not concrete. It focuses on a few fundamentals having to do with the properties of laws and the relation of people to law. This highly general conception points to what I take to be the basic properties of a situation in which the governance of law – the rule of law – subsists, and leaves out what I take to be inessentials.

One advantage of working with the idea of liberal – law-like – legality is that it becomes pretty evident that this general prescriptive conception, well understood, might be realized in the conduct of legal practice different ways. And this is a main claim of the book: that there are alternative ways of realizing law-like legality in the doing of liberal law, each of which is actively pursued in our legal practice.

0.2 COMMITMENT UNFOLDS

The aim of the present study is to show that a powerful governing commitment, in charge of the activity of legal argument and decision, generates salient features of our practice of law.

The method of the inquiry to come is to draw lines of connection between basic commitment and consequent undertakings. I want to show how the general commitment of liberal law leads to particular facets of legal enterprise. Analysis connects general and particular.

My hope in this study is to illuminate central features of actually existing legal activity, our practice of legal argument, but the method of the book is not one of inference from the concrete. We will not start with phenomenology of law – law described in concrete terms – and proceed to infer general properties and aims. Rather, we will start with highly general commitment, to carry out a conception of legality, and go on to see how the general commitment gives rise to fundamental aspects of legal enterprise which are features of our law. In this way, we may see that foundational aspiration unifies what otherwise may seem to be disparate undertakings of observed legal endeavor.

The method of deriving features of practice from basic commitment to realize law-like legality, even if evidently successful, might be challenged as follows. Suppose the procedure of derivation does – as an exposition – succeed. We see that certain general ideas about legality, taken as premises, do fit the main features of our legal practice, presented as derived conclusions. However, maybe the premises were made to fit. Perhaps the general ideas used as premises, stated by themselves, don't start out sharp enough to generate specific conclusions about the features of legal practice. Maybe the premises have to be sharpened and toughened – reverse engineered – in order to yield the features.

Even so, if we end up with a set of statable general ideas that do fit a range of observed attributes of law, and are able to account for the attributes in an economical way, that would be interesting. Elegant premises that make sense of diverse particulars are worth discovering. But I believe that the idea of law-like legality is more than an elegant abstraction able to fit details of our legal practice. It is the source of the lineaments of practice. It is the driving force that impels liberal legal argument. It shapes the practice to its design.

I hope that the analysis to come will show that the conception of law-like legality, when entrenched in legal practice, is very powerful. It says what, in particular, to do. It has a sharp edge. It rules things out. It says what not to do.

The main purpose of the book is theoretical. My aim is to show that important features of our legal practice can be traced to – because they are determined by – a basic conception of what law ought to be. By tying constituents of practice to controlling conception, we produce a unified theory of the elements of law. This is a framework for understanding the enterprise of liberal law. A fundamental framework defining the elements of law answers, in a way, the perennial question of legal theory: what is law? It tells us how law is defined by law itself.

Our method for showing that law's general commitment gives rise to particular features of law is to imagine law's unfolding. First we suppose that commitment to bring about law-like legality is entrenched in the controlling canons of legal practice. Then we go on to identify the kinds of argumentative pursuits and assumptions that emerge within a legal practice so controlled.

Practice of legal argument is constituted by canons of good argument. Such canons are criteria that say what counts as a proper legal presentation. Liberal practice of law is formed by incorporating a specific conception of legality – liberal legality – into the canons of good and sufficient legal assertion. In liberal practice, judges and other practitioners are instructed to conduct argument and judgment in such a way that legality is sustained.

The method of imagining law's unfolding starts by assuming the existence of a legal practice constituted by canons of good argument that incorporate the liberal conception of legality. Then the method is carried out by a narrative of legal development which tells us how a variety of undertakings and admonitions arise in the doing of law, as diverse consequences flowing from common starting conception, and shows that they arise smoothly, without a hitch.

0.3 UNIFIED UNDERSTANDING

In the main body of this book, which starts after the present prolegomenon ends, we will trace law's unfolding, in the conduct of legal practice, from its starting point in commitment to liberal legality, step by step. We will follow a flow of ideas from general conception to particular entailed projects and assumptions. By connecting particular features of legal striving to a basic idea of what law ought to be, we show how those features fit together as a whole. We arrive at a unified understanding of diverse elements of our legal practice.

According to ensuing analysis, two notable unifications arise in the unfolding of commitment to liberal legality. My claim is that general ideas about law's aspiration generate two groups of closely connected features of our law. One group comprises positive projects of legal argument. The other group includes cautionary assumptions, warnings telling argument what to avoid. These are the projects and assumptions briefly noted earlier in this introduction as salient features of liberal law.

The two groups of features are manifest properties of liberal legal practice. Each of these aspects of law, taken by itself, is pretty familiar. But the several features, considered one by one, seem to be separate properties, quite distinct. My claim is that appearances of separateness are misleading. The seemingly independent attributes of law, when each is traced to its source, turn out to be various ways of realizing the same thing. They are consequences of common – unifying – commitment.

In other words, there is a way to axiomatize liberal law such that, when a few ideas in the nature of postulates are well understood, a rich array of particular entailments, in two groupings, positive and negative, may be seen to follow as derived consequences of fundamental commitment.

The first unification emphasized in this book has to do with various ways of arguing legally. The ways of arguing legally are positive projects. They are argumentative pursuits undertaken in legal practice in order to establish law's meaning and so answer legal questions.

Three positive projects are persistent undertakings of liberal legal argument. Two of the three projects are contrasting kinds of legal reasoning. We noted these two kinds briefly early on in this introduction. On the one hand, law-like legal argument makes use of rules as grounds of judgment. On the other hand, law-like argument invokes practical moral aims – principles and policies – as legal grounds.

The third project cuts across the other two. Law-like argument undertakes to make law's elements cohere. Coherence-seeking is a manner of working with law's rules, on the one hand, and with law's principles and policies, on the other. The third project is to make law's elements of whatever kind fit together.

The three ways of arguing – invoking rules, invoking principles and policies, making things cohere – are pretty evident features of our legal practice. The kinds of reasoning plus coherence-seeking are familiar ways of doing law. But the three seem to be pretty distinct, indeed disparate. The two kinds of reasoning are very different in nature. Reasoning based on principles and policies is practical moral argument; reasoning based on established legal rules is not. The third project, coherence-seeking, is not by nature particularly related to either one of the other two – or so it seems.

As we will see, the three positive projects all arise from the same root. They are the varied fruit of singular purpose. The two contrasting kinds of reasoning are kindred – while contrary in their relation to morality, they are complementary, not contradictory. Each process is generated by aspiration to achieve law-like legality. The project of coherence-seeking is as well. All three positive projects are direct entailments of the formative commitment that stands at the center of liberal legal practice.

The second unification established by the book's analysis has to do with cautionary assumptions put to use in the conduct of legal practice. The assumptions say what legal argument ought not to do, what it should steer clear of. They are directives of a negative nature.

Two lines of directive assumption address law's morality and law's language. In the terminology of the book, law's morality is the sum of practical moral principles and policies used as legal grounds. Law's language comprises classifications and distinctions established by law's rules. Cautionary assumptions identify two kinds of pitfalls – perils – standing in the way of successful use of principles and policies on the one hand, and successful use of rules on the other hand, in legal argument.

Along one line of admonition, legal arguers are instructed to be careful in use of moral grounds. It is bad for legal decision to depend on personal moral judgment; practical moral grounds used in law must not be the same thing as morality embraced outside law. Along the other line of exhortation, arguers are told to watch out for imprecision. It is bad for law's categories to be irreparably vague; classifications and distinctions used in law must be sharper than those of common language outside law.

The two sets of admonitions are pretty unexceptionable. Their advice is familiar. Legal arguers should develop terminology having greater clarity than ordinary language – yes, indeed. Arguers should avoid getting embroiled in moral debate going on outside law – again, sure enough. But what does the one thing have to do with the other? Advice about avoiding moral conflict, and advice about linguistic clarity, address altogether different aspects of legal endeavor. The two suggestions seem unrelated, separately warranted, quite independent.

As we will see, the two sets of cautionary assumptions, about language and morality, arise from the same source. The source is liberal law's understanding of the relation between law and other realms of discourse. From the standpoint of liberal law, disorder exists in intellectual realms beyond law. Law's language and morality must do better than nonlegal language and morality. The admonition to do better is a consequence of law's view of discourse outside law, and that understanding is a consequence of the conception of legality that stands at the center of liberal legal practice.

0.4 OUR LEGAL PRACTICE

The thesis of this book, it is by now abundantly clear, is that the liberal conception of law-like legality is the controlling aim of our law. This means that the liberal aspiration defines the fundamental features of legal practice, its main projects and basic assumptions. It doesn't mean that the liberal commitment, by itself, controls everything.

Our practice of law is a liberal practice. The aspiration to secure law-like legality, here called liberal, is our vital aim, deeply entrenched in the discursive canons of existing legal practice. The idea of law-like legality and the canons of good argument that embody it are quite familiar, as we shall see in detail when the conception and its prescriptive entailments are elaborated later on. This well-known conception works powerfully to give shape to argument and decision, hence to form law's logic. I believe that it is the central commitment of our law, that it establishes the basic logic of the legal argument we do, and that in it may be found the distinctive character of the law we develop.

At the same time, actual practice is a motley proceeding. By no means are all its notable aspects readily assignable in full to the unfolding logic of any singular aspiration, however complex. Society's legal practice comprises an enormous number of performances enacted over time by a large cast of characters in a wide range of settings. Real practice by human beings is full of impurities. Governing canons of argument are sometimes executed rather strictly and skillfully, and sometimes not. More important than evident laxity or straying from the prescribed path is the apparent eclecticism of legal striving. Rhetoric of legal arguers about law's purposes is diverse. Legal practice seems to pursue a plurality of aims, to follow a variety of argumentative canons, hence to display many logics. In addition to the liberal conception, participants in practice invoke other ideas about legality – ideas of law's excellence, right resolution, good judging – not expressed in the standard vocabulary of liberal aspiration.

The other ideas of legality that appear to operate in argument may turn out upon careful examination to be equivalent to liberal dedication. Or maybe not. They may be elaborations or specifications of the idea of law-like legality, or largely compatible conceptions kept in tutelage. Or they may be truly divergent ambitions for law, straining to move law in directions different from the path indicated by liberal protocol, if often in practice suppressed. It is possible to point to numerous aspects of practice that seem discrepant in terms of the liberal commitment, better understood by light of some further or other commitment. Certainly, alternative construals of the point of the practice are possible, and any imputation is contestable.

But for purposes of the inquiry of this book, divergent aspiration – non-liberal motives in addition to liberal ones – ought not to be thought to be among the governing aims of the practice we study. We should assume that the formative commitment of legal practice is the liberal aspiration to achieve law-like legality, and none other. We ought not to assume that any significantly divergent conception of legality is operative in legal argument.

The thesis of the present study is that liberal commitment is the source of the major features of our legal practice. Major features are the main projects and assumptions which constitute the basic pattern of legal pursuit. Minor features of practice, matters of comparative detail, are not our interest. If we find that the major features of our law are indeed accountable to liberal aspiration, then any non-liberal motives pursued in practice are left with a relatively minor role, and so are outside the focus of the inquiry.

The method of the book is to trace the unfolding of specifically liberal commitment within legal practice. Its project is to see how liberal ambition itself works out. It is beside the point that actual practice may be governed in minor part by non-liberal aspiration. For the object of the inquiry is to investigate the development of the liberal commitment that lies within our law. Divergent commitment may safely be bracketed.

To see how commitment to seek law-like legality unfolds, we should imagine a liberal practice in unremitting pursuit of its own defining aspiration. We should posit a practice governed quite stringently by the conception of law-like legality, and then see how argument proceeds within that legal enterprise. This program of inquiry is the procedure of a thought experiment. We posit initial conditions under which an envisioned activity takes place. These conditions are the canons of argument that constitute law-like legal practice. Then we ask, taking such a practice as given, what follows. We figure out – work out – what argumentative pursuits within law, and what assumptions about discourse beyond law, take shape in the operation of the stipulated practice.

This procedure is a protocol of philosophical investigation, involving use of imagination. However, at the same time, the initial conditions we posit for law in this procedure are not imaginary, merely hypothetical, but rather are quite real. Practice of law under these conditions is not just a thought experiment we – author and reader – might dream up. Rather it is the way we – people in our society – have arranged to have law done.

Of course, the imagined practice will be different from actual practice to some extent. Actual legal argument is no doubt not so single-minded, not so fastidiously liberal. But we can also be sure that a specifically liberal legal practice is not an arbitrary invention. Liberal commitment surely operates – liberal canons are surely operative – within the legal practice we've got. So an inquiry into the development of liberal legality is more than the speculative investigation of an abstract logic.

So far as our own practice is concerned, to whatever extent it is in fact controlled by the liberal conception of law-like law, it is then subject to the specific discovered logic of liberal legality. This is a very great extent if, as I believe, the imagined practice differs from the one we've got only in the posited purity – not in the preeminence – of its liberal ambitions.

1

The Idea of Law-Like Law

Our topic, in the pages that follow, is the unfolding commitment of liberal law. The aspiration of liberal law is to realize the conception of liberal legality. This is a high ambition, high in its hope and high in the demands it makes on legal practice. Our task is to conduct a focused study of liberal commitment, and to specify – define – the liberal practice of law in terms of its aim.

I want to begin by sketching preliminarily, in a rather general way, the nature of the conception of legality that gets instituted in liberal practice. This is the idea of law-like law, or, as I will also call it, the nomological conception of law.

What are some salient aspects of the idea of law that governs liberal practice? And what does it mean to say that a practice of legal argument is governed by a particular notion of legality? What does a conception of legality say to us? Ask of us?

Before getting put into practice, a conception of legality is a disembodied idea of what might be and ought to be. At this initial stage of its career, the conception is a call for action, a social plan not yet implemented.

When a conception of legality gets entrenched in legal practice, it is embedded in the definitions of institutional positions that anchor practice, and in the operative canons that govern myriad argumentative performances. A well-embodied regulative conception of law becomes second nature for practitioners. It is the sea in which practitioners swim, whose existence at times seems just a matter of inference.

But an instituted conception of law does not come to be wholly tacit, secreted in professional detail. Legal practice is an articulate, reason-giving, self-justifying affair. Its formative aspiration is a constant point of reference, a template used to guide daily endeavor. So an entrenched conception of law never loses the directive power it could display when, as an uninstituted idea, it spoke to everyone, not just to legal personnel.

A conception of legality is an idea telling how law, legal argument, and legal decision ought to be. It may be stated as a model, as a prescription, and as a criterion of measurement.

First, it provides a model, a pattern of something to be made, that may orient practical striving. A conception of legality is an image of law's perfected condition.

This is the state of affairs in the legal realm and in social life brought about by law's due operation. Second, it serves as a prescription, a spur, a precept urging people to produce the dispensation of law's fulfillment. It is a political preachment addressed to people generally within political society. It commands that all who make up a polity ought to establish and maintain a legal enterprise that works rightly. Third, it offers a criterion of measurement, a basis for assessing whatever legal formation does exist in social life. A conception of due legality is a gauge for judging the performance of extant law, both overall and in detail. It is a yardstick that may be used to find the distance, if any, between what is and what ought to be. In each of its aspects, and all together, such a conception is an ideal of legality, a notion of what law ideally ought to be. It is an ideal for law in general, pertaining not just to this or that law, nor this or that field of law, but to all law: law as such. An idea of legality articulates the due form and right operation and sought condition of law and legal argument.

1.1 NOMOLOGICAL LEGALITY

The conception of legality I wish to explore in this book is the idea of law-like law. This conception insists that laws should be law-like. Its defining slogan is that the law should be fully law-like in form and operation. Law-like form is sought in order to achieve legal entitlement and legal justice, good states of affairs which are sustained through exercise of law-formed rationality.

I will call this complex conception the nomological conception of legality. Here I follow the usage according to which something nomological is a thing that has the nature of a law: something law-related, law-evincing, law-filled, law-full. Accordingly, nomological legality is law-like legality. Nomological entitlement and justice are law-constituted states of affairs. Nomological rationality is law-governed reasoning working with law-like grounds. And so on.

Nowadays, hardly anybody claims to be a nomologist actively doing nomology. If undertaken, nomology would be the science of law or laws. So, a nomology of some subject is the study of the laws of that subject.[1] An analytic nomology of legal laws would, I suppose, sift properties of laws generally to discover common distinguishing features. Now I am not proposing to launch any such inquiry. The prescriptive notion of law-like legality is not the product of an analytical project that seeks to explicate what, if anything, is specifically law-like about laws in all types of legal practice. Rather, the conception seizes upon certain very basic nomological

---

[1] See Hamilton (1861), p. 122: "If ... we analyze the mental phaenomena with the view of discovering and considering ... the Laws by which our faculties are governed ... we have a science which we may call the NOMOLOGY of MIND"; Mill (1865), approving Hamilton's distinction between phenomenology and nomology; and Anonymous (1886), pp. 143, 156: "nomology" in the study of politics is "the inductive science of law," which seeks "the discovery ... of the true statical laws which are actually operative in societies."

attributes – generality, impersonality, accessibility to reason, regularity, joint coherence – and prescribes that legal argument should realize these qualities in order to bring about legal entitlement and legal justice. So-called nomology has passed from the intellectual scene, and I do not mean to revive it. Nonetheless, things nomological remain plentiful.[2] I wish to appropriate the adjective for use as a label that may designate a particular prescriptive conception of law.

Up to now I have called the nomological conception by another name. I have been speaking of the liberal conception of legality. That label too is entirely apt, since law-like law is intimately related to liberty. Flourishing liberty requires legal argument able to uphold law-like entitlement and justice. The association between the notions of equal liberty and law-like law, an internal connection, will be discussed in some detail later on.

I will continue to speak of law-like law as liberal law. Nomological legality is indeed liberal legality. The nomological conception of law's perfected condition is a liberal conception of what law should be. The liberty-serving aspect of law-like law is vital. Devotion to human liberty is a powerful generator of prescriptive commitment to law-like legality. Still, it is the nomological aspect – law-likeness – that is of the essence. What is most striking about law-like law is its self-absorbed, self-inspiring, autotelic character. Such law finds its mission in its nature. It strives to be like itself.

The nomological conception of legality is an ideal for law in general. Its content may be expressed positively in two ways, which are largely equivalent but involve different emphases. First, nomological legality has to do with properties of laws: due qualities of nomological form that are necessary for law-like operation. Second, nomological legality has to do with relations of people to law: sought conditions for persons subject to legal imposition. Law-like qualities and law-like conditions both require rationality in the development and application of legal norms. The nomological conception can also be stated negatively, in terms of contrary qualities and contrary conditions that pertain when legality is absent.

Nomological legality requires that laws be general, accessible, and coherent. By extension, generality, accessibility, and coherence are aspects of the kind of rationality that ought to characterize legal argument and legal judgment. Laws should be general propositions applicable to classes of situations, yielding the same prescription for all members of a general class. Legal judgment should not depend on a grasp of the full particularity of situations unique in their concreteness. Laws should be norms accessible to reason, apprehensible and statable by exercise of common rational capacity. Judgment should not depend upon use of a faculty of

---

[2] In philosophy of science, Carl Hempel defines the "deductive-nomological" model of explanation. According to this model, causal explanation makes use of general laws, which are "nomological" or "lawlike" statements, and shows that a given phenomenon "conforms to a general nomic pattern" (Hempel 1962, pp. 101–102). For related usage of "nomological" and "lawlike" in philosophy of science, see also Nagel (1961), pp. 21–22, 49–51, 56–59, 69–71.

special insight thought to be possessed by some but not all. And laws should be coherent, rationally connected, consistently applicable. Together, law-like laws should be the sufficient basis for rational resolution of legal contest.

Nomological legality is a dispensation in which legal entitlement and legal justice are ensured to people in society. Legal entitlement exists when valuable positions of persons in social life are constituted by law and depend just on the content of the existing laws. The opposite of legal entitlement is dependence on official say-so, the irregularly exercised sway and grace of the powers that be. Legal justice exists when persons subject to collective authority are judged by general laws that are able to support consistent treatment. The opposite of legal justice is to be dealt with, not by virtue of shared characteristics, but uniquely, to be singled out for special treatment. The existence of legal entitlement and legal justice depends on the operation of rational legal argument. Entitlement and justice are sustained by nomological rationality.

The nomological qualities and conditions that make up liberal legality will be examined more closely in due course. In the meantime, the foregoing expressions may serve to indicate the nature and basic content of the conception of law that is entrenched in liberal legal practice.

When entrenched in practice of law, a conception of legality appears as an idea addressed mainly to practitioners of legal argument. It becomes a conception that animates, controls, and warrants the practical striving of judges and other participants in argument. It serves as aspiration, regimen, and justification.

Its model of law's excellence becomes the formative aspiration of overall practice. Its prescription that legality should be established becomes the operative regimen of daily practice. And its criterion of measurement becomes an available basis for the self-justification of practice as a whole and bit by bit.

1.2 ENTRENCHED ASPIRATION

A particular conception of legality may be so entrenched in legal practice that it motivates and directs all the performances that constitute argumentative practice of law. The internalized conception then formulates the organizing aspiration of legal pursuit. It states the overall aim – the mandatory goal – of the whole of legal endeavor. It amounts to a broad instruction or ground rule binding practitioners. The instruction is to strive to realize the dispensation of legality: always pursue legality. The model of law's fulfillment now serves as a regulative conception. It is a compass that directs self-regulating legal practice toward its end. Practice so governed is a project, a quest. Aspiration to secure legality forms the practice and argument within it.

When fully entrenched, the conception operates as a regimen, an argumentative discipline. The foundational prescription that legality should be honored develops to become a regime of stricture that speaks insistently to practical performance.

The regimen of legality is a set of particular instructions telling how to achieve a right understanding of the laws; proper argument; good resolution. The regimen says how the laws should be conceived and constructed, and how argument and decision should be conducted. Practitioners of argument are required to grasp legal grounds, and connect grounds with one another and with legal results, in a certain way.

And the entrenched conception provides a basis for the self-justification of legal practice. Its criterion of measurement is an available standard that might be used to defend practice as a whole and each of the resolutions which arise within it. Self-justification of practice is the justification of legal performance in terms of the same aspiration that animates and directs legal pursuit. If argument follows instructions, and thus is able to carry out its regulative conception of legality, then the conception provides a justification of the decisions that argument produces. Then practice of argument may be vindicated in terms of the very aim recognized within it as its governing commitment.

The alternative to self-justification is self-defeat. This above all, from the standpoint of practice, must be avoided. So, in practice, the entrenched instruction to pursue legality includes a negative complement, an admonition to avoid the conditions of legality's failure.

Legality may be defined positively, in terms of good states of affairs that constitute it, or negatively, in terms of the evils that occur in its absence. Aspiration to achieve legality is aversion to failed legality. To heed the negative, cautionary directive to steer clear of self-defeat is to be motivated by fear of legality's failure. Practice of argument is driven by fear as well as aspiration. Argument is doubly directed, as the positive regimen of practice implies a negative discipline. To pursue legality is to embrace modes of law, argument, and decision which will bring right resolution. It is at the same time to reject ways of doing law which will issue in failure. Commitment to legality gives rise to positive and negative impulse. Practice is formed alike by motive aspiration and motive fear, propulsion and recoil, and so is law's logic within it.

The objective of the present study is to find out how legal practice goes forward when practice is governed by the aspiration to realize nomological legality and by fear of its failure. The aim is to see what follows when argument is conducted subject to the regimen of nomological pursuit. Our approach is to think of a practice thoroughly controlled by the nomological conception of legality, and ask how it proceeds.

In the practice we consider, participants undertake to pursue the project constituted by nomological stricture. By participating they accept nomological regimen as their own. Everyone inside practice tries to realize law-like legality. Judges try to fashion arguments that sustain legality. Everyone else tries to fashion arguments that judges might adopt. Legal argument generally is crafted by insiders to meet the tests of nomological performance.

Thus we imagine an argumentative realm defined in terms that provide the constant aim and discipline of participants in its argument. This is a circumscribed world, a particular sphere of discourse, within which practitioners go forward, operating on knowable premises.

In the chapters that follow, our job is to provide a systematic exposition of the nature of liberal legal practice, the discursive activity under investigation. This expository effort involves a lesser task and a greater task.

The lesser, and prior, task is to describe the defining features possessed by any instituted practice of legal argument, whatever its aim. The subsequent, and larger, task is to delineate the distinctive content and basic implications of the formative aspiration of liberal law in particular.

Both the process of argumentative practice and the substance of nomological commitment need to be worked out in much greater detail than we have achieved so far. Matters of process are important, but introductory. Above all, our concern will be to articulate substance: to define liberal legal enterprise from the standpoint of the idea of legality that impels its argument.

The conception of law-like legality is multifaceted and ramifying, a complex of elements. It is a generic commitment that subsumes more specific undertakings, both positive and negative. The basic commitment branches to yield the components of a network of interrelated pursuits and aversions. We need to trace the development of the generic conception, identify its elements, lay out its derivatives, and show how the ensemble amounts to a liberal project. Thus we may specify the character and the constituents – guidelines and guideposts – of nomological practice, the forum within which liberal legal argument unfolds.

Our setting up of guidelines and guideposts for argumentative practice is like the activity of preparing for the presentation of a dramatic performance. Before the play can begin, the players must get acquainted with the arena within which their toing and froing will transpire. And direction needs to be given to the cast of performers. So the object of the whole drama is outlined. The motivation of each member of the company is established. The players receive general instructions which they must keep in mind during continuous action and must in performance render concrete. When the stage is set, and roles are learned by heart, the play of argument may commence, which the critics will observe.

2

Argument in a Legal System

According to the terminology of this book, legal practice is the activity of using society's laws as reasons for decisions. The inquiry of the book focuses on the process by which existing laws are used to judge situations in life. Herein, this process is called the practice of legal argument. The practice of legal argument of a society like ours takes place within an established legal system.

When we think of a legal system, we picture a set of ongoing, law-related agencies that function in relation to one another. These are institutions that have to do with the making and applying of law. In a nutshell, a legal system is made up of a legislative process plus a mechanism of adjudication – a legislature plus courts. The courts are the essential institution of the practice of legal argument.

In the discussion that follows, we will briefly consider the institutional context within which the practice of legal argument takes shape. We will canvass the basic features of a legal system emphasized by British legal philosopher H. L. A. Hart.[1] Hart's account of "the conditions necessary and sufficient for the existence of a legal system" is very influential, and it is quite useful – so far as it goes.[2]

As we will see, Hart's inventory of the constituents of a legal system is incomplete. He leaves out an essential feature of the process by which existing laws are brought to bear on cases. This omission has serious consequences. In the end, it disables Hart's analysis of what goes on in the courts. On account of it, Hart is unable to show how the courts function as parts of a system.

In the courts, judges listen to claims of lawyers on behalf of litigants, and render decisions, giving reasons for their judgments. In an established legal system, presentations made in the courts are crafted in line with commonly accepted criteria of good and sufficient legal argument. Accepted criteria tell the legal professionals how to argue legally. Canons of proper argument are an important part of a legal system. By virtue of shared canons, the activities of advocates and judges are coordinated. Arguers making claims and giving reasons appeal

---

[1] For H. L. A. Hart's account of the basic features of a legal system, see *The Concept of Law*, 2nd edition (Hart 1961, pp. 91–117). Hereafter in this chapter, *The Concept of Law* (2nd edn.) is cited as *CL*.

[2] *CL*, p. 116.

commonly to law upheld by the system. Arguers occupying institutional roles function as parts of the same system.

2.1 FEATURES OF A LEGAL SYSTEM

H. L. A. Hart undertakes to specify the basic features of a legal system. These basic features are said to be the "minimum conditions necessary and sufficient" for the existence of a legal system.[3] Hart presumes that a particular human community may or may not have a legal system. Whether a legal system exists in society is an empirical question. Some societies have legal systems; some don't. Modern societies do. Hart's project is to state the conditions that must exist as a matter of social fact in order for a legal system to take shape in social life.

Hart starts by imagining a "primitive" community in which behavior is subject to pervasive social control, and yet a legal system does not exist.[4] In the imagined community, social rules exist – Hart calls them rules of obligation.[5] People within the community accept a set of rules as standards of behavior; in their interactions, they justify conduct that adheres to the rules, and criticize conduct that violates the rules; by and large, members of the community comply with the rules as a matter of fact. Given this pattern of behavior – use of rules in social exchange, compliance with the rules for the most part – we may say that the designated rules are upheld by the society in question, though there is no official mechanism for their enforcement. In the primitive community, "punishments for violations ... and other forms of social pressure ... are not administered by a special agency but are left to the individuals affected or to the group at large."[6]

We might conceivably call the social rules upheld by Hart's imagined community "the law" of that community. We would be making the point that "law" might exist in society though a "legal system" does not exist. Hart himself does not speak that way. In his primitive society, there is no differentiated legal realm. There are no legal officials. A society with no specifically legal institutions – no legislature, no court system – is, according to Hart, a "prelegal" world.[7]

A legal system emerges when three developments occur. The three developments involve the establishment, within society, of three kinds of institutional rules.[8] First, what Hart calls "rules of change" are adopted. These rules constitute a lawmaking power for the society – a legislature. Second, "rules of adjudication" are adopted. These rules constitute a court system. Third, the judges, and other legal officials, embrace what Hart calls "the rule of recognition." This is Hart's name for the set of criteria that identify valid laws, the existing legal rules that are to be enforced by the courts.

First, a legislative arrangement is established. Institutional rules authorize persons occupying official roles to enact binding laws. The legislative institution exists in

---

[3] *CL*, p. 116. [4] *CL*, p. 91. [5] See generally *CL*, pp. 82–91. [6] *CL*, p. 93. [7] *CL*, p. 94.
[8] *CL*, pp. 94–98.

society when society's officials accept its constitutive rules, and ordinary citizens by and large comply with its products: legislated laws.

Second, a mechanism of adjudication is established. Tribunals authorized to hear and decide legal controversies are set up, and proceed to issue binding decisions. Courts of law exist socially when judges and other officials accept the rules that confer jurisdiction, and citizens by and large comply with the judgments of courts.

So far, Hart's account of the features of a legal system is not very surprising. The first two constituents posited by Hart – a legislative process and a mechanism of adjudication – are pretty basic. When an ongoing legal system exists in society, these institutions, over time, generate a growing stock of standing laws: statutory rules enacted by the legislature and rulings established as precedents in the courts. Hart's third condition for the existence of a legal system calls attention to this stock of rules and rulings.

Third, in order for a legal system to exist, a fundamental rule, what Hart calls "the rule of recognition," must be accepted and put to use by legal officials.[9] The system's rule of recognition is its conclusive test for identifying – "recognizing" – the valid laws of the system. The valid laws are the rules in force as law, the existing laws enforced by the courts. The criteria that identify existing – enforceable – law point to the sources of law. Hart often speaks of "the" rule of recognition, but he acknowledges that the tests used to identify valid laws of a modern legal system are plural and complex. "In a modern legal system ... the criteria for identifying the law are multiple and commonly include a written constitution, enactment by a legislature, and judicial precedents."[10]

Hart says that the rule of recognition is the "ultimate rule" of the system.[11] Its fundamental criteria define the realm of the legal. It provides criteria for assessing the legal validity of all other rules, but "there is no rule providing criteria for the assessment of its own legal validity."[12] The rule of recognition is an institutional rule which exists in fact when it is "actually accepted and employed" by the judges and other legal officials.[13] Normally, when the judges use the rule of recognition to identify existing law, the rule itself is not explicitly stated. Rather its content is shown by "the way in which courts identify what is to count as law."[14] In their common acceptance of the same sources of law, the judges of an ongoing legal system are on the same page.

Having identified the basic rules necessary in order to constitute a legal system, Hart describes two kinds of rule-following behavior which must take place in order to establish the system in social life. On the one hand, there must be outward obedience to the system's laws by citizens generally: "those rules of behaviour which are valid according to the system's ultimate criteria of validity must be generally obeyed." On the other hand, there must be willing acceptance of the system's basic rules by officials: "its rules of recognition ... and its rules of change

---

[9] *CL*, pp. 94–95, 100–117.   [10] *CL*, p. 101.   [11] *CL*, p. 107.   [12] *CL*, p. 107.   [13] *CL*, p. 108.
[14] *CL*, p. 108.

and adjudication must be effectively accepted as common public standards of official behaviour by its officials."[15]

Here, then, is a list of the basic features of an ongoing legal system, five in number, specified by Hart. The first three items of the list are institutional rules that together define the system:

(1) rules that constitute a legislative power for society;
(2) rules that constitute courts of adjudication;
(3) a rule of recognition stating the criteria that identify valid laws.

The last two features establish the social existence of the rule-defined system:

(4) acceptance of the institutional rules by legal officials, particularly the judges, of the society;
(5) compliance with the laws of the system, by and large, by the citizens of the society.

According to Hart, whenever these five conditions are found to exist together in social life, a legal system exists.

But something is missing from this list.

2.2 CANONS OF ARGUMENT

According to Hart, given a shared rule of recognition, the judges of a legal system commonly identify certain precepts as valid laws. But what happens then? The valid laws identified by the rule of recognition are, we assume, the starting points of legal argument by the judges in the courts. But from these starting points, argument might proceed in a variety of ways.

Legal argument by judges, leading to judgment, ensues – but what does proper legal argument look like? How are the judges expected to put the laws to use? How do they understand the rules they recognize as law? In administering the rules, what faculties do they bring to bear? Hart's idea of a rule of recognition raises – but it does not answer – these questions. Different historical legal systems, in addition to recognizing a wide variety of pertinent rules as law, answer these questions differently.

On the one hand, the recognized rules may be understood to be tentative guides for judges, at most pertinent points of possible reference. The rules may be regarded as isolated commands, narrow precepts applicable in past contexts of judgment, suggestive only in current contexts. Legal deciders may be instructed to come to judgment, not by reasoning based on abstract rules, but by exercise of wisdom.

Many historical legal systems have authorized administration of the various rules they recognize by use not of impersonal reason but of special insight on the part of

---

[15] The two quotes in this paragraph come from *CL*, p. 116.

the judges. In decisions enforcing the laws, wise judges may be expected to display special insight into the needs of a national group, the meaning of a religious text, the program of a vanguard party.

On the other hand, the judges may be instructed to come to judgment by exercise of logical capacities understood to be shared by humans generally. Judgment, then, is the fruit not of special insight, but of common reason. The found laws may be taken to be by themselves determining grounds of decision, widely applicable, for the most part hard and fast. The rules may be regarded not as isolated commands, but as interrelated prescriptions, which should be read to cohere.

Hart's account of the necessary conditions of a legal system leaves out something crucial. A crucial component of a legal system is shared acceptance of canons of argument. A legal system, properly so called, establishes criteria of good and sufficient legal argument. These criteria define proper judging, good reasoning, right resolution. Different systems establish different canons – or rather, different canons constitute different systems. A given system may be eclectic, embracing a variety of tests for proper argument, and the mix may change over time. But no legal order, operating as a system, lacks shared canons of good judging.

What would we think of a legal arrangement – we might hesitate to call it a legal system – in which all imaginable criteria of good legal argument are allowable, and in fact are embraced by one or another group of judges? One group of judges regards the found laws as determining grounds, seeks their coherence, and develops the law by articulate reasoning, rejecting any claim to exceptional acumen. Another group of judges rejects the idea that rules for past contexts dictate judgment now, rejects the idea that rules should be made to cohere, and appeals to superlative wisdom. For all the judges, a shared rule of recognition may get legal argument started, but cacophony soon reigns. A legal apparatus in which shared criteria of good legal argument are missing is not the sort of thing we think of as a legal system at all.

Disciplining Rules for Judging

H. L. A. Hart says that the activity of judges within a legal system is formed by common acceptance of criteria that identify the valid laws. Other legal theorists have suggested that the legal enterprise, well understood, is constituted by common acceptance of canons that go well beyond identification of valid laws. These larger directives say what to do after the valid laws are identified. They are basic canons of good legal argument. They define proper judging.

According to legal scholar Owen Fiss, the judges in the courts, engaged in interpretation of law, are members of an interpretive community.[16] The legal judges,

---

[16] For Owen Fiss' definition of an interpretive community, see "Objectivity and Interpretation" (Fiss 1982, hereafter cited in this chapter as "O&I").

by virtue of their office, are bound by "disciplining rules" which constrain interpretation.[17] The disciplining rules constitute the interpretive community. That is, the community of legal interpretation consists of "those who recognize the rules as authoritative." The disciplining rules of the legal community say how the activity of legal interpretation ought to be conducted. They provide standards by which the correctness of interpretation is to be judged. Through the disciplining rules "the law is defined."[18]

Fiss notes that, in particular hermeneutic activities going on outside law, there may be many different interpretive communities vying with one another. For example, there are "many schools" of literary interpretation, which employ rival methods for reading works of literature. But "in legal interpretation there is only one school and attendance is mandatory."[19]

Fiss says that disciplining rules for law "constitute the institution . . . in which judges find themselves." These institutional rules define the aspiration of the judges: a legal judge must "engage in rational dialogue"; "the judge must justify his decision in terms that are universalizable." The basis of the disciplining rules for legal interpretation is commitment to the rule of law. "Judges . . . belong to an interpretive community . . . by virtue of a commitment to uphold and advance the rule of law itself."[20]

Fiss emphasizes the vital role of disciplining rules in forming the practice of legal interpretation, but he doesn't show how different sorts of disciplining rules would form different interpretive practices. Fiss focuses on the disciplining rules that control judging in contemporary American law. His characterization of these rules is accurate so far as it goes. As he says, they require rational and universalizable argument that serves the rule of law. But he doesn't go into the content of our law's constitutive canons in any detail.

Legal philosopher Ronald Dworkin, in his analysis of alternative ground rules for legal enterprise, does both of the things Fiss doesn't do.[21] Dworkin shows how different sorts of legal enterprise are constituted by different ground rules. And he states the specific content of an important ground rule which is, he says, at the center of legal enterprise in the United States and Britain "and no doubt elsewhere."[22]

Ground Rules of Legal Enterprise

According to Ronald Dworkin, judges in the courts make legal assertions in line with established "ground rules."[23] Judges controlled by the same ground rules are

---

[17] "O&I," p. 744.   [18] "O&I," pp. 745, 752.
[19] The two quotes in this paragraph come from "O&I," p. 746.
[20] The four quotes in this paragraph come in sequence from "O&I," pp. 745, 754, 754, and 746.
[21] Ronald Dworkin discusses alternative ground rules for legal enterprise in three writings: (1) *Taking Rights Seriously* (Dworkin 1977b); (2) "No Right Answer?" (Dworkin 1977a); (3) A *Matter of Principle* (Dworkin 1985). Hereafter, in this chapter, these three writings are cited respectively as *TRS*, "NRA?", and *MP*.
[22] *TRS*, p. 288.   [23] *TRS*, p. 284.

engaged in a common "legal enterprise."[24] The ground rules of legal enterprise state the truth conditions for propositions of law. Dworkin underscores the vital role of the ground rules of legal argument by imagining alternative enterprises within which different truth conditions for legal assertion are accepted. Judges in the alternative enterprises come to judgment in different ways.

Dworkin's method of presenting varying ground rules for argument is to start by describing two different forms of literary interpretation.[25] After describing alternative interpretive methods in the literary realm, Dworkin goes on to identify parallel practices of legal interpretation.

Dworkin imagines that members of a group of literary scholars try to answer interpretive question about a particular literary text: Charles Dickens' novel, *David Copperfield*. This "group of Dickens scholars" adopts, successively, two different ground rules to govern their interpretations.[26]

First, the Dickens scholars adopt a fairly rudimentary ground rule. It authorizes assertions about the title character, David Copperfield, as follows: "Any proposition about David may be asserted as 'true' if Dickens said it, or said something else such that it would have been inconsistent had Dickens denied it."[27] This rule restricts interpretations to direct entailments of the text, and so limits the number of assertable propositions about David rather sharply.

Second, the Dickens scholars adopt a more permissive ground rule. It says that "a further proposition about David is assertable as true ... if that further proposition provides a better ... fit than its negation with propositions already established."[28] This rule authorizes complex readings of Dickens' text in order to find the interpretation that best fits the text as a whole.

Two contrasting forms of legal argument run parallel to the two modes of literary interpretation described by Dworkin.[29] According to Dworkin, the alternative forms of legal enterprise stipulate "different truth conditions for propositions of law."[30] On the one hand, legal interpretation might focus on particular entailments of the laws. On the other hand, legal interpretation might seek overall coherence.

In the first sort of legal enterprise, judges undertake a simple sort of interpretation. They scan the existing laws to find out what their direct entailments may be. Interpretation focuses on the particular laws taken one by one. Judge adhere to the

---

[24] *TRS*, p. 288.   [25] See "NRA?," pp. 73–84; *MP*, pp. 134–145.   [26] *MP*, p. 134.   [27] *MP*, p. 134.
[28] *MP*, p. 136.
[29] Discussion of Dworkin in the text is drawn from three writings (*TRS*, "NRA?," and *MP*). In these writings, Dworkin contrasts two forms of legal argument which differ from one another along two lines of distinction. One mode of argument is (a) simple and (b) formal. The other mode of argument is (a) complex and (b) ideal. In the text, the first axis of distinction (between simple entailment and complex coherence) is emphasized. The second axis of distinction (between formal argument and ideal argument in law) will be developed later on in this book. See Chapter 5, pp. 77–87. See also Chapter 6, pp. 94–95.
[30] *TRS*, p. 288.

following ground rule: "A proposition of law may be asserted as true if that proposition may be derived from settled law ... simply by deduction."[31]

In the second sort of legal enterprise, legal judges seek overall coherence. In a given area of law, legal reasoning works to develop an organizing framework – "a theory of the relevant law."[32] General ideas of the theory show how the particular laws fit together. A good theory makes a "good fit with the relevant legal materials."[33] Then, in deciding legal questions, judges adhere to the following ground rule: "A proposition of law may be asserted as true if it is more consistent with the [relevant] theory of law ... than the contrary proposition of law."[34]

In short, in the second sort of legal practice, canons of good argument require coherence-seeking throughout law. Good legal argument is complex. Dworkin says the second form of legal striving is the "judicial enterprise" of our law.[35] That is, he claims that the ground rule establishing coherence as a truth condition for propositions of law is a feature of "the legal enterprise actually in force in, for example, Britain and the United States."[36]

As we will eventually see, Dworkin is right that a canon of coherence is an important part of our law. However, he doesn't trace a requirement of coherence-seeking to its root.[37] The imperative of coherence, while vital, is not ultimate. It is an entailment of more basic criteria of good argument which control our legal practice. Later on, we will see that quest of coherence comes into being as a consequence of fundamental commitment to uphold nomological legality.

For present purposes, the important point to keep in mind is simply that, as Fiss and Dworkin affirm, canons of good reasoning and proper judging – whatever their content and provenance – are necessary constituents of the practice of legal argument going on in the courts.

2.3 WHAT FOLLOWS

A central assumption of this book is that legal argument in an established legal order takes place in a particular context. The context is a differentiated practice of social life, a practice of argument and judgment. The practice of legal argument is an

---

[31] *TRS*, p. 288. [32] *TRS*, p. 284. [33] *MP*, p. 145.

[34] *TRS*, p. 283. The quotation from Dworkin given in the text speaks of "the [relevant] theory of law ..." Dworkin's own text, without elision, says: "the theory of law *that best justifies settled law.*" The elided phrase (in italics) indicates that the theory in question is an ideal – not a formal – framework. On the distinction between formal argument and ideal argument in law (both of which seek coherence), see Chapter 5, pp. 77–87.

[35] *TRS*, pp. 287–288. [36] *TRS*, p. 288.

[37] The canon of coherence emphasized by Dworkin focuses on ideal – not formal – argument. This is argument that "justifies settled law." See *TRS*, p. 283. According to the analysis of this book, fundamental commitment to nomological legality gives rise to a wider requirement of coherence-seeking: one that addresses all argument in legal practice, formal and ideal alike. See Chapter 5, pp. 77–87. See also Chapter 6, pp. 94–96.

intellectual realm in which a certain discussion takes place, and it is an institutional arrangement, by which social life is coercively controlled.

In the chapter that follows, our objective is to conduct an analysis that defines the basic features of this intellectual and institutional phenomenon – an established practice of legal argument – with great care. We may say that our objective is to state the necessary and sufficient conditions for the existence of a practice of legal argument. Here we follow H. L. A. Hart, who sets out to state the necessary and sufficient conditions of an ongoing legal system, but as we have seen, comes up short. Hart is right that shared acceptance by judges of criteria that identify the enforceable law is necessary in order for courts to play their institutional part within an ongoing legal system, but, as discussion above indicates, it is not sufficient. More in the way of regimen is required. Directive canons of good argument, proper judging, right resolution – disciplining rules according to Fiss, ground rules according to Dworkin – are necessary.

More precisely put, our objective in what follows is to formulate, step by step, an analysis that does, in sequence, two things. First, our aim is to develop a generalized understanding that states the constitutive features of any sort of practice of legal argument. Second, we will go on to say how a particular sort of practice – liberal practice of legal argument, or, as we will also call it, nomological practice – gets formed.

First, our aim is to show how a practice of legal argument, constituted by canons of good argument, takes shape. As noted a moment ago, the practice is an institutional arrangement and an intellectual realm. The realm is a kind of extension of the institution. As we will see, the practice comprises argument by judges, advocates, and litigants in courts, and argument by others – law teachers, legal commentators, legislators, ordinary citizens – going on beyond the courts. The unity of the practice lies in the governance of all these legal arguers by the same canons.

Second, we will go on to consider how a specifically liberal practice of legal argument is formed. Liberal practice is formed when the canons of good argument that direct legal endeavor come to incorporate a particular conception of law's excellence. This is the liberal conception of legality – or, as we will also call it, the nomological conception. Entrenchment of that conception, not another, in the canons that control argument, constitutes a distinctive legal practice. That practice is the object of our investigation in the remainder of this book.

3

Practice of Legality

The first step toward specifying the nature of a liberal practice is to specify the nature of a practice, liberal or not. Nomological practice of legality is first of all a practice of argument and decision. Before conducting a detailed examination of the substance of nomological commitment, by parsing it into elements and charting their implications, we should ask what sort of realm it is within which that or some other commitment might set up shop. How shall we define the sphere within which nomological commitment holds sway? What is a practice of legal argument?

A good approach is to start at a distance from our subject and come closer by a sequence of steps. On this approach, we seek first to establish the general character of an instituted practice of legal argument, without regard to the particular conception of legality that animates it. We keep our focus wide, and ask generally what it is for such a practice to exist. Next, we ask what happens when the nomological conception in particular is implanted within the practice. We consider the specific character of nomological practice as a whole. And then after that we may sharpen our focus in order to scan detail, to see how the component parts of nomological commitment take shape within the practice of legality.

To have an instituted practice of legal argument is to have a certain amount of differentiation in intellectual and societal life. A practice of legal argument is an intellectual realm in which arguers undertake reasoning and offer reasons in line with accepted criteria of sufficient demonstration. This realm is bounded, differentiated from other discursive activities, by the argumentative criteria that form it. A legal practice is also social machinery for the rendering of coercive decisions by judges in courts. When an instituted practice exists, power of legal judgment is concentrated in a judging institution that is differentiated from other social formations.

The combination of a somewhat airy intellectual activity and very earthly social machinery yields the following arrangement. First, a practical apparatus for the rendering of judgment is established in social life. At its center are judges in courts. Second, this institution is a forum in which the activity of legal argument is conducted. The job of judging is taken to include the giving of reasons that justify results. Third, a wider discourse of law exists wherein discussants present the same sorts of arguments as those that lead to judgment. This wider discussion takes in much, but not all, of the law-related talk or disputation that goes on in society. Not every society has such an arrangement – differentiated courts, judges who give arguments, a wider discourse of the same sort.[1] Our society does. We do law within a practice having these characteristics.

Assertion within a practice of legal argument is directed by one or another prescriptive conception of law. Argumentative criteria say what laws set in motion as reasons should look like, and so formulate an idea of law realized. Canons of good argument reflect one or another conception of law's excellence. I have said that, for the purpose of investigating how nomological commitment unfolds, we should imagine a practice thoroughly controlled by a particular conception of legality.

In the practice we imagine, doers of law are instructed to try to realize a certain kind of legality. And, we assume, in crafting arguments practitioners heed this instruction. Participants make argument having in mind a common image of law perfected. All are guided by the same conception. Each can see others are so guided. So we may impute to practice as a whole a constant aspiration to realize legality. Pursuit of legality is the undertaking of the whole practice.

But this characterization of pursuit within a practice poses an obvious problem. How does aspiration to achieve legality come to be so widely embraced? How could the undertaking to try to bring about a perfected condition of law become the commitment of the whole practice?

It is not difficult to see how judges might be obligated to work to produce only certain kinds of arguments to justify their judgments. But what about others who participate in the discourse of the practice? Litigants and lawyers choose lines of argument on grounds that are highly interested, hardly devotional. Legal scholars

---

[1]   In terminology of legal anthropologist Paul Bohannan, a differentiated legal system is the consequence of "double institutionalization" of norms in social life. "'[D]ouble institutionalization' … comprises all legal systems …" First, social norms are instituted as custom. "Custom" is a body of precepts upheld in social interaction; customs form societal institutions. Second is differentiated law. "Laws" are norms of social institutions that have been institutionalized a second time – "doubly institutionalized norms." Law is "custom that has been restated" by legal institutions "so that the conflicts within nonlegal institutions can be adjusted by an 'authority' outside themselves" (Bohannan, "The Differing Realms of Law," 1973, pp. 306, 308, 309, 310).

All societies have institutions formed by norms of custom – "primary institutions" – and also procedures for settlement of disputes arising in social life. In stateless societies, procedures of dispute resolution produce "compromises" instead of "decisions" (Bohannan 1973, pp. 308–309, 311, 313).

In some societies, a differentiated legal system exists. There "customs … are *re*institutionalized at another level: they are restated for the more precise purposes of legal institutions." "[T]he device most commonly utilized to carry out the secondary, or legal, institutionalization" is the political state, "a 'sovereign.'" In societies with states, "it is possible to have judicial decision and a recognized mechanism of enforcement …" Law is "specifically" stated by "the court," a body of judges "representative of the political power." Resolution of disputes is "decision-based" (Bohannan 1973, pp. 308, 309, 312, 313, 314; emphasis in original).

and commentators may inquire about law in a spirit quite aloof from practical commitment, or feel detachment is their obligation. The problem is to show how a conception of legality binding judges may come to operate as a general regimen for practice, so that the aim of all of practice's argument is to realize that conception. I have said we should imagine that all practitioners heed the instruction to pursue legality. But how does this instruction, the thing to be heeded, run beyond the judges and demand the adherence of other practitioners in the first place? In short, how can it be that the many lines of professional advocacy and scholarly inquiry in legal practice are convergent?

The answer lies in the nature of the practice of argument. A practice of legal argument is both institution and discourse, a discourse anchored in an institution. The institution of judging governs presentations by litigants and lawyers as well as reasoning by judges. The whole discourse of practice extends beyond the judging institution, but is tied to the institution, governed by its instituted canons of good reasoning. The line that connects argument by judges first to argument by lawyers, and then to argument by other participants in a broader discourse of law, is the path along which the instruction to pursue legality is conveyed to all practitioners.

3.1 INSTITUTED DISCOURSE

A practice of legal argument, as I shall use the term, is an instituted discourse. The practice of argument is an ongoing inquiry into what the law prescribes. Its point is to make explicit law's content and implication. Argument within instituted discourse of law aims to articulate the joint meaning of the laws in order to come to legal resolutions and warrant them.

Practice of legal argument is a discourse about law plus an institution of legal judgment. The institution is society's system of courts. It is a relatively compact arrangement of offices, roles, and tasks that produces binding legal decisions. The discourse is a considerably broader undertaking that rests upon the institution, with its edges projecting well beyond its base.

Where the two coincide, the discourse takes place within the institution. There, practice is institutional, and its argument is decisional, talk leading directly to decision. Where the discourse overhangs the institution, jutting out beyond it, practice is discursive only, not institutional. There, the practice proper is just talk, or talk leading to more talk. But the projecting discourse is anchored, cantilevered, continuous with institutional deliberation at its center. So the whole of the discourse may be said to be instituted, though not all of it is strictly institutional.

Practice's Instituted Canons

The practice of argument in its widest extension is discursive interaction. It is a discourse anyone can engage in just by submitting to certain tests of good argument. The matter in discussion is the purport of the law. Participants put forward views about what the law requires.

Legal discourse is governed by canons of good argument. Discursive practice is formed by common acceptance of criteria that say what legal argument properly is and is not. Canons of argument specify what is entertainable and persuasive by way of demonstration and reasoning in law. Law's discourse is a particular realm of discussion by virtue of the set of disputational ground rules that define and delimit it.[2]

But the practice is not simply a freely entered, internally governed discourse. Practice's canons are not just what some free-floating congregation of discussants takes for the time being to be suitable tests of legal assertion. The canons of appropriate argument are specifically the canons of good judging. They are the discipline of an operative institution of legal judgment, tests put to use by judges endeavoring to give good justifications for decisions in cases before them. So the whole discourse, wherever it takes place, is tied to a specific institution. The discussion ranges far from the institutional forum at its center, but always on a tether running back to the institution.

The practice in its central precincts is an institutional formation. Its core is an institution whose executors are specially empowered to produce legal judgment in social life. This judging institution is social apparatus meant to bring controversy to conclusion in judgment backed by force. Discourse within the institution is the same as the discussion without, but decisional practice is a lot more than a conclave of reasoners invoking common canons. Argument in the judging institution views the laws as grounds of decisions that stick. There the discussion wields an ax.

The heart of practice is the activity of judging. At the center are the tribunals empowered to hear and determine. Judges in courts sit to decide cases. By virtue of institutional role, the judges are obligated to render good judgment under law rightly understood. They seek to find right legal resolution, and offer justifications for dispositions made.

Litigants and lawyers also occupy positions within the judging institution. They try to find appropriate reasons for the decisions they seek. Lawyers and litigants present legal arguments meant to be fit for judges to embrace. So, all

---

[2] For Ronald Dworkin, in order to understand law's logic, it is important to identify the disputational ground rules that control legal assertion in a particular legal enterprise. Law's logic will vary depending on what ground rules have been established (Dworkin 1977b, pp. 283–289).

  A particular legal enterprise "stipulates certain truth conditions for propositions of law"; its ground rules say when a formulated proposition "may be asserted as true" or "may be denied as false." It is easy to imagine different judicial enterprises "with different ground rules of assertion and denial." Whether there is "a single right answer to complex questions of law" depends on which ground rules by stipulation control legal argument (Dworkin 1977b, pp. 279, 283, 288). See also Dworkin (1978) ("The issue of whether there is a right answer ... will crucially depend upon which form of the legal enterprise is in play"). For more on Dworkin's idea of ground rules, see Chapter 2, pp. 23–25.

the basic roles and tasks in institutional practice – those of suitor, advocate, deciding officer – are defined in relation to argumentative resolution. Claimant and counsel look to judge. Litigant's demand and representative's plea look to pronouncement of decision.

The rest of legal practice occurs beyond the judging institution, but is rooted in it. Instituted discourse extends well away from the institutional sphere. Practice as an extended discourse encompasses all argumentation subscribing to the same criteria of good legal justification that are entrenched in the judging institution.

Suppose the discourse of practice first exists just as argument inside the courts. This discourse is controlled by certain criteria, established tests of good resolution.[3] Now if a legal assertion made outside the courts purports to be the kind of presentation that satisfies instituted tests of good argument, then that assertion affiliates itself with the discourse of legal practice. By submitting to the canons that discipline legal reasoning in court, argumentative activity annexes itself to the practice. Affiliated argument views the laws as fit grounds of judgment by courts and accepts the instituted discipline as its own regimen. Such assertion is as much a part of the discourse of the practice as the pronouncements of the judges.

Three Zones

We may view instituted discourse of law as something that takes place within three spheres. That is, considered as argument, legal practice is tripartite. The argument of practice occupies three zones of activity, which are related as concentric circles, from innermost to in-between to farthest ambit.

The central zone is the locus of argument by a judge in a judging tribunal or court. Here the primary argument of decisional practice renders the law to answer questions and decide cases according to tests of right resolution.

Next is the middle zone of argument before a court, to a judge, meant to be fit for the judge to embrace. Such argument is derivative activity in that its proper nature depends on the nature of primary argument by judges. Argument in the second zone invokes the canons of legal justification lodged at the center. Together the first two spheres make up the institutional practice, arena of the role-defined activity of judges, litigants, and lawyers.

Beyond is the third zone of affiliated argument subscribing to the instituted regimen of practice. This is the area of the extended practice larger than the judging institution, open to discursive participation without regard to institutional status.

---

[3] According to Owen Fiss, the practice of legal argument is controlled by "disciplining rules." These rules "constrain the interpreter [of law] … and they furnish the standards by which the correctness of the interpretation can be judged" (Fiss 1982, pp. 739, 744, 745). The disciplining rules that control legal interpretation "constitute the institution … in which judges find themselves and through which they act," and they demarcate "an interpretive community consisting of those who recognize the rules as authoritative" (Fiss 1982, p. 745). For more on Fiss' idea of disciplining rules, see Chapter 2, pp. 22–23.

Argument in the outer zone accepts the same strictures that control institutional judgment, and so might be advanced as well within the inner circles. Thus the practice includes any legal presentation that might be repeated in court – that is, any presentation meant to be fit to be argued in a court before a judge, because it is crafted to be fit to be argued by a judge.

Legal argument within the practice then is the sum of primary argument by courts, plus derivative argument by lawyers and litigants in courts, plus affiliated argument by anybody anywhere else meant to be fit for the courts to adopt. All three types belong to the instituted practice, though only the first two are institutional argument.

The image of three concentric circles suggests rightly that instituted discourse of law is always limited, defined by an outer perimeter. But such discourse also always might grow larger. Argumentative practice is bounded yet extensible.

The practice is indefinitely expansive because it is open to participation by all. Anyone may enter legal practice by submitting to its constitutive regimen. To come inside the practice is to embrace a certain measure of the success of one's argument. Discursive practice grows as large as common acceptance of its discipline. The practice swells to receive any submissive presentation. It enlarges by additions to its outer zone, the accretion disk of instituted discourse, from which argument may swirl inward, moving to the center, since reasoning in any zone of practice is interchangeable with reasoning in any other. There is in principle no limit to the amount of law-related discourse that may be drawn into orbit within the practice of legal argument.

The third zone of practice takes in a wide range of official, academic, and lay assertion about law. Affiliated discourse encompasses argument by many sorts of arguers in many settings: by judges not in court; by lawyers advising clients; by legal scholars and commentators; by teachers and students of law in the moot legality of the classroom; by office holders talking about law that exists; by legislators talking about law in the process of becoming; by members of the public discussing legal subjects, or citizens in social life appealing to law.

But while extensible, the practice as a whole is always bounded, and its outer zone might conceivably shrink, all for the same reason. The outer boundary of practice is set by the extent of acceptance of practice's discipline in legal inquiry and social life. The instituted canons enclose a particular realm of discursive exchange. Not every assertion or description of law is part of that realm.

There are very many ways of comprehending and invoking law. Not all presentations of and about law are crafted to satisfy the same discursive tests that are embedded in institutional role and task. Legal talk going on daily in the contexts of society – the exhorting, reproaching, and warranting that appeal to understanding of legal laws – may be heedless of the restrictions that control instituted practice. Reflective reconstructions of law – recoveries of its past, expositions of its present workings, imaginings of its future – may not submit themselves to the regimen that constrains the judgments of the current courts. So, the practice of argument, however effective institutionally, is not coextensive with every sort of disputation concerning law. Much lies outside it within a still wider, more diffuse activity of legal understanding.

3.2 ENTRENCHED PURSUIT

So far, we have surveyed the elements that define instituted discourse of law. Something more is needed in order to produce a discourse of law-like law. Our object now is to see how specifically nomological practice is formed.

The nomological practice of law is an argumentative realm possessing all the properties of instituted legal discourse. Its inner circles circumscribe argumentation going on within a judging institution established in social life. Its outer sphere includes all other discourse adhering to the canons that govern argument in the inner zones. It is a bounded practice, a realm of inquiry delimited by criteria of reasoning that direct inquiry.

In short, the general character of nomological practice lies in this set of features: argumentative canons, institutional argument, wider discourse, discursive bounds. Then the specific character of such practice comes from the conception of legality that is lodged within it.

Nomological practice is formed by the entrenchment of the idea of law-like legality within bounded practice of law. Sufficient entrenchment may be accomplished by a single operation.

In order for practice to become nomological practice, all that is necessary is for the notion of law-like legality to be embodied in the disputational tests that control legal discussion. After a particular idea of legality has been made the basis of the canons of legal argument, that idea will work itself into all the performances and exchanges of instituted discourse. In short, entrenchment of the liberal conception within legal canons yields liberal practice of law.

Conception Put into Canons

A conception of legality, as discussed earlier, is a model of law's excellence: an image of law's perfected condition. Such a conception states what qualities law should display and what dispensation law should sustain in the world. The nomological idea of legality says that law should be law-like in form and operation. This conception teaches that the fulfillment of law is the realization of legal entitlement and legal justice through rational legal resolution.

The canons of legal practice are directives pointing out the kinds of arguments legal discussants should try to produce. Argumentative canons are criteria of identification. They indicate what good legal assertion is, and is not; what proper legal reasoning amounts to; what qualifies as sufficient legal demonstration. And argumentative canons are instructions telling arguers how to do things. They tell us how to understand legal propositions, how to grasp the laws for use as practical reasons, how to make a presentation that leads to right resolution.

The incorporation of nomological conception into canons of good argument is done by formulating the canons in terms of the conception. This is not difficult, since conception and canons are complementary. The nomological conception amounts to a set of prescriptions, and is readily canonized. For their part, canons need to be spelled out in terms of some conception of law, in order to provide substantial direction.

When nomological conception is lodged in argumentative canons, practice's indicia of good legal assertion point to nomological reasoning, and arguers are instructed as follows. Laws should be understood as the sorts of reasons that manifest law-like qualities. What counts as good argument is reasoning in which grounds are general, accessible, and coherent laws. Argument should be conducted in a manner that upholds conditions of law-like legality.

Since argument in every zone of practice is governed by the same canons, the coupling of nomological conception and discursive canons produces a generalized directive telling all practitioners always to argue in line with the idea of law-like law. It is worth adding that the identical situation – everyone guided by a common conception – may be seen to come into being by another, somewhat less direct route. The alternative pathway starts with argument by judges.

Let us suppose the nomological conception is initially inserted just into canons of good judging. That is, initially we consider in isolation the criteria of due judgment that speak to judges at the heart of practice. We suppose the idea of law-like law provides the substance of practice's tests for proper judging, and so the pronounce-ments of courts are directed by that idea. This limited mating of nomological conception with canons of judging yields instructions addressed specifically to judges in courts. Judges are to fashion arguments connecting grounds and results in a way that honors legal entitlement and ensures legal justice. The laws should be regarded and rendered by courts such that legal justifications invoking them exhibit law-like rationality.

When the conception of law-like legality comes to be embodied in canons of judging, it follows that the same notion will control discourse generally within legal practice. The discourse of practice encompasses all construals and invocations of the laws that are meant to be fit to be embraced by a court. The kind of argument fit for the judges is the kind required of all participants. So, when a requirement is put in operation in the inner zone to direct argument by courts, it will migrate to the middle zone of practice and shape argument by litigants and lawyers in courts, and will go on to patrol the outer zone as part of the regimen for all other discourse anchored in the judging institution. Whatever conception is implanted in canons of judging will extend its sway to govern institutional and discursive practice as a whole.

Now the putting of conception into canons, in either of the ways just described, is quite sufficient to constitute nomological practice. All we need assume is that legal canons are formulated strictly in line with the nomological conception, so the canons speak in the terms of that – not another – notion of legality, and the result is a practice of argument governed completely, in all its precincts, by nomological commitment. The basic story of the coming into being of nomological practice is pretty short.

Of course, the story has been abbreviated in one respect. We have not yet explicated the idea of law-like law in detail, so the expressions of nomological canons given above are necessarily rather rough. But this sketchiness doesn't matter. We may assume that the full content of nomological conception, to be explicated later on, is what gets plugged into the canons of practice. For present purposes, we need only keep in mind the fundamentals of nomological preachment: that laws should have qualities of generality, accessibility, and coherence, and should sustain conditions of entitlement, justice, and rationality.

But still the basic story is, I think, too short. It lacks texture. More needs to be said about how canons of argument, once formulated in nomological terms, get their grip on legal practice. What is it that induces people to adhere to them? Why do arguers heed the canons?

In fact, canons gain adherence one way inside the courts – that is, inside institutional practice – and another way in discursive practice beyond the judging institution. In what follows I will describe, first, how the conception that is put into canons becomes more deeply institutionalized within courts. Then I will pose this question: why should people arguing outside courts accept the canons at all?

Deeper Entrenchment

Inside institutional practice, in the zones of argument by judges and by litigants and their lawyers, what happens is this: the conception of law-like legality that is incorporated in argumentative canons will dig itself deep into the roles and tasks of practice. So entrenched, the conception is a command, and pursuit of legality is compelled.

Canons are not straightforward commands. Rather, canons of argument identify and instruct. They say good argument is such and such, and if you want to make good argument you should do so and so. Yet it seems natural to state canons as imperatives for courts and counselors, because what is embodied in canons becomes embedded in institutional obligation and definition.[4] Obligations do command, and definitions in a way compel.

---

[4]   John Searle connects constitutive rules and institutional obligation. See Searle (1969), pp. 33–42, 50– 53, 175–191. "'[I]nstitutions' are systems of constitutive rules" which include "rule(s) of the form 'X counts as Y in context C'"; "when one enters an institutional activity by invoking the rules of the institution one necessarily commits oneself in such and such ways ..." (Searle 1969, pp. 51–52, 189).

The process of further institutional entrenchment proceeds by stages. First, the canonical conception of legality fixes the role obligation of the judges. Second, it specifies the derivative role obligation of lawyers and the craft of good advocates. Third, it enters the definitions of positions and performances generally within the judging institution. Fully entrenched, pursuit of 'legality is part and parcel of institutional endeavors inside courts.

Judges in courts execute the decisional authority of institutional practice. The job of a judge comes with a constant duty. Someone who occupies the institutionally constructed position of a judging officer is, by virtue of occupancy, obligated to try to reach right resolution and render due judgment. This role obligation, when stated so generally, is a blank waiting to be filled. Its content depends on how notions of right resolution and due judgment are spelled out. When the conception of law-like legality supplies canons – criteria – of right judging, the same conception fills in the blank in the positional duty of a judge. The obligation is to judge rightly; right judging involves pursuit of law-like legality; so such pursuit is obligatory. Judges must always aspire to achieve the dispensation of legality.

Lawyers in courts are obligated by virtue of institutional role to try to give arguments, on behalf of their clients, that judges might accept. Again, the positional duty contains a blank needing to be filled. The nature of a lawyer's argumentative duty is contingent upon the nature of judges' argument. Given this contingency, the same conception that supplies criteria of good argument by judges, and so forms the obligation of judges, will enter and form the institutional obligation of lawyers in the courts. Advocates are bound to try to fashion arguments fit for judges to make, and these are arguments that would sustain legality. Aspiration to sustain law-like legality, then, is the derivative aspiration of the lawyers. Pursuit of legality is incumbent on advocates as a matter of duty and craft – contingent duty, instrumental craft.

Institutional Definition

In the final stage of institutional entrenchment, the pursuit already lodged in obligation becomes further entrenched in definition, as follows. The office of a judge is a norm-constituted position: it is defined by established norms that say what judges must do. As we have seen, a vital norm of obligation, when filled in, says that judges must always pursue nomological legality. Plainly this norm is part of the institutional definition of proper judging. So, inside practice, it becomes true by definition that someone who engages in conscientious judging is someone who tries to realize law-like legality. It would be a kind of inconsistency to purport to act properly as a judge and at the same time disavow the project of realizing legality.[5]

---

[5]   The text says it would be inconsistent to announce, while acting as a judge, that one will not try to achieve legality. This is not to say that it is inconsistent to declare, in judging a case, that one has tried but found it impossible to succeed.

Once a conception of legality becomes part of the established definition of judging, it will enter the official definition of other activities. It will come to define the roles of lawyer and litigant, suitor and defender, and the tasks of advocating, claiming, and defending. All the main positions and performances within the judging institution are definable in terms of their relation to judging. A conception that defines what it is to judge also defines what is asked for by a prayer for judgment. So, in institutional practice, the communication that one is making a claim or defense is received in a particular way. To present a claim in the courts is to ask for due judgment, which, by official definition, is a judgment that sustains law-like legality.[6]

The process of institutionalization just sketched – whereby nomological conception put into canons is put into obligations and definitions of interrelated activities – forms the hardened mass at the center of legal practice, the institution occupying practice's first two zones. The rest of practice is an airy affair, much less densely constructed.

Adherence Beyond Obligation

The third zone is the sphere of affiliated argument, a vast extension of instituted discourse running beyond the judging institution. There discussants are not engaged in tasks of claiming, advocating, or judging in courts, and are not bound by the same obligations that command argument in courts. Activity in the outer zone is a discourse constituted by common acceptance of argumentative canons institutionalized elsewhere. Formative canons operate by virtue of acceptance, adherence, submission. The common activity just is the use of the canons. So the initial, simple incorporation of conception into canons suffices to make nomological commitment part and parcel of all argument in the outer sphere.

In the third zone, different sorts of participants undertake the same sort of reasoning that goes on in the inner zones. Affiliated argument takes place at two removes from primary argument by judges. Still it takes place inside the practice, since it is crafted to be twice repeatable. Such argument, wherever stated, is meant to be fit to be repeated in a court before a judge, because it is fit to be adopted as a judge's own argument.

Why would someone not bound to do so submit to the regimen of legal practice? Nobody in the outer zone is arguing in a court, so no one is caught up in the specific duties woven into definitions of institutional activity. Of course, there are many practical motives for making arguments fit for judges, not least of which is anticipation that one's own affairs, or one's employer's, or one's client's, may end up in court.

---

[6] According to Charles Fried, "[L]awyers and litigants ... argue to the judge to grant them a right that they claim they already have. They appeal to principles that they take to be binding on the judge, and expect from him not an act of legislation or of will, but an act of reason, an argument and conclusion based on principles of law" (Fried 1981, p. 68).

But consider the large and voluble corps of legal arguers who are not advising or advocating in particular cases but rather are trying – avowedly anyway – just to throw light on law. Why should they come inside the practice?

Legal scholars and commentators may participate in legal discourse for reasons mainly intellectual. Such discussants are not bound to accept practice's canons. For them, the practice creates no compulsion to conduct legal inquiry one way or another, unless they accept the canons of practice, and acceptance is not compulsory. It is entirely possible to inquire legally, and abstain from instituted discourse. But there are difficulties, costs and risks posed by abstention.

Practice offers a definition of legal argument, a specification of how to argue legally, something very important in social life. Instituted canons are criteria that identify just what it is to engage in legal reasoning. The definition that practice formulates, in terms of a particular conception of legality, is not the only one available to intellect. Human reflective capacity and linguistic resource are sufficiently great that it is possible, with enough effort, to pry one's presentation loose from instituted conception. Still it is a difficult undertaking to purport to reason legally and yet to reject the established criteria of what that is.

One problem is irrelevance, the price of disengagement. Legal practice is the only official game in town. Being officially beside the point is an unavoidable cost of severing the connection between one's own arguments about law's meaning and presently permissible advocacy in courts. Legal intellectuals have a choice. The alternatives are to break the link between legal exposition and institutional judgment, or to enter the practice – to stay outside, and suffer a kind of argumentative irrelevance, or to come inside.

Also, there is the problem of misunderstanding, a specifically intellectual hazard. Not to accept the instituted understanding of what legal discussants do is to risk misappreciation, since the vocabulary of abstention is not made readily available by practice. Someone who announces legal cogitation is forthcoming, but then proceeds to offend the instituted canons that govern such reasoning, appears from the standpoint of practice to be doing not deviant legal argument, but botched legal argument. The problem is not that practice's definitions are inescapable, but rather that they are enticing, and ready to work retribution. To go with the definitional flow is always the line of least resistance. Practice exerts a gravitational tug upon reasoning about law, to induce if not logically compel an in-gathering of intellect along the lines of established conception.

By the proffering of legal argument meant to be fit for judges to embrace, an arguer enters into discursive practice of legality. Affiliated argument is legal assertion fashioned to satisfy established tests. Any sort of presentation in the outer zone of practice, however detached or academic, is reasoning kept in line with entrenched conception.

In order to make argument fit for judges to make, one must heed the strictures that bind judges. Judges try to make arguments that would secure legality. Anyone else, trying to give arguments that judges might adopt, likewise must try to make arguments that would sustain legality. So the aspiration of primary argument by judges transfers to every entrant. It is the derivative aspiration of advocacy by lawyers in courts, and it becomes the assumed aspiration of affiliated argument – meant to be fit to be repeated in court – by all other legal insiders.

So the outer sphere of practice, like the inner zones, is governed by a ground rule prescribing that argument ought always to be crafted in accord with legality. The entrenched conception of law's excellence exists as an ordinance for all practitioners. Directly or mediately or by extension, it tells each how argument and decision ought to be conducted and the laws conceived and constructed. It addresses every reporting and reading of the laws as the repository of grounds for due resolution of legal contest. Anyone engaged in argument within the practice is directed to strive – aim, seek, try – to realize legality.

3.3 SELF-CONCEPTION

By now it would seem that the question posed at the outset of the present chapter has been amply answered. There we asked, how can it be that all practitioners receive the same instructions? We have seen how this coordination happens, and how a nomological practice of law gets formed.

Our exploration of nomological enterprise has shown that in fundamentals it has a unitary character. Indeed, such a practice is enough unified in commitment that it is legitimate to speak of the practice itself as an actor, an entity that does things.

The kind of unity we have encountered so far is performative in nature, a unity of doing, endeavor, pursuit. We have seen that practice as a whole is a project. It is an undertaking to bring about and maintain law-like legality. Aspiration to achieve legality directs the entire enterprise. It gives rise to operative modes of law, argumentative techniques used to come to legal resolution. Nomological aspiration is formative of the logic of argument and decision, law's logic, in practice of law. Argument is driven along the path of law's imperative ambition.

In addition to the performative unification just noted, nomological enterprise has a subtler sort of unity that remains to be explored. This is a unity of outlook or perspective, a oneness having to do with seeing and understanding rather than aspiring and acting. Inside nomological practice, arguers share a common awareness.

Legal practice is self-conscious, aware of itself. Legal discussion is conducted having in mind an instructive model of good legal discussion. Argument meant to accord with a guiding image of argument is a reflexive, self-referring activity. Law imagines law, as law is developed with reference to a regulative notion of law.

Self-regulating practice is conscious of itself as a whole. The idea of law-like legality is an image of the right operation of the whole of law for all in society. A particular performance of law is done having in mind a conception of the proper nature of law as such including this instance. A formative idea of law in general stands behind law in the particular.

And nomological practice comes to acquire a self-image. It gets its view of itself from its formative conception, the model of law entrenched as law's inner aim.

Self-Image of Law-Like Law

Practice's self-conception is the characteristic view of legal enterprise that is embraced in the doing of law-like law. It is how law is viewed inside nomological practice of law, how law views itself. Instituted discourse of law-like law conceives itself to be a singular quest, a necessary instrumentality, the one way of realizing a vital mission. Significant consequences flow from this self-image, as we shall see.

Self-conception is made up of presuppositions about legal activity that are taken as true – accepted as premises – from the standpoint of liberal practice as a whole. Following is an exposition of main constituents of liberal law's self-understanding.

Inside liberal legal practice, legal argument is understood to be a very specific sort of argumentation. Argument considered to be specifically legal is, of course, nomological. Nomological argument says what legal laws prescribe. It seeks to state the meaning of the standing laws and to confer due judgment under law. It looks to resolution by society's judges. It is governed by a defining regimen. From the standpoint of the doing of law, argument having all these aspects takes place within a particular realm. All such argument falls within the bounded practice of law. So argument in the realm of law is different from argument outside it.

Inside practice, an ongoing process of argument and judgment is understood to be required – necessary – in order to bring about the substance of legality. The substance of legality has to do with legal entitlement and legal justice. In order for entitlement and justice to exist throughout society, legal judgment for the society must be controlled by a systematic discipline. Legality requires law-like argument issuing in law-like decision in case after case. Thus, the nomological conception of law contains the image of a specially formed process that is essential in order to realize law-like substance.

Since legality requires a certain kind of argument, and since this kind of argument happens only within law's own realm, it follows that legality can be brought about only inside legal practice. Law-like legality can arise only given a discursive endeavor devoted to its production. Legality is a contingent condition manufactured within a particular realm of discourse. It will not happen without a specific effort to make it happen. Thus, self-understanding of law-like law includes the invigorating idea that constant pursuit within legal practice is needed to attain the substance of legality, and the cautionary idea that legality fails absent dedicated pursuit.

The exposition of practice's self-conception just given boils down to two key notions, having to do with what liberal law is and what it does. Liberal law is seen to be different from other things, and to be the sole producer of something vital.

Liberal law's insistence on its own differentiated character and productive character is very pronounced, and rather urgent.

Distinctive and Constructive

The self-conceived character of nomological enterprise may be summed up in a pair of propositions. First, practice of law-like law is a distinctive activity, a special realm of rational inquiry. Second, such practice is a constructive agency, an endeavor to build something that would otherwise not get built.

First, legal practice is a distinctive process. It is different from all other practical and intellectual activities.

As understood within practice, the instituted discourse of law-like law is a singular undertaking within society. It is a particular sphere of argument having its own canons, performative strictures, and criteria of success. Thus legal argument is a rational realm, not a province of a more far-flung realm. It is not simply a branch of some larger communicative or prescriptive endeavor constituted by more highly general criteria of rationality.

In this connection, it should be recalled that the quality of law-likeness is itself a property specific to law. Nomological aspiration is peculiarly domestic, inward-looking, home grown. The nomological view of law is a quintessentially legal conception. The model for law is law. Quest of nomological legality within the realm of law aims at a sort of self-realization of lawfulness. Law finds its excellence in its own outstanding qualities, its own diacritical mark. Law's specificity is its virtue.

Second, legal practice is a constructive process. Practice is a process of building, and nomological legality is built legality.

As understood within practice, the dispensation of law-like legality is a state of affairs that may be achieved only by dint of an effort of active construction. Legality is a contrived situation, something made, fashioned, brought into being. Intent pursuit is necessary to its achievement, pursuit within a practice dedicated to the unremitting making of law-like law and decision.

In short, according to the self-understanding of nomological pursuit, law's rational perfection is the product only of legal practice. Law-like law is fashioned by legality's own processes within the realm of law. Law must rely on its own resources. All other argumentative processes in other intellectual spheres are by themselves insufficient to develop and sustain the sought nomological conditions. Law-like legality, creature of legal discourse, does not arise as the by-product of other discursive undertakings having other canons, strictures, aims.

Modern Liberal Law

Now the foregoing needs to be put in a larger perspective. We have been listening to the voice of a particular practice's self-understanding. And the self-advertisements of law-like law – propositions about law's nature embraced inside liberal practice – should not be mistaken for universal truths.

Nomological enterprise may present itself as the one way to law's fulfillment, and its motto that law should be law-like may seem a truism, but still such practice, seen from outside, is just one way of doing and understanding law.

The object of the present study is to investigate the unfolding logic of nomological commitment, so attention will be kept on law-like law throughout. But it should be borne in mind that legal activity guided by nomological commitment is hardly inevitable. However familiar and seemingly definitional the guiding conception may be, it remains but one conceivable starting point for practical formation of law. There are many other kinds of legality. Other starting points lead to practices organized by different canons of judgment, or to ways of doing law that do not fit the pattern of a self-consciously bounded practice at all.

Two broad labels, appropriately attached to nomological pursuit, help to locate the sort of thing it is. The nomological idea of law is, first, a liberal conception, and second, a modern conception of law.

Because of the intimate connection between nomological law and liberty, the nomological commitment and its practice may properly be labelled liberal. Law-like legality is liberal in substance. Liberality lies in the service to freedom provided by law-like entitlement and justice. The nexus between liberty and legality – a dimension of polity and a type of law – will be examined a little later on.

Because of its identification of law with a specially differentiated effort of production, the nomological conception may aptly be called modern. Nomological legality is modern in process. Modernity lies in the two key aspects of practice's self-conception that have just been discussed. The nomological idea of legal pursuit is modern in that it affirms the differentiated and the productive character of legal activity – law's particularity and law's artefactuality.

Law-like law is a particular pursuit. In the self-image of practice, legal enterprise is specialized, distinctive. Law's guiding commitment is, in a way, circular: it draws a circle around law.[7]

And law-like law is an artefact. Legality is devised, manufactured, achieved. Seen from the standpoint of practice, law's law-like nature is the artefact of a specific project and no other.

---

[7] On the differentiated character of modern legal activity, see "The Categories of Legal Thought" in Weber (1925), p. 657 ("the peculiarly professional, legalistic, and abstract approach to law in the modern sense" leads to development of "definitely fixed legal concepts in the form of highly abstract rules"); Habermas (1979), p. 158 (law in "the modern age" undertakes "conflict regulation from the point of view of a strict separation of legality and morality"; law is "general, formal, and rationalized"); Luhmann (1982), pp. 122–123 ("in modern legal systems … special importance is conceded to organizations where legal questions are handled professionally, uninterruptedly, and … by means of a division of labor"). See also Hart (1961), pp. 91–94, 113 (in a "developed" legal system, "rules of adjudication" constitute an "agency specially empowered" to decide legal matters, and "rules of recognition specifying the criteria of legal validity" are accepted by officials of the system).

This self-conception is a modern understanding of law's character. The notion that law is a product of human manufacture, and is produced within institutionally differentiated processes, is, generally speaking, a modern view of law. So nomological legality is properly characterized as a modern legal formation. What we are investigating, then, is legal pursuit of the modern liberal type – modern liberal practice of legal argument.

4

Pursuit of the Rule of Law

We have seen how liberal legal practice is formed. As we know, the great aspiration of law in liberal practice going forward is to realize the condition of law-like legality. In the operation of liberal practice, a vital question arises: what kind of legal argument – what sort of legal reasoning leading to judgment – is needed in order to realize legality? What are proper legal grounds? What is proper argumentation? Practitioners in quest of legality need to know. What kind of reasoning based on law arises within a legal practice in quest of legality?

Another name for the sought condition of law-like – liberal – legality is the rule of law. That is, the rule of law is another name for the legal dispensation, governance of law in life, prized by political commitment that prizes liberty. So another way of asking the vital question is this: what sort of reasoning based on law is necessary in order to achieve the rule of law?

There is a well-known tradition in thought about law which gives a definite answer to this question. The answer given is that the rule of law is secured by one kind of law and associated reasoning, and only that kind. According to this tradition, the vitally important kind of law is formal legal prescription. Formal means nonmoral. Formal laws are rules that exist as law as a matter of fact. Meaning of a formal rule is knowable without the conduct of a moral inquiry. The kind of reasoning needed in order to sustain the rule of law is argument based on laws stated as formal – nonmoral – rules.

A major figure within the formality-affirming tradition is Max Weber, the German sociologist, author of an influential social theory of law. According to Weber, a fundamental distinction among kinds of legal order is the division between formal justice and substantive justice. "Formal" reasoning, for Weber, happens in legal discourse sharply differentiated from moral and political argument outside law. "Substantive" judgment, by contrast, appeals to considerations of practical morality which are not specifically legal. Specifically legal rationality is displayed by formal law alone. The tradition that affirms the vital importance of law's formality is, we may say, Weberian.

The Weberian assumption that formal law is paramount becomes, in the hands of other theorists, the assertion that the rule of law, the aim of liberal legal enterprise, is realized by formal – and only by formal – law. The great aspiration of liberal political commitment, to achieve the rule of law, becomes the quest for formal law. Quest for formality is rejection of moral argument in law. It is understood that nonformal law – law governed by practical moral aims – defeats the rule of law. In discussion below, we will consider this identification of the rule of law with formality exclusively in two renditions, following Weber.

The identification of the rule of law with formality – and only formality – is a mistake, according to analysis of this book. Our consideration of the Weberian tradition will show that, in its understanding of the rule of law, it is half-right. Yes, formal law is a way of realizing the rule of law. But it is a mistake to say that, when law is not formal, the rule of law is in abeyance. The Weberian tradition is wrong when it says that nonformal argument, by its nature, defeats legal rationality and the rule of law. It is instructive to see how and why it is wrong about that.

4.1 FORMAL AND SUBSTANTIVE JUSTICE

Max Weber's legal sociology, formulated early in the twentieth century, has been widely influential.[1] Weber's delineation of contrasting types of law, based on study of many historical legal orders, is perhaps his best-known contribution to legal thought. The key to the typology is its definition of formal law. Weber's characterization of formality in law – formal grounds, reasoning, judgment, justice – is very helpful.

The basic distinction of the Weberian typology is the separation between formal law on the one hand, and substantive justice on the other hand. There are two kinds of law and justice, formal and substantive. Formal law is legal prescription divorced from morality. For Weber, law is either formal or nonformal; nonformal law aims at substantive justice, while formal law does not; substantive justice is the working out of moral postulates. Formal argument, which doesn't try to achieve substantive justice, is specifically legal. It is detached from practical moral discussion going on beyond law.

Formal justice makes use of established rules as grounds of judgment. "[F]ormalistic" legal reasoning maintains the "separation of law from ethics." Law is developed by "a strictly professional legal logic," which leads to "the self-contained and specialized 'juridical' treatment of legal questions." A formal rule is a general precept, applicable to indefinitely many concrete states of affairs. The "abstract propositions" of formal law are brought into systematic interrelation by "logically consistent formal legal thinking." For Weber, statement of law as formal rules, plus alignment of the rules as parts of a system, produces the "specifically modern form" of legal development.[2]

---

[1] See generally Weber, *Economy and Society*, vol. 2 (1925). Hereafter, in this chapter, *Economy and Society*, vol. 2, is cited as ES2.
[2] The seven quotes in this paragraph come, in sequence, from ES2, pp. 657, 810, 885, 810, 885, 885, 656.

By contrast, law in quest of substantive justice makes use of moral precepts as grounds of judgment. Substantive reasoning in law invokes "ethical imperatives, utilitarian and other expediential rules, and political maxims." Argument inside law based on such premises is not sharply distinct from practical moral discussion conducted outside the legal system. According to Weber, the law of theocratic regimes and traditional monarchies is "substantive in character." Also, substantive justice in law is demanded by champions of "propertyless masses" seeking to "equalize . . . economic and social life-opportunities."[3]

Weber's distinction between formal prescription and substantive prescription is not just a clarifying discrimination between alternative types. The line of division is a battle line. Formal law and substantive justice are at war. Each term of the distinction negates the other. According to Weber, pursuit of substantive justice undermines formal law; sticking to formal law defeats substantive justice.

There is a fundamental opposition between "an abstract formalism of legal certainty" on the one hand, and on the other hand, "desire to realize substantive goals." For Weber, the "conflict between the formal and the substantive principles of justice" is both "inevitable" and "insoluble." ". . . [F]ormal justice, due to its necessarily abstract character, infringes upon the ideals of substantive justice." "[T]he system of formal justice . . . must time and again produce consequences which are contrary to the substantive postulates of religious ethics or of political expediency."[4]

By its nature, formal law in operation constantly thwarts achievement of substantive goals for society. But at the same time, also by nature, it succeeds in bringing about a valuable state of affairs in the world, legality in life.

Weber calls attention to formal law's service in securing two vital conditions of legality in life. First is legal justice, equal treatment under general laws: "'Equality before the law' and the demand for legal guarantees against arbitrariness demand a formal and rational 'objectivity' . . ." Second is legal entitlement, dependence on law, not on the will of the powerful: "Formal justice is thus repugnant to all authoritarian powers . . . because it diminishes the dependency of the individual upon the grace and power of the authorities."[5]

Legal Disaster

Franz Neumann, Marxist legal and political thinker, left his native Germany when the National Socialists came to power, and observed legal developments under the Nazi tyranny from afar. In 1944, almost a quarter-century after Weber's death in 1920, Neumann put forward a diagnosis of the disaster that befell law in Nazi Germany.[6]

---

[3]   The four quotes of this paragraph are from ES2, pp. 657, 810, 980, 980.
[4]   The seven quotes in this paragraph come, in sequence, from ES2, pp. 811, 811, 893, 811, 893, 813, 812.
[5]   The two quotes in sequence are from ES2, pp. 979 and 812.
[6]   See Neumann, *Behemoth: The Structure and Practice of National Socialism, 1933–1944* (2nd edn. with appendix, 1944).

At the center of his analysis is Weber's distinction between formal law and moral reasoning. For Neumann, the collapse of formal law is at the root of legal disaster.

In his study of law in the courts of the German dictatorship, Neumann notes some continuities. The courts remain open. Many, many cases are decided according to established rules. Law in myriad routine applications exists. But commitment to "the rule of law" – governance of law in life, as a bulwark of liberty – is altogether missing. "National Socialism completely destroys the generality of the law ..." "Nothing is left of the principle of *nulla poena sine lege* ... (no punishment without a law ...)."[7]

For Neumann, the most important component of the rule of law is law's generality, "the general character of law." Generally operating laws, applied to classes of situations, establish "legal equality." General laws able to support consistent decision are a necessary condition of liberty. "Voltaire's statement that freedom means dependence on nothing save law has meaning only if the law is general in character."[8]

Law's generality in the service of equal treatment, the aspect of the rule of law emphasized by Neumann, is the condition of law called, in the vocabulary of this book, legal justice – which is conferred when like cases are judged alike under general laws, and is denied when cases are understood to arise in incomparable circumstances and are judged in isolation from one another.

For Neumann, the rule of law requires that laws be formulated as nonmoral rules. It is secured by "the restraint of predictable rules." Neumann distinguishes two kinds of prescription which might be used in law: formal rules on the one hand, and moral precepts on the other hand. Formal – nonmoral – rules, not moral precepts, are "true legal norms." Law's generality depends on "the formal rationality of law."[9]

Neumann gives an example of a moral precept found in Nazi law. It says that an act "which is deserving of punishment according to ... healthy racial feeling shall be punished." This precept is not a general rule able to support consistent decision. There is "no agreement in contemporary society" about what healthy racial feeling requires. Despite its general formulation, the precept is "only a shell covering individual measures."[10]

At the heart of the disaster of Nazi law is the destruction of law's generality in favor of individual measures. An individual measure is a legal decision based on assessment of the full particularity of a concrete case in its unique context – an ungeneralizable judgment. "Absolute denial of the generality of law is the central point in National Socialist legal theory ... There are no two people and no two cases in which the same rule applies."

---

[7] The three quotations in this paragraph are from Neumann (1944), pp. 442, 447, 454.

[8] The three quotes in this paragraph come in sequence from Neumann (1944), pp. 441, 452, 444.

[9] The three quotes in this paragraph come from Neumann (1944), pp. 453, 446, 446.

[10] Quotes of the paragraph are all from Neumann (1944), p. 442.

Take the example of theft. Traditional criminal law defines a burglar both by his acts and by the intent. [National Socialist legal thought] defines him by his personality. A burglar is one who is a burglar 'in essence.' The judge must decide by intuition whether to convict or not. There could be no more complete negation of the rationality of law ...

In the terminology of the present study, resort to individual measures is failed legality, the absence of law-like judgment.[11]

Descent of law into imposition of individual measures happens when the "dividing line between law and morality is destroyed." Recourse to morality by the Nazi legal system is, for Neumann, the inevitable cause of disintegration of law. "[E]very act of the judiciary is invested with the halo of morality." Legal deciders are told to "deal with each specific case as you think fit." The supposedly moral judges use "extra-legal values" as grounds of decision. The upshot is not governance of law but "arbitrary decisionism."[12]

Neumann acknowledges that the general formal law, the opposite of moral prescription, does itself have an ethical function. "Paradoxically ... this ethical function lies in the rigid divorce of legality from morality." The rule of law in support of freedom is achievable only by avoiding moral judgment and sticking to the rules. Looking forward to restoration of the liberal rule of law, Neumann declares: "The lasting achievement of liberalism is that it freed legal judgments from moral evaluations."[13]

The Rule of Law and Formal Reasoning

In his commentary[14] on what he calls the "liberal" way[15] of doing law, Roberto Unger, writing some thirty years after Neumann's dissection of the evils of Nazi law, acknowledges that two modes of law and argument are widely practiced in the courts of the "Western" democracies.[16] The two modes of law are formal reasoning on the one hand, and, in sharp contrast, nonformal argument and judgment.

Formal argument is appeal to existing legal rules. Formal justice, Unger says, lies in "the uniform application of general rules." "Legal reasoning is formalistic

---

[11]   Quotes in the paragraph, and indented, are from Neumann (1944), pp. 452, 453.
[12]   The five quotes in this paragraph are from Neumann (1944), pp. 454, 454, 453, 446, 453.
[13]   Quotes in this paragraph are from Neumann (1944), p. 443.
[14]   See Roberto M. Unger, *Knowledge and Politics* (Unger, 1975); Unger, *Law in Modern Society* (Unger, 1976). Hereafter, in this chapter, *Knowledge and Politics* is cited as K&P; *Law in Modern Society* is cited as LMS.
       In later writings, Unger drops the Weberian distinction between formal law on the one hand and nonformal law on the other hand. Unger continues to acknowledge that there are two modes of legal argument: rule-based argument and argument appealing to practical moral principles, policies, and purposes. But he comes to call both of these modes "formal." Apparently, the term "formal" for Unger comes to refer to any sort of argument which is, in the vocabulary of this book, "law-like." See Unger (1983), pp. 564–565.
[15]   See K&P, p. 63; LMS, p. 200.   [16]   LMS, p. 192.

when the mere invocation of rules and the deduction of conclusions from them is believed sufficient for . . . legal choice." In formal decision-making, the reasons for judgments "under rules" are different from "the justification for the rules them-selves." The reason for decision under a rule is formal; it is simply that the rule, by its terms, applies. The reason for the rule itself – a lawmaking reason – is nonformal.[17]

Nonformal argument is appeal to practical moral principles, policies, and purposes of law. In contrast to "formalistic legal reasoning," Unger speaks of "purposive" or "policy-oriented" legal argument in which rules are "interpreted in terms of ideals." "Legal reasoning . . . is purposive when the decision about how to apply a rule depends on a judgment of how . . . to achieve the purposes ascribed to the rule."[18]

According to Unger, one of the two kinds of law and legal reasoning subserves the great ideal of the rule of law. This is formal law and reasoning. The other kind does not. The rule of law requires formal rules in law. It is disserved by reasoning appealing to practical moral aims. From the standpoint of commitment to the rule of law, nonformal argument, while it abounds in modern law, is under a cloud. Preeminence of nonformal reasoning in law leads to "disintegration of the rule of law."[19]

For Unger, the rule of law requires that law be "general and autonomous." Generality of law establishes "the formal equality of the citizens" and protects citizens from "the arbitrary tutelage of government." Autonomy of law exists when law's "rules are applied by specialized institutions" and when "legal reasoning has a method . . . to differentiate it . . . from moral, political, and economic discourse." Together generality and autonomy require a specific arrangement of the law-related institutions of the state. "Administration must be separated from legislation . . . ; adjudication must be distinguished from administration . . . These two contrasts represent the core of the rule of law ideal."[20]

A reason for the affinity seen by Unger between formal reasoning in law and the rule of law in society is that both phenomena are constituted by rules. Formal reasoning in law, by definition, is a rule-governed activity. And the institutional order of the rule of law, at the center of which is a state defined by general laws, is, likewise, rule-constituted.

According to Unger, in modern times, two developments running in parallel undermine both the rule of law in society and the preeminence of rules within law. First, the state increasingly undertakes the purposeful ordering and reordering of social life. "[T]he state becomes involved in the tasks of overt redistribution, regula-tion, and planning . . ." Second, in tandem with changes in the state's projects, law becomes more and more nonformal. The enlarged undertakings of the state

---

[17] The first two quotations in this paragraph are from LMS, p. 194. The last two quoted phrases are from K&P, p. 89.
[18] Quotations of the paragraph are from LMS, pp. 194, 195.   [19] LMS, p. 192.
[20] The six quotes in the paragraph come in sequence from LMS, pp. 52, 54, 54, 53, 53, 54.

"influence the legal order" by fostering "the turn from formalistic to purposive or policy-oriented styles of legal reasoning."[21]

The net effect of the changes in the state and the changes in law is to undermine "the generality and autonomy of law." "The cumulative impact ... is to encourage the dissolution of the rule of law ..." Formal rules are in eclipse in law; the rule of law is in eclipse in life.[22]

Nonformal Law

There are two basic modes of law and legal argument regularly conducted in legal practice. One mode is the formal kind of law and reasoning affirmed by Weber, Neumann, and Unger: rules and rule-based reasoning. The other mode is nonformal. Nonformal argument in law uses practical moral considerations as grounds of legal judgment. Unger acknowledges that nonformal argumentation is routinely undertaken in modern law. The question is whether this sort of law and argument comports with the rule of law.

Nonformal argument in liberal legal practice is appeal to practical moral aims that underlie law's rules. Moral aims that underlie law's rules are legal ideals. These are precepts that say what law ought ideally to bring about, used to guide and shape formal law. Legal ideals are practical moral purposes of law, principles embodied in formal rules, policy objectives served by the rules.

The ideal aims of law fit and justify law's existing formal norms. The principle behind a legal rule fits and justifies the rule; so does a policy served by a rule, or the purpose of a rule. An ideal aim fits a rule when the two are in prescriptive accord – when what the ideal says ought to be is in accord with what the rule prescribes. An ideal that fits serves to justify. It is a good practical reason for the rule it fits, the rule's rationale.

Consider, for example, the modest ideal aim served by a workaday legal rule.[23] A rule of law says that it is prohibited to bring a vehicle into the public park. The purpose of the rule – the policy it serves – is, let us say, to maintain peace and quiet in the park. The policy aim behind the rule – peace and quiet – runs in line with the no-vehicles rule, and provides the rationale for the rule. It fits and justifies the rule.

Here is another example of a legal ideal, not so modest. Basic rules of contract law, in a nutshell, say: an offer of terms of agreement, followed by acceptance of the terms, results in a binding contract. A principle of contract law says: freely willed

---

[21] The three quotes in this paragraph come from LMS, pp. 193, 193, 194.

[22] The two quotes in this paragraph come from LMS, p. 200.

[23] A hypothetical rule barring vehicles from coming into the park was used as an example by H. L. A. Hart in his article, "Positivism and the Separation of Law and Morals" (Hart 1958, p. 607). Lon Fuller discussed this hypothetical rule in his reply to Hart (Fuller 1958, pp. 662–663). Later, Hart returned to the matter (Hart 1961, p. 123), and Fuller also revisited vehicles in the park (Fuller 1968, pp. 57–59).

obligation ought to be honored. This principle – in Latin, *pacta sunt servanda* – is a practical moral imperative. The principle is in harmony with the rule that says an offer followed by acceptance results in a contract, and it gives a good reason for the rule. It fits and justifies.

Ideals that fit and justify law-like rules support the rules in law-like operation. Ideals which are formulated in such a way that they serve to support rules in law-like operation are themselves law-like in form and operation.

Mistaken Identification

It is a mistake to identify the rule of law with formality and only with formality. As we have seen, identification of the rule of law with formal law exclusively arises within the Weberian tradition of thought about law. We may call this mistaken identification the Weberian mistake.

To be sure, Weber's distinction between formal and nonformal ways of doing law is very helpful. His definition of formality, which opposes formal argument to moral argument, is pretty fundamental. But Weber puts nonformal – ideal – argument under a cloud. He suggests that ideal argument leading to judgment in law, by nature, is not law-like – not regular, consistent, generalizable. This disparagement is a mistake. Franz Neumann and Roberto Unger, following Max Weber, make the same error, albeit in different ways.

Weber is wrong about nonformal – moral – assertion in law. Weber thinks that nonformal considerations necessarily subvert formal rules. But ideal considerations are not, by nature, anti-formal. To the contrary. Inside nomological practice, law's ideal aims and law's rules are not at war. In nomological practice, the ideal aims invoked in legal argument are formed to fit and justify the rules. The justifying ideals uphold the rules. In prescriptive accord, the ideals and the rules work together.

Neumann is wrong about the lesson to be learned by studying Nazi law. The evils of Nazi law don't show that moral argument in law necessarily defeats the rule of law. What they show is that moral argument within a legal practice that does not aspire to attain the rule of law will not achieve law-like disposition. And that's hardly news. Nazi law abhors the regimen of the rule of law. How ideals are formed in such a practice is a far cry from what happens in liberal law.

Finally, Unger is wrong about what the rule of law requires. He defines the rule of law narrowly. He says the rule of law requires a specific institutional order. He doesn't go deeper to articulate, in general terms, how people are to be treated by law within any society in which the rule of law exists. Narrow understanding of the rule of law misconceives the commitment of liberal legal practice. It fails to capture the full sweep of the conception of legality which, entrenched in practice, forms its aspiration, defines its projects, and sets its pursuits in motion.

4.2 OUR VOCABULARY

Going forward, our task is to formulate the aspiration of liberal practice with care, and then to work out what sort of argumentative striving might carry out that aspiration in the doing of law. We want to avoid the mistake of the Weberian tradition – its narrow understanding of the kind of law and argument that might comport with liberal commitment to the rule of law. To that end, we will revert to the standard parlance of this book which, for the most part, doesn't talk about the rule of law.

According to the vocabulary of this book, the fundamental commitment of liberal law is to bring about law-like legality. The idea of law-like legality is a highly general conception. The purpose of the jargon of the present inquiry is to capture the content of that vital conception. Going forward, we will use a vocabulary that speaks of nomological legality, the properties of law-like law, and the sought conditions of entitlement, justice, and rationality – rather than the rule of law.

If we consider a situation in which the rule of law is said to exist, and we focus on the basic elements of the indicated situation that define the relation of people to law, while leaving out other features that construct the specific institutional embodiment of the rule of law, we are left with the fundamental devotion of liberal legal enterprise – the idea of law-like legality. In the discussion following below, that devotion – its content, its unfolding – is our topic.[24]

Starting with the highly general conception of law-like legality, we may readily see that aspiration to realize legality gives rise to a dual impulse. It leads to pursuit of two kinds of law and argument, not one kind – formal and nonformal law alike, argument based on rules and argument based on ideals, alike law-like in nature. Also, we may see that both of the modes of law-like law, formal and ideal, are impelled to develop in the same way, as each is shaped by coherence-seeking, the quest for coherence in law.

---

[24] For a view of the institutional embodiment of the rule of law, in addition to Unger's, see Hayek, *The Road to Serfdom* (1944), pp. 72–87; Hayek, *The Constitution of Liberty* (1960), pp. 193–249. Like Weber and Unger, Friedrich Hayek also makes the mistake of equating the rule of law with formal rules. See Hayek (1944), pp. 72–73.

5

Aspiration and Impulse

From now on we should take for granted that the enterprise we are studying has all of the characteristics of a legal practice emphasized in the analysis of the chapter before last. The object of our inquiry is an instituted discourse of liberal law.

A liberal practice of law is, we imagine, a continuous concentration of argumentative endeavor, legal assertion and legal resolution going on in social life, controlled by a constant objective. The inner aim of practice is the aspiration to realize the conception of law-like law. Legal practitioners are directed by governing canons to try to realize nomological legality, and, as we assume, they heed this directive in self-conscious pursuit.

Now we should take up the deferred task of examining nomological substance in detail. Our task is to inquire into the content, nature, and implication of nomological devotion. What is the substance of the formative ambition that drives the argumentative process of law-like law? In what precise sense is this a liberal commitment? And how does the basic idea of law-like law come to generate a set of instructions and admonitions specific enough to steer legal argument?

So far, the central idea of nomological practice has only been roughly sketched, in terms of a number of easy slogans. At various points we have noted that nomological legality has to do with entitlement, justice, and rationality, and that such legality is liberal because of an association with liberty. Mainly we have adverted to the end or goal of nomological striving by means of some adjectives and catch phrases. The full ambition of liberal legal argument has not yet been worked out. Both the content of the nomological conception, and its liberal character, remain undeveloped.

The aspiration to bring about and maintain the state of affairs of law-like legality is a complex commitment. The conception of law-like law itself comprises multiple interrelated elements. It is a liberal commitment in virtue of its connection to liberty when liberty is understood to be a complex normative position. That is, the complex regime of legality is required to secure a complex system of equal liberty. Both of these complexities need to be addressed, in a systematic exposition. We need to focus on the separate elements of legality, and also draw them together, and then identify the systemic aspects of liberty that demand law-like law.

Once the idea of liberal legality – the situation to be achieved – has been explicated, our job is far from done. We need to specify the practical implications of nomological adherence. The next step is to derive the complementary idea of failed legality, the situation argument fears and tries to avoid. And next, abstract governing conception must be made concrete. A bare summons to strive to achieve law-like law is hardly sufficient to inform and direct argumentative activity. The highly general idea of law-like law needs to be translated into operable procedure. In order to set argumentative practice in motion, we must establish the directional signals and warnings that guide nomological pursuit day by day.

Aspiration to bring about legality is a ramifying commitment. The commitment to law-like legality unfolds to produce an array of directives, both positive and negative. Motive commitment branches to include fear as well as aspiration, and then branches again as general impulsion takes particular forms. In the main line of development, the conception of realized legality implies a complementary conception of failed legality, and the generic aspiration to achieve law-like law points to specific modes of argument and decision. Nomological aspiration may be seen to evolve by stages in a process of specification, to the point that its broad invitation has become sufficiently concrete to organize practical pursuit.

In the four sections of the present chapter we will examine the content, character, and ramifying implication of nomological commitment. In a series of four steps we will draw out its practical meaning. Below is a brief overview of the four topics to be discussed, presented by way of main propositions to be developed.

First, the idea of law-like law in people's lives is composite. Sought legality is a compound of three separable but interdependent conditions. Triune aspiration to legality includes commitment to a kind of practical status in social life, commitment to a kind of practical treatment of persons under law, and commitment to a particular kind of reasoning in the conduct of legal judgment. Law-formed status implies the happening of law-governed treatment, and both presuppose the operation of law-like reason.

Second, law-like law is liberal because of its intimate connection to liberty conceived as a system. When equal liberty is understood to comprise multiple liberties that are secured by reciprocal duties, defined in relation to one another, and buttressed by prerequisites, then liberty requires legality. Law-like law is both the perfected form of flourishing liberty and the essential form of minimal freedom. It is the kind of law prized by a polity that prizes equal liberty of individuals and seeks to realize liberty in law. Liberal political allegiance yields embrace of rational nomological legality.

Third, nomological commitment undergoes a branching development. It ramifies to reveal a negative as well as a positive aspect, a minus as well as a plus. Thus it exhibits polarity. The animating idea of law-like law includes both the conception of a sought situation of legality realized, and the conception of an evil condition that arises when legality fails. Argument in practice is animated by fear as well as aspiration, and fear impels aversion, flight, the opposite of pursuit. Negative undertaking seeks to avoid the evil of arbitrariness, which exists absent a sufficiency of law-like reasoning. Arbitrariness exists given too little law or too many possibilities. Nomological argument fears the plenum and the void.

Fourth, the nomological commitment branches again. Affirmative undertaking to seek legality divides as it develops and looks in two directions. Positive endeavor exhibits duality. Argument in practice is committed to pursue whatever specific mode of law and reasoning may be able to achieve its governing aim. There are two such modes of nomological legality. Each mode is a type of law that possesses law-like qualities, plus an associated type of reasoning which, if carried out in practice, would sustain legality. The two approaches represent specific interpretations of the generic situation of entitlement, justice, and rational resolution. Thus aspiration to legality yields a dual impulse to pursue each of two argumentative projects. As we shall see, nomological practice strives constantly, first, to formalize law, and second, to idealize law.

I should note that all the topics just broached – definition of legality, relation to liberty, negative commitment, dual impulse – are best addressed by focusing chiefly on argument and decision by courts. The reason is that courts sit at the center of practice of law-like law, and, so far as realization of legality by legal practice is concerned, everything hinges on what happens there.

Judges in courts occupy the inner zone of the instituted discourse we are investigating. When a practice of legal argument exists in society, the courts constitute society's main agency of legal judgment and its primary arena of legal justification. Judges in courts of law are specially empowered to decide legal questions based on good and sufficient argument. Their institutional performances produce binding legal resolutions, and their discursive offerings set the direction for the whole extended discussion of law that revolves around the courts.

The judging institution at the center of the practice of legal argument is also at the center of the drama of liberal legality. However the laws are made, the moment comes when they are brought to bear on persons. The drama of legality has to do with coercive enforcement of the laws. The conception of law-like legality speaks to a situation in which the decisions of legal judges are backed by the force of the collectivity. Legality, when all is said and done, is the mediation of power. It depends on the success of law-like argument yielding legal resolution in cases brought to judgment.

When nomological argument by judges succeeds, exercise of coercive authority over persons by courts is fully formed by law. Then legal judges are able to transmute raw power into law-like reason, and subjection to judgment is subjection to the law. But when nomological argument fails, yet decision ensues, coercive power over persons is unmediated by law-like law. Then power remains power, and decision is – by the lights of legality – sheer imposition.

So the hopes and trepidations of pursuit of legality focus their attention on the forum of legal judgment. Here is where we should look to find out what we need to know about the fundamentals of liberal practice: what's sought, what serves liberty, what's feared, what argumentative impulses arise.

5.1 NOMOLOGICAL LEGALITY

At its simplest, the nomological conception of law puts forward a prescription about the form of legal pronouncements. The prescription is that the laws should have law-like qualities. Laws should be formulated as general propositions, statable precepts accessible to common reason, consistent with one another in their joint operation, together the sufficient basis for rational resolution of legal contest.

In a word, the laws should be law-like. This simple slogan may seem to suggest that law's excellence lies in its existence, or that the laws must be law-like for otherwise they would not be laws. The nomological prescription for law, while not in terms a definition, seems oddly circular.

But the list of law-like qualities required by the nomological conception is not meant to be an enumeration of defining properties of laws, such as might be compiled by the now forgotten science of nomology. Law in liberal practice aims to be law-like not because of any sort of definitional compulsion, nor because of some esthetic sense that in the nature of things it is fitting or meet for law to be like law. Instead nomological commitment in the legal realm fastens on basic qualities of law-like form for entirely substantive reasons. The motive of the commitment is quite practical.

The laws should be law-like in order to bring about a situation of legality. Law-like form is for the sake of the nomological status and treatment of persons. Nomological status is entitlement under law, which exists when standing general law alone is the basis for certain valued positions of persons in social life. Nomological treatment is justice under law, which exists when law-like law alone is the basis for dealing with persons subject to collective imposition. Such entitlement and such justice depend on the operation of law-like reason, or nomological rationality. So the point of the slogan that laws should be law-like is given by the formula for legality – entitlement, justice, and rationality – already incanted many times in these pages.

Nomological legality has three components. The three conditions that make it up are legal entitlement, legal justice, and legal rationality. Law-like legality is a situation that exists when the law does realize all three conditions.

In the present section, we will look at the three constituents of legality seriatim, though in fact they implicate one another. The first requires the second, and each of the first two implies the third. So, strictly speaking, the full meaning of none will have been indicated until all have been presented. But we will take them one by one.

Law-Formed Entitlement

Legal entitlement is the first element of an achieved situation of legality. For nomological legality to come into being, standing general laws must be able to sustain the entitlements of persons. And everyone must be significantly entitled by law.

Legal entitlement is a law-formed position with respect to something valued. Entitlement by law to do or seek or receive or protect something is a sort of status in the social world, a dependence just on law.

A simple image of the context of entitlement is the image of many people, undertaking projects and interacting with one another, in social life within a polity. Everyone has some capabilities and resources that are put to use in pursuit of desired associations and sought ends. Each faces the possibility that the others may withhold needed support. The others may diminish the one's holdings and chances, while advancing their own aims or those of the collectivity. Now suppose some particular person is, in some important respect, assured of favorable action by everyone else. The person is in the desirable position of being able to protect an important acquisition or involvement or prospect from dominating interference by others. This beneficial position could arise in a number of ways. For example, it could come about because the favored person happens to be the beneficiary of power, that is, happens to be the recipient of favorable treatment by officials who presently command the power of the collectivity. Or it might come about because legal entitlement exists.

Legal entitlement is secured in social life when many valued positions of persons depend just on the meaning of the standing laws, not on power unmediated by law, the grace or favor of the authorities. It occurs when standing laws contain general propositions whose meaning, accessible to shared rational capacity, is alone sufficient to constitute advantageous holdings and options for people. Law-constituted positions are not dependent on somebody's say-so, fiat, or will.[1] Entitlement is

---

[1] Two great maxims of legal entitlement posit opposition between "law" on the one hand and "man" or "men" on the other hand. In the rhetoric of advocacy of the rule of law in the polity, the terminology "man" or "men" refers to an agency of arbitrary – despotic – judgment. So understood, the slogans say that, when the laws rule, a member of the polity is not dependent on the lawless will of the powerful.

The first maxim declares, "not under man but under God and the law" (*non sub homine sed sub Deo et lege*). Edward Coke in 1607 invoked this expression in a speech objecting to King James I's pretension to be the voice of law, to the King's displeasure; Coke cited Henri de Bracton (c. 1250) as the maxim's author (Coke 1607, p. 282).

The second maxim endorses "government of laws not men." This characterization appears in a provision, written by John Adams and adopted in 1780, of the Constitution of Massachusetts, which requires separation of powers of the branches of government "to the end it may be a government of laws and not men." See the current Mass. Const., Part the First, Art. XXX (Adams 1780).

John Locke explicates the sense of slogans contrasting rule by law and rule by men. "[F]reedom of men under government is to have a standing rule to live by, common to every one of that society, and made by the legislative power erected in it; a liberty to follow my own will in all things, where the rule prescribes not; and not to be subject to the inconstant, uncertain, unknown, arbitrary will of another man …" (Locke 1689, ch. IV, s. 22, p. 13).

bestowal by law. To invoke one's legal entitlement is to attempt a kind of rational compulsion of social consequence. To the extent of one's entitlement, the element of personal sway over one by others, or one's subjection to personality, shrinks to a vanishing point.

An obvious precondition of legal entitlement is the existence of a body of standing laws whose prescriptions constitute valued positions for persons. Laws governing the mutual dealings of people and their relations to the collectivity must be extant. Extant laws preexist judgments under them. The legal grounds that sustain an asserted entitlement must be available prior to the assertion. Entitlements are positions formed by generally applicable legal norms that authorize, require, and prohibit identified conduct. The content of legal entitlement must be discoverable by an inquiry that asks what is the law in force around here.

In a situation of legality, everyone is entitled to protection against lawless physical coercion by the governing officials. This core entitlement will be discussed later on as an aspect of liberty. Beyond that, everyone is entitled to legal justice, to be discussed in a moment. For justice is an aspect of law-like entitlement. Beyond that, everyone is entitled to whatever the standing laws provide. The most general entitlement is the diffuse right to legal results, whatever they are, just as such. A regime of legal entitlement need not try to assign title to everything good about life, and may exist though this or that good thing is unprotected. Still it cannot exist unless a number of facilities and expectancies significant to humans are formed just by general law. A social life of entitlement is a significantly legalized social world.

Above all, in order for entitlement to exist, laws and legal judgments must have a certain character. Laws must be commonly intelligible. Their meaning, available to common human intellect, must be fully communicable. Legal directives must be knowable and statable apart from reference to the particular volition of the current authorities. In legal judgment honoring entitlement, law's meaning is grasped by exercise of common reason, and applied to events of common experience. This is not to say that systematic study is unnecessary in order to learn law well, but rather that the faculties put to work in such study, and in application of law, are common ones.[2] Knowledge of law must be accessible to shared rational capacity. Legal judgment is not a matter for special insight or uncommon wisdom, had by a gifted few. It is not the preserve of ineffable prudence or sense or discernment. In a regime of entitlement, no one can be presumed to possess exceptional faculties of

---

[2] In 1607, Edward Coke told the King that legal judgment calls for special knowledge. "... [T]hen the King said, that he thought the law was founded upon reason, and that he and others had reason, as well as the Judges: to which it was answered by me, that true it was, that God had endowed his Majesty with excellent science, and great endowments of nature; but His Majesty was not learned in the laws of his realm of England, and causes which concern the life, or inheritance, or goods, or fortunes of his subjects, are not to be decided by natural reason but by the artificial reason and judgment of law, which law is an act which requires long study and experience, before that a man can attain to the cognizance of it ..." Colloquy between Edward Coke and King James I (Coke 1607, p. 282).

heightened legal understanding. Legal grounds are common ground. Legal judgment is nomistic, not gnostic.

In a world where everyone always complies with law, entitlement might be fully honored without convening courts. But when law-breaking is anticipated, and provision is made for enforcement of law by judges who render coercive decisions, then entitlement requires a specific sort of judging. The idea of a judging tribunal that exists to enforce entitlement is the idea of a completely legal agency. This is the pure conception of a court of law. The sole duty of a judge in such a court is fidelity to law. Decisions of the disposing court are judgments fully formed by law. Reasons for decisions are laws. The job of judging authority is to pronounce whatever the standing laws prescribe. Courts of justice are the forum of entitlement, epicenter of legality.

Law-Like Justice

Legal justice is the second component of the dispensation of legality. For nomological legality to exist, laws and judgments under them must be able to confer law-like justice. And everyone must be accorded justice under law.

Legal justice has to do with the handling of particular contests by resolving legal judges. It is a way of treating or acting upon persons in the disposition of cases, a fully law-constituted way.

A simple image of the context of legal justice is the image of a mass of cases that have come to courts of law for decision. Cases involve contested application of the laws in particular circumstances. A discrete case is carved out of the innumerable relations of life when the courts take up the question of the legal meaning of a designated state of affairs. Cases are subject to coercive resolution. Each contest culminates in judgment, an exercise of the decisional authority of the judging officials, one way or another. People involved in these controversies receive favorable or unfavorable treatment at the hands of collective authority. The whole mass of past and current cases is a continuously growing aggregation. When legal justice exists, a particular pattern may be seen – and shown – to link all the cases.

Legal justice is conferred when the treatment anyone receives at the hands of judging authority is the same as that received in a recognizable class of cases. Handling of any case is accountable to its falling within a discernible class, all of whose members share certain qualities. Differential handling of any two cases is accountable to their falling within different classes, whose common features are mutually exclusive. In a series of judgments honoring legal justice, each resolution is in virtue of general qualities, and treatment is the same for all who share the same characteristics. Everyone receives like treatment. This is the defining precept of legal justice: like cases should be judged alike.[3]

---

[3] According to John Rawls, "The rule of law ... implies the precept that similar cases be treated similarly ... [T]he criteria of similarity are given by the legal rules themselves ..." "This impartial and consistent administration of laws and institutions, whatever their substantive principles, we may

The pattern of like judgment, observable in a situation of legal justice, is specifically the law's pattern. That is, the set of propositions that fully captures the pattern of the cases is equivalent to a statement of the law. Shared characteristics are the ones picked out by law. The classes of cases are the law's categories. Differentiations are those of the law. So like treatment is the same thing as completely law-formed treatment.

Justice lies in demonstrable relationship of judgment to law. The requirement of justice says that all particular impositions by the judging authorities must line up in a configuration wholly accountable to the general terms of law. It is silent about the content of legal materials. Legal justice is indeed a very legal sort of justice.[4] Like judgment means that cases alike within the terms of the laws are judged alike, whatever those terms may be. Properties of justice are evenhandedness, consistency, regularity.

Legal justice requires that laws have a form sufficient to sustain regular judgment. Laws must be generalized directives able to yield consistent resolution. Generality of law and regularity of decision go together. Laws should be formulated as prescriptions addressing generally defined categories of persons, actions, circumstances. Each law, and all laws in their joint application, should operate so that multiple particular judgments under them are consistent with one another.[5] Generally applicable laws are the grounds and the tests of regular resolution. They supply the criteria of alikeness and unlikeness, sameness and distinction, that sort the cases.

Justice requires that persons and situations subject to judgment be conceived in a certain way. When justice is honored, law's view of the world to be judged is abridged, filtered, abstracted. Only so much of any case is to be considered as is necessary to fix its character in terms of the law's general precepts. Not everything

---

call formal justice." "Formal justice is adherence to principle, or as some have said, obedience to system" (Rawls, *A Theory of Justice*, 1971, pp. 58, 237).

[4] John Rawls notes that, "because [the precepts of the rule of law] guarantee only the impartial and regular administration of rules, whatever these are, they are compatible with injustice." He concludes: "There is no contradiction in supposing that a slave or caste society, or one sanctioning the most arbitrary forms of discrimination, is evenly and consistently administered, although this may be unlikely" (Rawls 1971, pp. 59, 236).

Rawls is right that many practices of unjust dependency and discrimination could be conducted compatibly with the rule of law. However, there is a contradiction in thinking that a regime of slavery which gives the master unlimited dominion over a chattel slave could be so conducted. Such a regime is the very opposite of a *rechtsstaat*. The precept "no penalty without a law" means nothing when the only "law" is this: "do as I wish or suffer." On the opposition between the rule of law and slavery, see Chapter 5 note 14.

[5] See Hart and Sacks, *The Legal Process* (1958), pp. 145–148. Henry Hart and Albert Sacks discuss the argumentative task of "an official who is charged with the duty of resolving a controverted issue about the meaning of a general directive arrangement." The judging official "must elaborate the arrangement in a way which is consistent with other established applications of it." "[C]onsistency with other established applications ... is an expression of [the] pervasive principle ... that like cases should be treated alike ..." (Hart and Sacks 1958, pp. 146–147).

about a case can be relevant to decision, however complex an assessment of circumstance may be needed to establish its legal meaning. Law's categories must be determinable in the particular apart from a review of the whole concrete state of the world. Legal assessment must be structured, bounded, closed to all but a specific subset of possible considerations. Each situation is to be judged only in terms of features that are illustrative of shared qualities. A case is always a case of something, a member of a class. Persons subject to judgment are to be viewed abstractly, as entities made up of representative attributes. Like treatment is treatment as an instance. Relevant particularity is but a specimen of something general.

No case, in a regime of justice, is understood in its full specificity. No case may be regarded as a unique plenitude of features, an inexpressible totality, beyond classification. Judgment responding fully to the uniqueness of each situation, embodying a truly individual measure regardless of any other, is the antithesis of legal justice.[6] Judging that celebrates the concreteness of life, seeing each case in its incomparable context, is the singling out of people for special treatment. Justice, by contrast, is impersonal treatment. To do justice is to achieve explicable regularity. Justice requires a grasp of the general residing within the particular, in order to exhibit a rational relationship among all the cases.

Nomological Rationality

Legal rationality is the third – and pervasive – feature of the situation of legality. Legal rationality is evinced in law-like legal reasoning. Liberal legality is, in the end, a kind of rational argument, a way of setting the laws in motion as reasons that yield and justify results.

To be sure, there are many different kinds of rationality and rational activity in the many precincts of human life. Rationality in general has to do with exercise of reason. It is the quality of being rational, and something rational is something that manifests reasoning.

The context of legal rationality is the activity of legal argument. Legal argument is a type of practical reasoning. It is prescriptive, decisional, and justificatory in nature. It invokes prescriptive grounds that say what ought to be, and assembles chains of reasons that may generate decisions, and offers rationales to justify conclusions reached.

---

[6] According to Franz Neumann, in his study of Nazi law, "Absolute denial of the generality of law is the central point in National Socialist legal theory … There are no two people and no two cases in which the same rule applies. Every man and each concrete situation must be dealt with by a particular rule, or … by individual decisions" (Neumann 1944, p. 452). "In the liberal era, the general character of law is that element which alone embodies reason. The reasonableness of law … becomes … a rationality that is formal and technical, that is to say, predictable and calculable." "'When I say that the object of laws is always general,' wrote Rousseau, 'I mean that law considers subjects *en masse* and actions in the abstract, and never a particular person or action …'" (Neumann 1944, p. 441).

By legal rationality I mean specifically nomological rationality, evinced by nomological reasoning. Accordingly, rational legal argument possesses nomological qualities. It employs general, impersonal, and coherent laws as grounds for resolution of legal issues. Put another way, legal rationality is a property of the successful use of laws as law-like reasons leading to law-governed decision. To say legal argument is rational is, in effect, to say it succeeds as law-like reasoning.

Legality stands or falls depending on whether law-like legal argument succeeds or fails. The status of entitlement and the treatment of justice are products of the rational rendering of standing general laws able to support consistent disposition. Entitlement exists when legal argument is able to form valued positions of persons. Justice exists when legal argument is able to yield like judgment. In short, the nomological status and treatment of persons rest on the success of law-like reasoning. Everything comes down to rational legal argumentation.

In order to sustain legality, legal argument must do two things. First, argument must achieve rational resolution of legal controversy. This requirement is particularly a demand of entitlement. Second, argument must achieve rational connection of law's elements. This requirement is particularly a demand of justice. Rational argument is both terminable and associative, able to resolve and able to connect.

Rational Resolution

First, successful argument brings about rational resolution of legal contest. Rational resolution occurs when reasoning based on the meaning of standing law is capable of resolving legal dispute in an examined case. Rational resolution is the same thing as the determination of a specific legal entitlement by means of dispositive legal reasoning.

In order to secure entitlement, argument from generally applicable prescription must present an explicit progression of connected reasons sufficient to generate and support judgment in the particular. Sufficient argument is the exercise of rational capacity to grasp and make manifest purport and connection. Argument's starting point is apprehension of extant laws, knowable grounds that preexist decision. Its route is along a path accessible to common intellect. Its terminus is a prescribed legal result. Here legal rationality resides in argument's capacity to conclude, to dispose, and to do so through the giving of reasons that provide a justification for the conclusion reached.

Dispositive argument involves more than a purely deliberative sort of resolution. Deliberative resolution happens when a disinterested judge reflects seriously on possible grounds of judgment prior to deciding which ground and which result to affirm. But careful deliberation does not amount to sufficient argument.[7] Rational

---

[7] For H. L. A. Hart, necessary but not by themselves sufficient qualities of nomological judging are the deliberative "virtues": "impartiality and neutrality in surveying the alternatives" and "consideration for the interest of all who will be affected" (Hart 1961, p. 200). See also Rawls (1971), pp. 238–239 (precepts of "natural justice" say that "judges must be independent … and no man may judge his own case").

resolution is not just an inward matter of thinking hard and impartially. It is an outward matter of presenting impersonal argumentation able to yield legal judgment. Nomological rationality is discursive, demonstrative, not just deliberative. Legality depends on the happening of a dispositive reasoning process that can be, and is, exhibited for all to see. Legal reason must display its reasons. Argument must be able to show, step by step, that extant laws prescribe the adjudged result – that these laws, in conjoint application, sustain this entitlement.

The Imperative of Coherence

Second, successful argument achieves rational connection. To begin with, rational connection means linkage of ground and result in a single case, and in this respect it overlaps rational resolution. It also means much more: consistency of result with result for all cases, and coherence of ground with ground for the whole of the law.[8]

Legal justice requires articulable regularity of all resolutions prescribed by the laws. Each disposition must be in accord with other dispositions. Justice lies in rational connection between this case resolved by this law, and that case resolved by that law – between this case and that, and this law and that. So, sufficient argument in any one case implicates a larger coherence. Reasoning that successfully connects a particular decision with the general law links a multiplicity of arguments, past and present. The legal precept invoked to justify decision in a given case should be compatible with outcomes reached in other cases. Likewise, precepts used in the other cases should jibe with the decision in the given case. All available legal grounds must be compatible with one another, in order to be the grounds of regular treatment. Law must be a body of rationally connected reasons.

Law-like legality is a situation of prescriptive accord. This is a situation in which the general laws join together and speak in harmony. The main operative command of legality is the imperative of harmony. All prescriptive elements of law must be made to cohere. Argument must always work to build and show coherence of part with part. The imperative of coherence is a constant dynamical force driving liberal legal argument toward concatenation, interconnection, union. Nomological ratiocination views each legal precept in light of the others. Operating on extant legal materials, connective argument strives to square one item with another item, to fit things together in patterns articulable through general propositions. Nomological-connective reasoning processes seek complex unity. Successful argument builds complex legal wholes. It brings multiple legal precepts into structured relations, and displays the structures it finds.

---

[8] According to John Rawls, "[T]he precept that like decisions be given in like cases ... forces [judges] to justify the distinctions that they make between persons by reference to the relevant legal rules and principles ... This precept holds also in cases of equity, that is, when an exception is to be made when the established rule works an unexpected hardship." "The requirement of consistency holds of course for the interpretation of all rules and for justifications at all levels" (Rawls 1971, pp. 237, 238).

Coherence is at the heart of nomological rationality. The connective impulse is a general tendency of law-like legal argument, more or less definitive of the aspiration to secure liberal legality.

5.2 LIBERAL COMMITMENT

Now the question is: why should this sort of legality be called liberal?

I have asserted a number of times already that the nomological conception of law's perfected condition, which we have just reviewed, is a liberal conception. Liberal commitment, I have assumed, prizes liberties of individuals; then nomological conception is liberal since the condition of law it affirms is intimately related to human liberty. In short, pursuit of entitlement, justice, and rationality in law is liberal in the simple sense that it serves liberty.

I suspect the relationship I am asserting – the liberal affiliation of law-like legality – is rather intuitive, and I don't want to belabor the matter. But I do wish to make my contention quite explicit, and then develop it enough to indicate how close the connection is between liberty and legality. In fact, my basic claim involves two connections, two linkages, among three main terms. First is the association between liberal conviction and equal liberty, and second is the association between equal liberty and nomological legality. The first connection involves a proposed definition of liberal commitment. The second connection involves a finding of what commitment to liberty entails for law.

First, liberal political commitment is, I take it, commitment to equal liberty. A prescriptive position saying how life in a collectivity ought to be ordered deserves to be called liberal if it presses the point that liberty should be prized. Liberal allegiance is the commitment to honor and secure individual liberties in collective living, including freedoms that constitute democracy.

Second, nomological legality is – I mean to show – the kind of legality prized by a political position that prizes equal liberty. If political belief calls for equal liberty, and imagines law, then it also prescribes the law-formed status and treatment of persons. Embrace of liberty yields embrace of law-like legality. Commitment to a dimension of polity yields commitment to a type of law.

I want to take some time to develop the line of thinking summarized above, which links liberal commitment to liberty, and liberty to legality. The first linkage is readily forged, by way of apt definition. The second connection is the vital point.

There is a very tight nexus between liberty and law-like legality. This juncture is an analytical connection. It may be established by working out a good understanding – a sufficient analysis – of the idea of equal liberty well realized in society. Law-like law is both the perfected legal form of flourishing liberty, and the essential legal form of minimal freedom. Both a maximum of liberty and a minimum of liberty entail law-like legality.

I should note at the outset that focus on liberty in what follows is for the sake of showing a progression of ideas. Liberty is the mediating term in an analytical chain that runs from liberal commitment to law-like law. Emphasis on liberty should not be taken to mean that liberty is the premier political value, much less the only one. We need not share liberal commitment in order to understand it. I confess it does seem to me that liberty of the sort discussed here is very important. To me, nomological aspiration has a nobility that comes in good measure from the liberty-serving aspect of law-like law. But it remains that our rating of liberty – as opposed to our analysis – is strictly speaking beside the point.

I should also note that the relationship I mean to show between commitment to liberty and commitment to legality is basically a one-way connection. The securing of liberty requires law-like legality, in full, but the reverse is not the case. Law-like legality does not necessarily uphold any particular table of liberties. Nomological practice of law might exist in a society, and yet the law-like laws of the society may not honor this or that or the other liberty. Such a one-way nexus is enough for our purpose, which is to establish that nomological legality is rightly called liberal. The point of the present discussion is not to find out what particular laws liberal conviction would recommend. We are considering liberal commitment in order to find out what it requires so far as the general nature of law is concerned.

Commitment to Equal Liberty

Now the first connection we must consider – between liberal commitment and liberty – is, I think, quite easily made. Liberal commitment is the conviction that equal liberty of individuals should be well instituted in social life. This is my assumption. The identification of liberal commitment with the promotion of liberty seems not just reasonable, but fairly definitional. How does liberal conviction get to be worthy of its name except by prizing liberty of persons?

We will assume liberal commitment prescribes equal liberty.[9] And equal liberty comprises a number of particular liberties. Liberties are rightful positions, permitted powers and required immunities – authorizations to do things, and protections from being done to. Equal liberties are generalized positions, uniformly permitted and required, for all people within a polity. Liberal belief prescribes equal liberties of free citizens in personal, civil, and political spheres. Modern liberal prescription encompasses entitled safety from collective interferences, and entitled involvement in processes of collective self-government. It includes freedoms that constitute democracy, as well as freedoms that limit it. In this book, by liberal commitment I mean the modern sort.

---

[9] A careful formulation of the central prescription of liberal political commitment is given by John Rawls' "first principle" of justice: "Each person is to have an equal right to the most extensive total system of equal basic liberties compatible with a similar system of liberty for all" (Rawls 1971, p. 250).

The foregoing is all we have to know about the content of modern liberal commitment. We should be aware that various nonequivalent schemes of freedom may all equally be instances of such commitment. Particular liberal programs may differ with respect to the specific liberties they propose, the ranking of liberties, and many other things. Our definition of liberal allegiance circumscribes a large class of programs conducting a family quarrel. We need not enter this debate. We don't need to know more than the broad contours of liberal conviction – what the rival liberal programs have in common – in order to find out what sort of law such conviction requires. All we need assume is that liberal belief prescribes that a number of individual liberties should be systematically instituted in collective life. Then the second connection – between equal liberty and law-like legality – follows by a train of general reasoning.

The System of Liberty

Nomological legality is liberal in the specific sense that it is required to secure the system of equal liberty. When equal liberty is understood as a system of liberties, and individual freedom is seen to be a complex position formed within a system, then the realization of liberty in life requires specifically nomological legality.[10]

In order for liberty to be well realized in a polity, the multiple equal liberties prescribed for people in the polity need to be practically specified. Prescriptions that articulate available liberties must be specific enough to guide practical activity, and the several prescriptions stating different freedoms need to be coordinated with one another. Well instituted equal liberty is a complex of interrelated directives worked out as a practical system. Equal liberty by its nature is general, extensive, and constant. Well-developed liberties are at the same time complex, refined, and integrated.

Liberty is a system in virtue of three practical necessities. That is, liberty gets worked out practically when three requirements are met: when each liberty is buttressed by reciprocal obligation, when the several freedoms are mutually defined, and when preconditions of liberty are prescribed. I think these requirements of a working system of liberty – reciprocal duty, mutual definition, prescribed preconditions – are pretty self-explanatory. The basic statement of each is a truism, if not a conceptual truth.

First, if one is at liberty to do something free of constraint, others must not be at liberty to behave in certain ways. Freedoms of individuals imply the existence of duties of forbearance on the part of other actors. Certain civil and political liberties, such as rights that constitute self-government, require the prior existence of

---

[10] For John Rawls, "A rather intricate complex of rights and duties characterizes any particular liberty." "… [A]rrangement of the several liberties depends upon the totality of limitations to which they are subject, upon how they hang together …" (Rawls 1971, p. 203).

collective arrangements, secured by obligation, within which the right in question might be exercised.

Second, given multiple liberties dealing with interrelated aspects of personal and civic life, the reach of any one freedom depends in part upon how the others are formulated. Knowable liberties, well established, need to be explicitly defined – elaborated – in relation to one another. To know the full content of a freedom is to know its relative extent, its place in a scheme of liberty.

Third, actual exercise of liberty depends on conditions for secure and successful social activity. Prerequisites for effective liberty, such as the essentials of social peace, must be prescribed – specified and required – in order for liberty to be well instituted. Liberty needs to be qualified in order to achieve conditions necessary to liberty itself.

Flourishing Liberty and Law

A system of liberty, for its full support, requires the medium of law-like law. Here is the connection we seek. Nomological legality is the best way of sustaining systemic freedom by law. It is the perfected legal form of equal liberty.

When a polity is one in which liberty is to be honored, and also one in which law exists, then the laws of the polity should include laws of liberty. Laws of liberty are legal precepts that embody the system of liberties meant to be accorded. The best way of formulating laws of liberty is through legal prescriptions that are knowable, statable, general, impersonal, jointly consistent, regular in effect, applicable by reason – that is, nomological. A legalized liberty should be a legal entitlement accorded with law-like justice through rational resolution. Laws that institute the complex of liberties should be law-like in form and operation.

So intimately related are equal liberty and law-like legality that it is difficult to conceive liberty by itself, quite apart from its legal expression, other than nomologically.[11] Equal liberty by itself, prior to its inscription in legal laws, is uniform yet qualified, generalized and also systematic – already law-like.

Think of how a system of liberty might be fully articulated prior to any attempt to formulate legal laws of liberty. A few broad, uncoordinated imperatives will not suffice. A system of equal freedom is a complex of normative statuses and relations that qualify one another and together constitute collective arrangements. Precepts stating equal liberties, in law or outside law, should be general grounds for even-handed judgment of similarly situated persons. Full statement of the content of a system of liberty, in law or outside law, must strive for rational connection of the parts of the whole. In other words, the medium suitable for practical specification of

---

[11] According to John Rawls, "Liberty, as I have said, is a complex of rights and duties defined by institutions." "[B]y an institution I shall understand a public system of rules ..." "[F]ormal justice ... is implied in the very notion of a law or institution, once it is thought of as a scheme of general rules" (Rawls 1971, pp. 55, 58, 239).

liberty is law-like prescription. Law-like expression is the native language of equal liberty.

In a polity organized to support liberty fully, all laws should be law-like, not just the ones that directly state what freedoms are available. Liberties have to do with the many areas of activity of free citizens: personal, societal, and governmental spheres. The laws that institute liberties, by working out correlative duties and associated arrangements and mutual qualifications and practical preconditions, will together amount to a large and complicated mass of legal stuff. The line between these laws of liberty and other laws is none too sharp. Liberty is strengthened when laws of liberty and other related legal provisions are rationally connected, jointly coherent, compatible with one another, not inconsistent in effect.

Liberty is strengthened when other laws like its laws are rationally applicable general grounds, law-like in character. Law as such should be law-like in order to provide a basis for the secure and effective exercise of accorded freedoms.[12] Liberty is buttressed by nomological regularity in the operation of laws that define the basic structures within which activities of social life take place, and laws that constitute and limit the state, whose powers impinge on freedoms of individuals.

Laws of whatever sort by definition impinge on freedom of action, as do legal decisions backed by the force of the collectivity. Wayward exercise of the power of legal judgment may disrupt and defeat the exercise of liberties. Law-like operation of all the laws, through law-formed resolutions that sustain entitlement and justice, increases confidence about liberty. Nomological legality is the best way of developing law meant to guard and support freedom fully. In short, nomological rationality of law in general is a necessary condition for the flourishing of liberty. Law-like legality is the proper form of a regime of maximum liberty.

Minimal Liberty and Law

Nomological legality is also the essential form of minimal liberty. That is, quite apart from its service in sustaining a system of maximally realized liberty, just described, law-like legality may also be seen to provide the bare minimum of equal freedom that might exist in collective life. I want to close the present discussion with some comments on minimal freedom, in order to develop a final connection between the form of legality and the promise of liberty.

---

[12]   In A *Theory of Justice*, John Rawls says: "Now the connection of the rule of law with liberty is clear enough ... [I]f the precept of no crime without a law is violated, say by statutes being vague and imprecise, what we are at liberty to do is likewise vague and imprecise. The boundaries of our liberty are uncertain. And to the extent that this is so, liberty is restricted by a reasonable fear of its exercise" (Rawls 1971, p. 239). "The principle of legality has a firm foundation, then, in the agreement of rational persons to establish for themselves the greatest equal liberty. To be confident in the possession and exercise of these freedoms, the citizens of a well-ordered society will normally want the rule of law maintained" (Rawls 1971, pp. 239–240).

Earlier I made the point that while equal liberty requires the form of law-like legality, law-like legality does not necessarily uphold any particular table of liberties. Practice of law-like law might exist, and yet the laws in force might fail to make provision for one or another freedom. This suggests the possibility of an extreme case in which laws are law-like in form and operation but, in their content, do not confer any specific liberties upon everyone in society, and so do not foster equal liberty at all. The extreme case would be a kind of paradox: liberal legality would exist, but not liberty. Is this extreme dissociation of the two things possible?

At first glance it would seem the paradoxical state of affairs is quite possible, since what freedoms are made available by law depends on the content of the laws, not just their form. Of course, from the standpoint of nomological commitment as such, law-like legality all by itself is still a good thing. But a condition of entitlement and justice under the standing laws, whatever their content may be, is not evidently the same good thing as a situation of extensive equal liberty under law. So it would seem that the form of legality might exist apart from the substance of liberty.

On second thought, the absence of legality produces what may be thought to be the absence of freedom. As we shall see in detail in the following section, the opposite of legality is a situation of arbitrariness. Absent legality, valued positions of persons depend on the grace of the authorities. The lawless judging of someone's legal case involves the subjection of that one to the arbitrary will of another.[13] Now, a condition of dependence on say-so, or subjection to personality, strongly resembles servitude, the opposite of freedom.[14] So there is a similarity between lack of legality

[13] Franz Neumann describes lawless judging in National Socialist Germany. "[T]he Reichstag fire decree [of 1933, suspending civil liberties] does not have a single concrete element that permits one to predict ... under what conditions ... a man may be deprived of his freedom. It simply says to the Gestapo: Do what you please; deal with each specific case as you think fit. Such a rule is not law but arbitrary decisionism" (Neumann 1944, p. 453). "Nothing is left of the principle of *nulla poena sine lege, nullum crimen sine lege* (no punishment without a law and no crime without a law) ..." (Neumann 1944, p. 454).

[14] Classical liberal expressions of commitment to a regime of legality regard reliance on law – the rule of law – as deliverance from servitude. Servitude is subjection to the personality of another – dependence on another's will. The classical writers lived in a world that, in many places, upheld slavery. They knew what they were talking about.

According to Friedrich Hayek, "The Rule of Law was consciously evolved ... during the liberal age ... as the legal embodiment of freedom. As Immanuel Kant put it (and Voltaire expressed it before him in very much the same terms), 'Man is free if he needs to obey no person but solely the laws'" (Hayek 1944, pp. 81–82). The words Hayek imputes to Kant are a rather free rendition of Kantian text. His reference to Voltaire is apt. Voltaire wrote: "Liberty consists in depending upon the laws only" (Voltaire 1752, p. 230).

John Locke states connections between liberty, servitude, and law more fully. "[F]reedom is not, as we are told, a liberty for every man to do what he lists (for who could be free when every other man's humour might domineer over him?), but a liberty to dispose, and order as he lists, his person, actions, possessions ... within the allowance of those laws under which he is, and therein not to be subject to the arbitrary will of another, but freely follow his own" (Locke 1689, ch. VI. s. 57, p. 29).

See also Montesquieu (1748), bk. 26, s. 20, p. 76 ("Liberty consists principally in not being forced to do a thing, where the laws do not oblige: people are in this state only as they are governed by civil laws; and because they live under those civil laws, they are free").

and loss of liberty. Given this negative affinity, can we conclude that the positive condition of legality and the positive condition of liberty are in some sense identical?

The answer is this: in general, legality by itself is not equivalent to liberty, but in one connection these two things are the same thing. Law-like laws, in order to be law-like, need not embody all equal freedoms but one. But in one important respect the form of legality all by itself is the meaning of liberty. So it turns out that the extreme dissociation mentioned above is not quite possible.

One very basic liberty of the person comes into existence just given the existence of law-like legality, regardless of the specific content of the laws. The irreducible minimum of equal individual freedom in collective life is definable entirely in the terms of nomological form and operation. This bedrock liberty is also the hard core of legal entitlement.

Whatever the content of the laws, even if the laws do not attempt to prescribe any of the particular liberties that would be bestowed in a perfected system of liberty, nomological form by itself ensures minimal freedom if it controls collective coercion. Minimum liberty has to do with the singling out of people for physical punishment by the state.[15] Here is a most exigent situation: the direct physical coercion, bodily restraint or worse, of some individual in the name of the collectivity. Nomological legality controls collective coercion if punishment occurs only when standing laws prescribe it, and only when the laws that prescribe punishments are law-like in form and operation, and only when the basis of any instance of punishment is a judgment fully formed by law.

Nomological governance of all collective coercion constitutes a generalized position of immunity from official tyranny. When such immunity exists, no penalty may be imposed except as provided by law-like law.[16] Nobody is left at the mercy of the unmediated physical power of the authorities. Nomological control of coercion ensures the law-like status and treatment of persons in that crucial connection. Given it, everyone is entitled to justice, secured by rational resolution, with respect to the incidence of force. Everyone may occupy a valued position of dependence on law only, not on the ungoverned will of the powers that be, in order to be safe from collective force.

Entitlement to coercive regularity is the core entitlement of law-like legality and also the fundamental liberty of any regime of equal freedom. Freedom from lawless

---

[15] According to Franz Neumann, "Voltaire's statement that freedom means dependence on nothing save law has meaning only if the law is general in character. The general law establishes personal equality." "Equality before the law is merely formal or negative, to be sure, but it does contain a minimum guarantee of freedom ..." (Neumann 1944, p. 444).

[16] John Rawls says, "The precept that there is no offense without a law (*Nulla crimen sine lege*) ... demands that laws be known and expressly promulgated, that their meaning be clearly defined, that statutes be general ... and not be used as a way of harming particular individuals who may be expressly named (bills of attainder) ... and that penal laws should not be retroactive ..." (Rawls 1971, p. 238). "Knowing what things [law] penalizes ... citizens can draw up their plans accordingly. One who complies with the announced rules need never fear an infringement of his liberty" (Rawls 1971, p. 241).

physical imposition is at the heart of the liberty of the person. Even if no specific laws of liberty exist, when everyone enjoys immunity from collective coercion except by nomological judgment, minimum liberty exists. To be sure, the freedom constituted just by law-like legality in the realm of coercion is limited. But being free from terror of official violence is a personal liberty without which all other liberties are in jeopardy.

In sum, the barest assurance of equal liberty in collective living demands law-like law, as does liberty's full development. Germ and flower require the medium of nomological legality. And so, in the terminology of this book, nomological legality is liberal – liberty-serving – legality.

The aim of the book is to investigate instituted discourse of law-like law. On account of connections I have stated, such law is rightly called liberal. Nomological achievement is a liberal ambition; nomological enterprise is the liberal pursuit of legality. Liberal legal endeavor is that practice of legal argument and decision which aspires to uphold law-like legality.

5.3 FAILURE OF LEGALITY

As we have just seen, the core entitlement of law-like legality – which is the same thing as minimal liberty – is a bulwark against a great calamity, a fearful tyranny. Here is an example of a general pattern: a constituent of legality, a sought aspect of law-like law, is needed in order to ward off something bad, which appears when the good thing is in eclipse.

We have encountered this pattern before: notably in the first section of the present chapter, and also at other points, when considering the qualities and conditions that make up nomological legality. A natural way of presenting a basic element of legality – entitlement, justice, rational argument – is by means of a positive statement in association with a negative one. The positive statement characterizes a good state of affairs that pertains when the element is achieved. The negative statement describes a polar state, an evil condition, which arises when the element is absent. Explication in terms of antipodal states, happy and unhappy, comes naturally because the conception of nomological legality is itself systematically negative as well as positive. The complex conception of legality is a conception of failure as well as a conception of success.

The idea of law-like legality includes the idea of failed legality, an imagining of what happens should legality give out. The notion of an unhappy development to be avoided is built into the very definition of each of the elements of the dispensation of law-like legality. Everything positive has a negative counterpart. Each good thing is specifiable negatively: that is, in terms of something bad that the positive thing operates to exclude. So, when something sought goes missing, something feared turns up.

Absence of Legality

Entitlement is dependence on standing law, not dependence on the grace of the authorities. Justice is consistent decision, not irregular decision of cases in isolation from one another. Entitlement and justice require rational resolution and rational connection in the conduct of legal disposition.

Absent rational argument connecting general grounds and particular results, judgment is the expression of power, not law, and legality ceases. Absent legality, valued positions of persons depend on the sufferance of dominating officials. Treatment of persons subject to authority becomes erratic imposition. Assertion of law-formed status gives way to beseechment of judges' volition, and like treatment gives way to individual measures.

It follows that fear is the inseparable companion of aspiration in practice of law-like law. Aspiration to achieve legality is fear-haunted. Since each positive aspect of legality has its negative counterpart, which is understood to develop whenever the positive state is not achieved, commitment to bring about the good thing is at the same time an urgent resolve to forestall the evil development. Avidity is coupled with aversion, rejection. Thus nomological commitment exhibits polarity. It yields negative as well as positive impulsion, avoidance as well as pursuit. Imperative pursuit of the situation of legality means imperative avoidance of conditions of failure. Argument within the practice of law-like law is the product of formative aspiration and also – equally – formative fear. What's feared, always, is failure of legality.

Failure of legality, understood by light of the nomological conception, is a definite situation characterized by a number of notable features. The nomological conception may be stated as a series of oppositions, between good things and bad things. Failure of legality is a derivative situation, a bad presence owing to an absence of the good of legality. The situation of failure may be described element by element, piecemeal, in terms of particular bad things that arise when specific constituents of legality do not occur. Or we may characterize it more generally, in terms of generic or pervasive evils that attend abeyance of legality.

The lexicon of legality is structured by specific equations according to which the lack of a particular sought condition is the same thing as the existence of something bad. Absence of a particular good equals the presence of a particular evil. Four specific equations, basic relations which we should bear in mind, are as follows.

Absence of entitlement is the presence of domination. Absence of justice is the presence of irregularity. Want of rational resolution is the happening of resolution by will, volition, choice. Nonoccurrence of rational connection is the occurrence of special treatment, the singling out of persons.

Viewed more broadly, absence of legality is an evil condition of arbitrariness. This is the generic condition that pertains when legality fails. The negative counterpart of legality as such is a regime of arbitrary power, power unmediated by law. In a word, arbitrariness is the common denominator of disentitlement, injustice, and failed rationality.

Arbitrary Judgment

Arbitrariness is an aberration of judgment. As we noted at the outset of this chapter, the central drama of liberal legality happens in the forum of judgment, in courts at the center of argumentative practice. Just as aspiration to sustain legality fastens on the operations of courts, so too does fear of legality's defeat focus on judging. Arbitrary judgment by those who exercise decisional power over others is the great fear of nomological practice.

From the standpoint of commitment to legality, arbitrary decision takes over when law-like law quits, quite apart from any corrupt motive, bias, spite, passion, or partisanship on the part of the decider. Arbitrariness is not the expression of a bad as opposed to a good personality. Rather, it is the negation of impersonality. When legality goes missing, both judging and being judged take on a personal, rather than an impersonal, character. One who decides exercises personal will, choice, sway. One subject to decision is singled out personally, dealt with uniquely.

There are different types of arbitrary assertion, to be distinguished in a moment. The types have in common a fundamental absence, want of lawfulness. Absent governance of law-like law, coercive legal judgment is exercise of raw power, unmediated assertion of self. Transmutation of raw power into law-like reason does not occur. Conceivably, someone possessed of the power of arbitrary decision may delight in its exercise, reveling in the moment of self-assertion, or might trade power for aggrandizing favors and deals. On the other hand, the empowered decider may resolve to be thoroughly self-restrained, and hew strictly to self-imposed procedure, always remaining incorrupt, benignant, elevated not base. But still, from the standpoint of nomological commitment, arbitrariness can be cured only by lawfulness. Judgment not law-full is arbitrary imposition, notwithstanding self-restraint. High-minded imposition is none the less high-handed.

Two broad types of arbitrariness may be defined by use of the negative terms of the nomological conception. I will call the first type of arbitrariness anomic, and the other type nomothetic. Anomic – or law-less – arbitrariness happens when there is a deficit of available law. Nomothetic – or law-giving – arbitrariness occurs when there is a surfeit of possible laws.

These two general kinds are different, though a given complex arbitrary event may display features of each type. In either situation, there is no established law to govern a case, and the decision that ensues is arbitrary. The basic difference has to do with the character of the judgment that is made. In the first – anomic – situation, the immediate basis of judgment is not a law-like proposition. In the second – nomothetic – situation, the immediate basis of decision is law-like, but it cannot be said to be extant law. So the two situations differ with respect to the particular element of legality that is most dramatically absent. Judgment of the first type enters a void of law-like law. Judgment of the second type draws at will from the plenum of law-like possibility.

In what follows I will give a description of each aberration, always from the standpoint of the nomological conception, whose parlance is structured by the fundamental opposition of the lawful and the arbitrary, and by the specific equations I have presented, according to which a particular evil arises from the nonoccurrence of a particular good. Also, I will indicate the sort of benign self-restraint that might be attempted in each situation. Associated with the two basic types of arbitrariness are characteristic ways of trying to make the best of a bad situation – different ways of failing in the end.

Anomic Arbitrariness

Anomic arbitrariness is judgment without nomological basis. Something anomic is something without law, or law-less. Anomic judgment lacks properties: it is unruly, disorderly, anomalous.

Suppose that judging has no nomological foundation, none at all. In the situation of anomic judging, a case comes up for decision, but there is no available nomological basis for decision. There is no applicable general precept, addressing a class sharing specified characteristics, able to control the case and serve as a ground of consistent treatment. A vacuum defined by the absence of controlling law-like law might be imagined to develop in different ways. For example, the judge may find an established law that seems pertinent, but the law may be incorrigibly vague in application to the case, the occurrence at issue, which is rationally classifiable as falling under the law and also as not falling under the law, so that the contrary readings of the vague law cancel each other out. Or there may be two laws that seem pertinent, but the two prescribe contrary results, and both apply equally well to the case, yielding divergent commands that cancel one another out. Or there may be any number of laws all speaking to somewhat similar circumstances, but none of them applies specifically to this occurrence, which then falls into a gap left by all available laws. Let us assume that, one way or another, an irremediable void of dispositive law has arisen.

Now suppose judging proceeds to decision, in as judicious and circumspect a manner as may be, as follows. Since available nomological resource has failed to produce sufficient law-like reasoning to govern the case, the judge handles it, we imagine, otherwise. In order to avoid sheer self-assertion, the judge adopts a regimen of immersion in the concrete problem at hand. The self-restrained judge is attentive to all facets of the contested occurrence in its context, deliberates carefully and impartially, and arrives at a well-considered decision. The resolution reached is the culmination of a careful retelling of the case, constructed by the judge, which incorporates features of the concrete problem seen to be important from the varying perspectives of all concerned. Judgment is particularized, individuated, responsive to the matter at hand. However well motivated and self-abnegating the judge, and no matter how sensitive or clever the resolving narrative, this is a situation of anomic arbitrariness.

Judgment proceeding in a void of generally applicable laws is anomic in nature. The fatal affliction of anomic decision is its want of the abridgement of view and the regularity of result that attend nomological judging. Judgment ungoverned by law-like reasons lacks law-like tests of relevance, which are also criteria of irrelevance, so legal assessment lacks a basis for stopping short of plenary consideration of circumstance. Law-less judgment also lacks legal criteria of sameness, so judgment is idiographic, or logically particular, and a pattern of equal treatment is quite impossible. At its best anomic deliberation does not achieve the abstracted, associative reasoning required of law-formed disposition. Accordingly, the epithets of failed nomological connection attach.

Seen from the standpoint of nomological commitment, anomic judgment is special treatment. Judgment does not turn on the presence or absence of distinguishing features of classes. Decision is not governed by reasoning from generally applicable grounds able to ensure consistent resolution. Thus, according to legality's equation, whatever decision arises is an irregular imposition. In a series of anomic determinations, each case is a singularity, where no laws hold, and each resolution is a unique disposition. Anomic judging looks out at a world of disconnected, unrepeated, incomparably contextual happenings. Persons brought to judgment are accorded individual, not like, treatment. The handling each person's case receives depends upon the particular characteristics of that person's concrete conduct. So legal imposition is unavoidably personal in character. People being judged are dealt with personally. To suffer anomic assessment is to be singled out, examined in isolation, fixed by the stare of disassociated judgment bearing down. Anomic judgment is injustice, failure of rational connection. By its nature the meting out of anomic results cannot confer like treatment upon persons subject to authority.

Nomothetic Arbitrariness

Nomothetic arbitrariness, the second type, is judgment based on freely selected law-like prescription. Nomothetic activity is law-making or law-giving activity, the laying down of nomic grounds. In nomothetic judgment, norm-creation occurs in the process of norm-application.

Suppose judges are quite free to select the nomological basis of legal resolution. In the situation of nomothetic judging, a case that comes up for decision is decided on the basis of some law-like ground, but there is no established stock of laws that the deciding officer is bound to use. Rather the judge is the law-giver, the nomothete. The decider, we imagine, may designate any precept at all to be the controlling ground of decision in a matter at hand, so long as the dispositive ground may itself be formulated as a law-like prescription able to sustain impersonal decision under it. Every generally statable precept able by its own operation to generate consistent decision is equally available. It is up to the judge, acting as a law-maker, to determine what in general ought to be required, authorized, or prohibited in the area of life addressed by legal decision. In short, the nomothetic decider is free in the case to be judged to embrace whatever law-like ground that particular judge determines then and there should be the basis of decision.

Let us imagine nomothetic judging proceeds to resolution, in as rational and dispassionate a manner as may be. By hypothesis, the judge is confronted with no given legal material from which a dispositive legal proposition must be derived. So the judging officer undertakes, we suppose, a careful moral deliberation, to find out which general prescription is on the whole morally best. Let us assume that, in a particular case, the practical moral inquiry has produced, for the inquirer, normative discovery. The judge has conducted an earnest search for an appropriate ground of decision, and the search has produced a law-like ground that the judge feels compelled to accept, all things considered, by law-making reason. After deliberation, the judge is convinced that pertinent legislative considerations, well understood, require the general norm now affirmed and applied. Though the ground affirmed may be law-like in the sense that it is general and impersonal and itself able to support consistent judgment, and though resolution of the particular case may follow easily from the ground of decision, this is a situation of nomothetic arbitrariness.

Judgment drawing grounds freely from the plenum of possible laws is nomothetic in character. The fatal affliction of nomothetic decision is its lack of a starting point in standing law. Decision does not begin by recognizing the givenness of legal material. Nothing is taken as the prior, extant, specifically legal, unavoidably given source of prescriptive grounds. The basis of judgment does not preexist the occasion of judgment. So, nomothetic ratiocination is not the specifically legal reasoning required of law-governed argument, and the epithets of failed nomological resolution attach.

Seen from the standpoint of commitment to nomological legality, nomothetic judgment is assertion of self. It doesn't matter that the judge feels compelled to adopt a particular ground of decision, compelled by the force of the judge's best legislative reasoning. Selection of the ground that governs decision is not governed by law. So, by legality's equation, it is an exercise of will, an act of positing, on the part of the particular officer empowered to decide. Law-giving judgment is resolution by say-so, unsupported volition, personal in character. The personal nature of judgment is not altered by casting the ground of decision as a generalized prescription that speaks impersonally to a particular case. Any law-like appearance of the ground is ersatz, a mask of self-assertion. Since the ground is the creature of the decider's will, it follows that its imposition to decide a suitor's case is subjection of the suitor to personality, not the law. It is a form of lawless sway, domination of one by another.

To have one's case submitted to nomothetic choice is to be made dependent on someone else's will. Nomothetic decision is disentitlement, the failure of rational resolution based on law. By definition it cannot uphold valued positions of persons that depend just on rational rendering of the meaning of the standing laws.

Negative Endeavor

Arbitrariness of some variety – anomic, or nomothetic, or a mixture, self-restrained or not – happens during any eclipse of decisional legality. Within the practice of law-like law, the abiding peril of arbitrary judgment serves as a constant stimulus to argumentative pursuit. The negative conception of failed legality is both a goad and a guide to positive striving.

To pursue legality in argument is to execute a positive operation and also a negative maneuver. The positive undertaking is to try to bring about a situation of entitlement, justice, and rationality. The negative endeavor is to try to avoid a situation of arbitrariness. The direction of striving is always along a line laid out between opposite poles. Argument inside nomological practice constantly seeks to find a way to accomplish complementary tasks at once: to steer clear of the conditions of legality's failure and advance toward the conditions of legality's success. Thus argumentative undertakings arise and develop with a view to negative as well as positive achievement.

5.4 DUAL IMPULSE

Now we should put negative endeavor to one side, and focus our attention on positive striving toward the good end of legality. What remains to be discussed, the last of the four topics of this chapter, is the specific nature – the dual nature – of the positive pursuit of liberal law.

The affirmative commitment to try to realize legality is a commitment to adopt, and try to work out, whatever particular mode of law and argument is able to sustain legality. Nomological aspiration is generic. It encompasses – and induces the pursuit of – specific argumentative projects which are ways of realizing legality concretely.

In the present section, my object is to show that nomological commitment gives rise to two specific projects. It gives rise to a dual impulse, the impetus to develop two different kinds of law, argument, and decision. The two kinds of legal endeavor are alternative ways of conceiving – formulating – law that exists, and different ways of reasoning legally. But the two modes of legal prescription are alike modalities of law-like law. Each, when carried out, is sufficient to sustain law-like legality.

Here is a remarkable, pervasively important aspect of law developed in liberal legal pursuit: its duality. Duality is the hallmark of law in liberal practice, a distinguishing mark of this kind of law. In dual impulse lies the richness of law-like legal argument. Duality is the way nomological aspiration becomes concrete.

Two Modes of Law

The conception of law-like legality is, we have seen, a considerable abstraction. The interrelated ideas of entitlement, justice, and rationality that make it up are terms of a very highly general vocabulary of commitment. All by itself, without more concrete expression, the nomological conception does not supply a practical methodology.

In order to direct workaday pursuit in legal practice, the generic idea of law-like legality needs to be made more palpable, more down to earth. It needs to be translated into a working understanding, a usable model of the thing to be built that includes a specification of how to build it. The product of a sufficient translation would be a specific conception of law-like legality that is suitable for the purpose of practical direction and is equivalent in scope to the generic original.

A sufficiently instructive conception of law-like law is the idea of an operable mode of legality. A mode of legality is a kind of law plus a method of argument: a particular type of law having features that include the nomological qualities, plus an associated process of reasoning – an argumentative procedure – which, if carried out successfully, would suffice to secure legality day by day. A mode of law-like law and argument is a manner in which legality might be realized throughout law. An operable mode of legality is the embodiment of generic aspiration in a particular project, which has the same reach as the aspiration it embodies.

There are two specific conceptions of law-like law suitable for use in nomological practice. That is, the generic condition of law-like legality is subject to practical interpretation in either of two ways. Each way is a rendering of the whole aspiration of legal practice: each rendering is applicable, in principle, to any department of law. The specific conceptions are alternative working understandings of nomological legal endeavor. They specify two basic modes of law and argument, either of which, if realized in practice, would sustain law-like legality.

So the formative commitment to pursue legality impels pursuit of each of the alternative modes. Aspiration to bring about legality yields a dual impulse to pursue two kinds of law-like law.

The specific conceptions of nomological law are, first, the idea of formalized law, and second, the idea of idealized law. The first sees law-like law to be made up of formal rules. The second sees law-like law to be governed by ideal aims that underlie rules – principles, policies, and purposes behind the rules.

Law-like legality may be understood in either of these ways, in terms of the notion of a formal rule or the notion of an underlying ideal. Associated with the types of law are two kinds of law-like legal reasoning: formal argument, the appeal to categories of extant rules, and ideal argument, appeal to ideal aims that the rules subserve. So there are two available modes of law-like law and law-like argument, formal and ideal, each an embodiment of the same generic aspiration. The modes of legality, when pursued in legal practice, are processes of active construction, ways of operating upon and working with given legal materials. Legality's concrete projects are formalization of law and idealization of law.

Now, I am aware that the assertions just made about formal and ideal ways of doing law amount to a presentation of labels, not a specification of their content, and that we seem rather on the brink of close definition. But we must maintain our perch for a little while. Before we go on to examine the variant types of law-like legality introduced above, we must first digress.

Presuppositions

Before we proceed to see how the formal and ideal conceptions of law – modes, processes, projects – would operate, we need to envision a stock of legal material upon which the constructive pursuits might operate. We ought first to posit the existence of an assemblage of standing laws and decided cases, and afterward consider how formal argument and ideal argument would go to work against this background.[17]

The standing laws, as we imagine them initially to be, have no particular form. Legal directives for society are, initially, conveyed by commands, by exhortations, or by descriptions of what's properly done. They may take the form of unqualified requirements, practical maxims, or ethical demands. Likewise, the teachings of decided cases might be stated as general pronouncements or as instructive examples. Normative items of varying kinds have, we suppose, been laid down as laws and judgments.

Law-like legal argument, we must assume, does not start from scratch. It begins by confronting a stock of given legal material, standing laws. So, we should imagine a social situation in which laws exist and a differentiated practice of legal decision by judges in courts has been going on for some time. Lots of legal norms have, we suppose, been established for society over time, and have accumulated to form a dense mass of extant legal prescription. Many cases in the courts have been decided by legal judges and have accumulated to form a train of remembered legal resolutions. It doesn't really matter where the laws administered by the judges first came from. What matters is that the laws, and resolutions, have come into existence, and must be taken by legal arguers of the present to be extant.

---

[17] That legal argument should be understood to take place in a context in which many standing laws exist, and many prior cases have been decided, is a commonplace assumption in jurisprudence. For example, according to analytical legal philosopher H. L. A. Hart, in order for a legal system to exist, rules constituting law-making and law-applying institutions must be "accepted" by legal officials, and rules of behavior which are legally valid must be "generally obeyed" by citizens – in other words, a mass of standing legal rules must exist (Hart 1961, p. 113). Likewise, Ronald Dworkin, when exploring law's capacity to achieve rational resolution, assumes that many standing laws, plus prior decisions under them, exist – he examines the workings of an "advanced" legal system "thick with constitutional rules and practices, and dense with precedents and statutes" (Dworkin 1977b, p. 286).

These assumptions are necessary because nomological legality cannot happen in full on day one in the history of legal enterprise. Legal entitlement is a position of dependence on standing laws, so the existence of a body of laws is a precondition of legality. Legal justice is a pattern linking a multiplicity of cases, so the realization of legality happens in a context of multiple remembered resolutions. Legality can possibly occur only when legal argument regards as given a stock of standing laws and established resolutions under them. Hence the existence of standing laws and decided cases will be our presumption throughout. We are investigating a differentiated practice of legal argument in which present laws and past decisions are taken as given.

In addition, we may make the natural assumption that practice of legal argument takes place in a broader institutional environment, and that societal lawmaking mechanisms exist outside it. Such external processes of legislation supply legal materials – statutes, constitutional provisions – to the practice of argument. In line with modern liberal commitment, which prizes freedoms that constitute self-government, we may assume that some mechanism of democratic lawmaking exists, and that judges are bound to respect the laws it produces, provided they are law-like. That is, legal judges have a responsibility, as officials in a democracy, to accept the legislative products of democracy, as well as – as part of – their fundamental responsibility to bring about legality. But apart from these slender presuppositions, we ought not to concern ourselves with the source of the stock of standing laws. Our focus will be kept on the practice of legal argument and judgment itself. The place of that practice within some larger institutional arrangement is beyond the purview of our inquiry. We ought not presume the existence of any particular constitutional plan, other than one that produces a concentration of decisional power in the agencies of legal judgment – the courts – at the center of the practice we are investigating.

Given a stock of legal material, the argumentative pursuit of law-like legality may go to work. Indeed, it must. Availability of standing laws and prior decisions is a necessary condition of nomological legality, but not a sufficient one. There must also be a process of law-like legal argument that grasps the laws and sets them in motion as reasons. Extant materials are the raw material of legality. Practice of legality is an active process of construction working upon and with the given stuff.

So now the question is how to proceed, how to regard the laws as reasons and how to use them as grounds, in argument. What is the model of law-like law that is to be employed in developing and applying legal material? How should the laws be formulated, and read, in order that their law-like qualities be fully realized?

Formal and ideal conceptions of law give different answers to these questions.

Formalized Law

The formal conception of legality identifies law-like law with rules. It conceives law-like law to be rule-like law.

A rule is a prescription that points to a class of actions, done by certain persons in certain circumstances, and indicates that acts of the class are authorized, or required, or prohibited. A legal rule gives a general description of a state of affairs plus an indication whether it ought legally to be. Formally realized law is made up of rule-like prescriptions, rules and resolutions arrived at under rules, readings and restatements of rules – for short, the R material of law.

Something formal is, in the context of legal argument, something nonmoral. A formalized category or proposition is one divorced or sealed off from the substance of moral debate. Here is a very simple definition of formality that will serve us throughout the present study: formal means nonideal. A formal precept – such as an extant legal rule – is a prescription whose content is knowable independently of an inquiry that asks what ideally ought to be. Formal law – rule-like law – is statable without reference to morality and applicable without reliance on moral judgment. Formal reasoning depends not on a moral faculty, but on common linguistic or communicative capacity to apprehend meanings, identify instances, and grasp logical connection.

The basic mental activity of formal legal decision is subsumption of particulars under available general categories. Simple formal resolution involves categorizing a situation within the general terms of a pertinent legal rule, and then applying the rule's prescription to decide the case. These are the operations of rule application: classification followed by indicated judgment. Formal argument succeeds when available legal rules sustain rational resolution of cases arising in the world.

Fully realized formality is a specific regime of law-like legality.[18] In formal law, entitlements are rights under established rules; justice means like treatment within the categories of rules; rationality lies in rule-governed reasoning. To pursue formal legality is to direct legal argument by the conception of law as rules. Formalizing argument first works to render the extant laws as formal rules, expressing law's content by means of propositions having a rule-like character, and then it uses the formulated rules as grounds of legal judgment. Formal pursuit hammers out law's precepts as rules and rests decision on rule-like grounds.

---

[18] A formal interpretation of law-like legality – the understanding that entitlement, justice, and rationality are realized by rule-governed judgment – is affirmed by some notable political theorists who otherwise embrace widely differing political views.

For Marxist political scientist Franz Neumann, the "rule of law" lies in "the rigid divorce of legality from morality" (Neumann 1944, pp. 442–443). Libertarian economist Friedrich Hayek identifies "the Rule of Law" with control of government by "general and formal rules" (Hayek 1944, pp. 72–73). Liberal moral philosopher John Rawls says that "the rule of law" is "formal justice, the regular and impartial administration of public rules" (Rawls 1971, p. 235).

However, Rawls later affirms a different view of the kind of legal prescription needed in order to realize the protections of the rule of law. See Rawls' *Political Liberalism* (1993), pp. 227, 236, 237 n. 23, where the rule of law is seen to be sustained by nonformal – practical moral – reasoning in the courts. For more on Rawls' two views of law in the service of the rule of law, see Chapter 6, pp. 90–93 and Chapter 7, pp. 116–119.

Idealized Law

The alternative way of realizing nomological legality is through nonformal – ideal – legal argument. Idealization of law starts more or less where we just left off, by taking as given a stock of legal materials of a formal nature. For ideal – or nonformal – legality has formal roots.

In order to picture the distinctive approach of idealizing argument, we should assume that the stock of legal stuff to be addressed by such argument has already been significantly formalized. That is, provisions of legislation, prescriptions of common law, and rulings in prior cases have been expressed in formal terms, without reference to morality. So now the given stock is a mass of formalized propositions. This imagined formality need not be thought to be fully perfected. Available formal expressions of law may be rough or partial or tentative. In any event, we assume that before nonformal argument gets going, a good deal of formalization has gone on. We might imagine that all the available formal stuff of law, such as it is, has been gathered and laid out on a table, and the question is what to do with it.

The simplest way of viewing the starting point of nonformal pursuit is as follows. We suppose that, at some time earlier, legal argument came upon a particular stock of legal materials, and proceeded to render the laws it confronted as rules, thus aiming to satisfy the formal conception of law-like legality. But there is another conception of law-like law, and this conception does not stop – rather it begins – when laws have been rendered as rules.

The ideal conception of legality sees law-like law to be governed by legal ideals that underlie legal rules. It says that law's meaning is dependent on the meaning of law-like ideals, the principles, policies, and purposes of law.[19]

A legal ideal is a prescription stating the general aim or point or object of some legal rule: what the rule is getting at. The ideal is the rule's rationale, the reason for the rule, the spirit behind the letter. A particular ideal states the object of a particular rule or, it may be, a group of related rules. Ideal aims invoked in legal argument include democracy, privacy, security of property, competitive markets, environmental protection, deterrence of crime. Within ideally realized law, the most important legal items are law's principles, policies, and purposes, the practical reasons that guide rules – in short, the P materials of law.[20]

---

[19] Frequently in the text the phrase "principles, policies, and purposes" is used to indicate the diversity of practical moral aims serving as grounds of legal argument. This useful mantra is particularly associated with the legal theory put forward by Henry M. Hart and Albert M. Sacks in their teaching materials for a course in applied jurisprudence, *The Legal Process: Basic Problems in the Making and Application of Law* (1958).

[20] According to Oliver Wendell Holmes, Jr., "The life of the law has not been logic: it has been experience. The felt necessities of the time, the prevalent moral and political theories, intuitions of public policy, avowed or unconscious, even the prejudices which judges share with their fellow-men, have had a good deal more to do than the syllogism in determining the rules by which men should be governed" (Holmes, *The Common Law*, 1881, p. 5).

An ideal underlying a rule is the practical justification of the rule. Unlike the rule, which tells us only what extant law happens to be, the ideal says what ought to be, what law ought to bring about. So the ideal is a proposition of practical morality. Legal ideals are moral precepts and goals that are anchored in existing law, rooted in formality. The ideal underlying a legal rule is a practical moral reason that fits and justifies the particular rule. Different ideals fit and justify different laws. Law's multiple ideals are notions of what ought to be in the many areas of social life addressed by law. Together they constitute a worldly morality embodied in the extant laws. Because of its rootedness, this morality is specifically legal, law's own morality.

The basic reasoning process of ideal resolution in law involves two operations. The first step is to state an ideal prescription that a given rule subserves, and the second is to guide and shape the rule in line with its ideal. Simple ideal argument attributes a practical aim to a formal rule and then uses the aim to direct the rule's application. In order to sustain legality, guiding legal ideals must be law-like in nature.[21] In nomological practice, policies as well as principles – ideal goals as well as ideal precepts – must be formulated as general directives able to support consistent, law-like judgment.[22] Ideal prescriptions that are generally expressed, specifically legal, and regular in operation, work to sustain entitlement and justice. Ideal argument succeeds when rational resolution in law is governed by law-like principles, policies, and purposes. To pursue ideal legality is to conceive law to be animated by the ideals it embodies. Idealizing argument fashions ideal propositions that fit and justify extant legal rules, and then gives voice to ideals as prescriptive grounds. Ideal pursuit develops law's ideal order.

In *The Legal Process*, Henry Hart and Albert Sacks declare: "Law is a doing of something, a purposive activity, a continuous striving to solve the basic problems of social living … It can be accepted as a fixed premise, therefore, that every statute and every doctrine of unwritten law developed by the decisional process has some kind of purpose or objective … This principle or policy is always available to guide judgment …" (Hart and Sacks 1958, p. 148).

[21] Ronald Dworkin, in his essay "Hard Cases" (1975), p. 1057, says that judges must decide cases consistently, ensuring "the fairness of treating like cases alike," and are obligated to give coherent reasons for their decisions – to practice "articulate consistency" (Dworkin 1975, pp. 1064, 1090). In *Law's Empire* (1986), Dworkin says that law's fundamental aspiration, which controls argument and judgment throughout law, is "integrity." In all his jurisprudential writings Dworkin affirms that use of practical moral principles and policies, which fit and justify formal rules, as grounds of decision, is necessary in order to realize consistency, coherence, and integrity in law.

In *Political Liberalism* (1993), John Rawls describes the kind of judicial reasoning needed in order to implement "constitutional essentials," including "the protections of the rule of law." "[T]he best interpretation" of law is the one that "best fits … and justifies" the relevant body of legal materials. "I doubt that this view differs in substance from Dworkin's" (Rawls 1993, pp. 227, 236, 237 n. 23).

For more on Dworkin's portrayal of the law-like character of legal ideals, and on Rawls' allied view, see Chapter 7, pp. 108–114 and pp. 116–119.

[22] See Dworkin, "Hard Cases" (1975), pp. 1085, 1086 (policy-based interpretation). Dworkin says that "policies" which are used, as in "rule utilitarianism," to justify general rules in regular operation, are admissible to law (Dworkin 1975, pp. 1072–1073).

Alternative Conceptions

The two contrasting working conceptions of law and legal argument sketched above are the two ways of realizing nomological aspiration. The sketches indicate how the alternative modes, in their different ways, satisfy the requirements of nomological commitment – that is, how formal law and ideal law each amount to law-like law.

Still I think it would be worthwhile to underscore the point that both prescriptive modalities have a sufficiently nomological character. Law-like law may be either a matter of formal prescription, or an affair of ideal prescription, because both of these types of prescription are equally – sufficiently – law-like in logic and legal in status.

In order for a type of prescription to be a ground of nomological argument, in the sense required by the generic conception of law-like law, two things must be true. First, the type of prescription must exhibit law-like qualities such as generality and regularity of application. It must be law-like in basic logic. Second, the type of prescription must be an expression of the meaning of the standing law. It must be specifically legal in status. Both formal legal prescription and ideal legal prescription meet these tests.

Both prescriptive kinds are law-like in logic: formal prescriptions are in the nature of law-like rules; ideal prescriptions are general directives able to justify and guide law-like rules in regular application. And each prescriptive mode anchors its argumentative operations in the standing laws. Formal argument casts extant laws as rules and uses rules as grounds; ideal argument formulates specifically legal ideals, practical aims that fit the rules in force, in order to establish the purport of the extant law.

The formal and ideal conceptions constitute alternative ways of looking at law. They are different ways of apprehending the meaning of standing laws and prior cases. When law is understood formally, the meaning of a legal norm is thought to be graspable without any reference to morality. When law is understood ideally, legal meaning is thought to be dependent on the practical moral point of a legal norm. On the ideal approach, but not the formal, quest for legal meaning is part of a discourse that considers what's right, good, just, prudent in the running of society. So, formalized law is stripped of moral rationalizations, while idealized law is controlled by practical moral grounds.

The two conceptions identify law-like law with different sorts of prescriptive items. Law's formality and law's morality reside in different sorts of legal stuff: R material and P material. The two modes develop two different kinds of controlling reasons: nonmoral and moral. From different types of reasons flow different types of reasoning, the articulation of categories of rules and the giving of voice to ideals, which lead to different types of rational resolution, by rule application or through ideal guidance.

Law-like law may be formal or ideal. Given nomological commitment, law may be regarded one way or the other way.

Laws are either understood formally, that is, quite independently of whatever practical moral grounds may justify them, or not – and if not, legality is ideal. Laws are either taken to have a moral dimension as well as a formal aspect, to be given voice by an ideal discourse of law, or not, and if not, legality is formal.

In a word, either law-like law has a moral character or it doesn't. When law is nomological but not moral, then legal argument is formal, meaning nonideal. When legal argument is nomological and also moral, then law is nonformal, that is, ideal.

The two ways of looking at law are, by definition, mutually exclusive. Thus, the two modes are, in a sense, competitors, rivals for the allegiance of legal striving. Just as the generic conception of legality speaks equally to all law, so do its offspring, the specific conceptions of formal law and ideal law. But the two specific modalities, since they are mutually exclusive, cannot be equally successful at the very same locus and moment of legal argument. If one takes hold at some time somewhere in law and succeeds, the other necessarily cannot. So, formal pursuit may displace ideal pursuit, and vice versa.

But still, in a larger sense, the two cannot defeat one another. For they are begotten of the same commitment and are allied in ultimate aim. Both seek to realize nomological aspiration. If one prevails, in a particular connection, the other can't; but the one that prevails does not defeat the large aim of the other. So far as nomological aspiration is concerned, it doesn't matter which prevails. The relation of each to the other, then, is that of a resource in reserve, or a backup system. If one of the sibling rivals fails, its ultimate aim might still succeed, carried out by its twin. Success of either suffices to sustain legality.

The two modes, necessarily, have much in common. Each sort of law is a manner of achieving legality. Despite differences, formal and ideal kinds of law are alike avatars of law-like law. Both conceptions interpret, and in different ways would confer, entitlement and justice. Each mode bases its operations on standing laws and prior cases, and works to secure the law-formed status and treatment of persons. Each type of law has nomological features. Both modes aim to supply general, accessible, impersonal, statable, regular, coherent prescription. Each is a mode of nomological-connective rationality.

Coherence and Development

Within each argumentative mode, the imperative of coherence operates powerfully.

A mighty endeavor to bring about rational connection is, as we have seen, more or less the signature of quest of nomological legality. Law-like argument draws legal elements together, builds coherence of part with part, shows how one thing jibes with another. The impetus to achieve connection – demonstrable unity, prescriptive accord – is the gravitational force of law's universe, working across great distances. It is a general force affecting law-like argument as such, therefore formal and ideal argument alike. Both modes are governed by the idea of things fitting together. Both pursuits develop to become complex, concatenating projects.

Legality's force of coherence magnifies legal endeavor. It enlarges the domain of legal attention. Small undertakings expand their scope, to achieve harmonious fit of ground with ground and judgment with judgment. The connective tendency leads to construction of unities. It gives rise to processes of overall interrelation and unification. Discrete resolutions are framed by wider operations aiming to construct ordered association of laws. Subject to the tutelage of the command of coherence, simple argument becomes complex. What starts out small and piecemeal and simple, ends up large and holistic and complex.

Both modes of liberal law undergo complex development. Both formal pursuit and ideal pursuit develop tectonic processes that produce structured wholes. Each starts with the elementary notion that a single propositional item, a formal rule or a legal ideal, is the exemplar of law-like law, and each develops to affirm a complex idea of many such items knit together in systematic union. Each pursuit struggles to bring about a kind of structure. Structuring operations aim to build and display the coherent disposition of multiple related legal elements. The idea of structure dominates fully developed formal and ideal argumentation.

Formal pursuit aims to achieve formal structure. Here, structure means rules working together, each read in light of the others. An achieved formal structure is a scheme of interconnected categories and propositions within which multiple, mutually qualifying formal norms stand in defined relations.

Ideal pursuit aims to develop ideal structure. Here, structure means the configuring of ideal prescriptions so that they speak together in harmony. A developed ideal structure is a construct of ideal precepts and goals in which the multiple aims are ordered with respect to one another and with respect to complex underlying formal material.

And so it is that particular argumentative undertakings arise and develop in parallel within a legal practice working to achieve nomological legality. The arisings and the developings are all impelled by the same motive: nomological commitment.

Deep Duality

The main point of the present discussion has been to show how the initial arisings take place: how aspiration yields impulse in liberal practice. We have seen that the formative aspiration of practice, which is abstract and generic, gives rise to concrete and specific impulsion. Following, by way of conclusion, is a brief restatement of the story.

Liberal practice, with nomological aspiration wired in, awaits further, specific instruction. The generic aim of practice is to bring about an abstractly defined situation of law-like entitlement, justice, and rationality.

Given an interpretation of the abstract situation that both captures its defining features and renders it concretely, argument in practice will strive toward the concretely formulated condition of law. Given an understanding of the generic aim that shows how it might be effected step by step through argumentative endeavor, practice will undertake to carry out the specified method of argument and decision. In short, aspiration to achieve legality yields impulsion to execute a working conception of law and argument which, if realized, would secure legality. An impulse arises within the practice to proceed in line with such a conception, to argue that way and make law so.

It happens that, for liberal practice, two working conceptions of nomological legality are equally available. Alternative understandings of law-like law are each able to fill in the coordinates of nomological arrival. So aspiration to realize law-like legality gives rise to a dual impulse to pursue each of two modes of law.

Two projects take shape within practice, each seeking to realize a particular understanding of law-like law. The dual impulse of liberal legal argument is, first, to formalize the law, and second, to idealize law. Each pursuit is an active process of construction working to develop a complex mode of legality. Formalization of law endeavors to express extant laws as rule-like precepts and build prescriptive schemes able to harmonize formal elements. Idealization of law strives to project ideal aims that fit extant rules and build unifying constructs that order ideal grounds in relation to one another.

These two broad projects are persistent undertakings of liberal legal argument. Each is a continuously operative process within argumentative practice. The duality of liberal law is constant, enduring. Practice's dual impulse is vigorous, powerful, deep.

6

Deep Duality: Formal Law

My claim that liberal aspiration gives rise to a dual impulse, developed in analysis of the prior chapter, is a claim about the logical implication of embrace of liberal commitment in doing of law, and it is a claim about the actual development of law in our legal practice. Two modes of legal argument are in fact undertaken in practice of liberal law – that is, in our law.

Now, at one level, the idea that our law displays duality is hardly debatable, indeed banal. Two ways of arguing legally – rule-based reasoning and policy-based reasoning – are both entirely familiar. Legal arguers persistently invoke rules as grounds of judgment, and they persistently invoke policies and principles as legal reasons. An attentive observer, if at all circumspect, can hardly miss spotting this superficial duality of our law.

My claim about law's duality is not just that two tendencies are apparent in law. The claim is much stronger than that. It is that formative commitment gives rise to deep duality. According to analysis of the prior chapter, there are two – and only two – modes of liberal legal argument; the two ways of realizing liberal legality are formal argument and ideal argument; the two are on a par.

In legal theory addressing liberal law, duality of law is widely acknowledged, up to a point. An account that offers a picture of liberal law as a whole typically recognizes the existence of two kinds of law, formal and ideal. But usually, a synoptic picture of law will emphasize one kind of legal development, and downplay the other. Emphasis on rules tends to relegate ideal argument to a minor role. Emphasis on ideals tends to regard formal argument as rudimentary.

For example, H. L. A. Hart says that formal rules are the basis of rational resolution in law.[1] Hart grants that ideal argument plays a minor – interstitial – role in law. But he portrays ideal aims operating in the gaps and gray areas of formal law as the kinds of factors that figure in discretionary lawmaking, not as law-like precepts. He does not show ideal aims to be the grounds of law's coherence.

---

[1] See generally H. L. A. Hart, *The Concept of Law* (1961), pp. 120–150.

Ronald Dworkin, in contrast to Hart, believes that ideal aims – principles and policies – are the basis of rational resolution in law.[2] Dworkin recognizes that formal rules play an important, if preliminary, role. Ideal principles and policies are grounded in the rules. But Dworkin portrays law's rules, by themselves, as separate items detached from one another. Formal argument does not produce law's coherence.

Such one-sided pictures of liberal law are, at best, half-right. While they recognize the law-like nature of the kind of law in primary focus, they do not fully affirm the law-like nature of the other kind. Deep duality is not recognized.

In deeply dual law, both of two modes of legal argument, formal and ideal, develop to become fully law-like. Each mode is law-like in two ways. First, each type of argument makes use of prescription that manifests law-like qualities in form and operation. That is, each type invokes precepts of existing law as grounds of regular disposition. Second, each type of argument works to organize related laws, so that separate laws fit together. That is, each type seeks coherence.

Deep duality is entrenched in the canons of good argument that direct liberal practice. Formative canons of practice say that formal argument should be law-like, and ideal argument should be law-like, and all argument should seek coherence. Formal rules of law should be formulated as general directives able to support evenhanded judgment. Ideal principles and policies of law should be formulated so that they fit and justify standing general rules, and so yield consistent resolution. Related formal precepts of an area of law should be read in such a way that they fit together and work together – the same for ideal prescription.

In the present chapter and the next, we will see what fully law-like law looks like, according to two legal theorists who take different aspects of law to be of primary importance. In successive chapters, our tutelary theorists will be Max Weber, legal sociologist, systematic analyst of formalization, and Ronald Dworkin, legal philosopher, premier exponent of idealization.

First, in the present chapter, we will focus on formalization of law. Here Weber's legal theory, which puts formal law in primary focus, will show what law-like formal law looks like. Then, in the following chapter, we will consider idealization of law. There Dworkin's legal theory, which emphasizes ideals in law, shows what law-like ideal argument looks like. If we put together the separate pictures of law drawn respectively by Weber and Dworkin, we have before us a comprehensive – unified – portrait of liberal law's duality.

We are in search of a comprehensive picture of law-like law. But such a picture is not to be found fully developed in the work of a single major legal theorist. Accordingly, we will put our comprehensive picture together by combining partial views. Our two tutelary theorists are the two halves of a whole. Neither Weber's view nor Dworkin's view affirms the whole. But

---

[2] See generally Ronald Dworkin, *Taking Rights Seriously* (1977b), pp. 81–130, 279–290.

together they affirm the fully law-like nature of law's formality, and the fully law-like nature of law's ideals: deep duality.

In addition to our study of views of Weber and Dworkin, in discussion that follows we will briefly consider ideas of another notable theorist, political philosopher John Rawls, who offers a curiously synthetic view. Rawls addresses both formalized law and idealized law. Unlike Weber and Dworkin, Rawls doesn't try to describe the operation of legal argument in depth or detail, but he does something the other two don't do. Unusually, Rawls affirms both modes of law, formal and ideal, equally.

John Rawls, liberal political theorist, undertook to identify the kind of legal argument that is needed in order to secure the governance of law in the polity. In different writings, Rawls showed that the rule of law is upheld by formal legal argument, and also by ideal argument. Curiously, Rawls' affirmation of formal rules in the service of the rule of law, and his affirmation of ideal principles and policies in the same service, came twenty years apart.

6.1 RAWLS' FIRST VIEW OF LAW

We will start our quest for a comprehensive picture of liberal law's duality by turning to ideas of John Rawls, philosopher of liberalism, because Rawls, at least in outline, constructs one. In his writings on political theory, Rawls traces the connection between liberty on the one hand, and liberal law on the other hand. According to Rawls, political justice requires liberty; flourishing liberty requires the rule of law; and commitment to the rule of law yields a dual impulse to develop two kinds of law.

Rawls builds a dualistic picture of law in two steps. First, in his book *A Theory of Justice*, he shows that the rule of law in society is served by formal – rule-based – legal argument.[3] This is Rawls' first view of law. Subsequently, in further writing on political justice, Rawls presents an additional view of law, which shows that the rule of law is also served by nonformal – ideal – legal argument. In the present chapter, we will focus on Rawls' first view. We will consider Rawls' second view of law later on.

John Rawls, moral and political philosopher, is not primarily a legal theorist, but he does address law – quite inevitably, given his starting points. In *A Theory of Justice*, Rawls puts forward – famously – two principles of justice. His first principle of justice says that a system of equal liberty ought to be instituted in society – "the most extensive total system of equal basic liberties."[4] Rawls' principle of maximum equal liberty in turn requires that the rule of law be maintained.

---

[3] John Rawls, *A Theory of Justice* (1971), §§ 10 and 38. Hereafter, in this chapter, *A Theory of Justice* is cited as *TJ*.

[4] *TJ*, p. 250.

The rule of law, says Rawls, "is obviously closely related to liberty." The rule of law is the governance of social life by standing general law. When the "boundaries of our liberties" are well-defined by law, "citizens can draw up their plans," and conduct their affairs, "confident in the possession and exercise of . . . freedoms." The rule of law – legality – is a necessary condition of liberty in the polity. Rawls sums up: "legality has a firm foundation" in commitment to "the greatest equal liberty."[5]

The Rule of Law Defined

The rule of law is a situation in which – in the terminology of the present study – law-like legality exists in the world. Law-like legality is secured when the laws exhibit law-like qualities – generality, impersonality, regularity – and together uphold legal entitlement and legal justice, the law-formed status and treatment of persons.

Rawls defines the rule of law by stating specific requirements. He calls these requirements "the precepts of the rule of law."[6] Rawls' requirements, when implemented, would constitute a regime of law in which, according to the jargon of this book, law-like legality is secured.

There are differences between Rawls' definition of the rule of law and this book's idea of law-like legality. The conception of legal entitlement used herein is broader than – a considerable expansion of – Rawls' corresponding requirements. Likewise, the conception of legal justice we have developed is larger than Rawls' corresponding notion. Still, Rawls' understanding of the rule of law, and this book's idea of law-like legality, are not at odds. So far as the sought operation of law in life is concerned, the two understandings come out the same. The requirements that constitute the rule of law in life, according to Rawls, suffice to establish a regime in which, according to our vocabulary, legal entitlement and legal justice are secured.

In the terms of our analysis, legal entitlement is a situation in which valued positions of persons in social life depend just on the meaning of the standing laws, not on the say-so of the authorities. Meaning of standing law is accessible to reason. In a regime of legality, legal argument achieves rational resolution under law. Argument based on general law sustains entitlements of persons, and everyone is significantly entitled by law.

According to Rawls, a central precept of the rule of law is that "there is no offense without a law" (*nulla crimen sine lege*).[7] A related precept says that law-breaking must be voluntary in order for a penalty to be imposed. Together Rawls' precepts establish negative entitlement: everyone is entitled to protection against lawless punishment. "One who complies with the announced rules need never fear an infringement of his liberty."[8] The negative entitlements defined by Rawls are,

---

[5] The six quoted phrases in this paragraph come, in sequence, from *TJ*, pp. 235, 239, 241, 240, 239, 240.
[6] *TJ*, p. 236.   [7] *TJ*, p. 238.   [8] *TJ*, p. 241.

according to analysis of this book, at the core of a much larger positive conception, which says that entitlement is dependence on the standing law only.

In the terms of our analysis, legal justice is a situation in which people whose cases come up for decision receive evenhanded judgment. Laws are generalized directives; particular resolutions under law are consistent with one another. In a regime of legality, legal argument displays rational connection among laws. Argument is able to state general propositions according to which the several laws fit together.

According to Rawls, the rule of law "implies the precept that similar cases be treated similarly."[9] This familiar maxim of evenhandedness requires "impartial and consistent administration of laws."[10] Rawls notes: "The requirement of consistency holds of course for the interpretation of all rules ... at all levels."[11] The requirement of consistency stated by Rawls is, according to our analysis, at the core of a larger imperative, which says that legal argument should build and display law's rational coherence.

Rules and the Rule of Law

What sort of legal prescription is needed in order to uphold the rule of law? What manner of formulating law's commands serves to secure the protections of the rule of law? What kind of legal reasoning?

In *A Theory of Justice*, Rawls says that rules – formal legal directives – secure the rule of law. The law that ensures no penalty is imposed without law is prescription in the form of "announced rules."[12] The reasoning that ensures that like cases are decided alike is "authorized public interpretation of rules."[13] In short, Rawls says that formal argument – rule-governed legal argument – is the essential means of realizing the rule of law. Indeed, Rawls not only identifies the rule of law with rules; he identifies law itself with rules.

First, Rawls equates the rule of law with rules. Requirements of the rule of law, he says, are "implicit in the notion of regulating behavior by public rules."[14]

Rawls believes that the rule of law depends on rules and rule-governed reasoning. Rule-governed reasoning confers formal justice; formal justice is the same thing as the rule of law. "[T]he conception of formal justice, the regular and impartial administration of public rules, becomes the rule of law when applied to the legal system."[15] The relation between rules and the rule of law is very intimate. The precepts of the rule of law "are those that would be followed by any system of rules which perfectly embodied the idea of a legal system."[16] In other words, the rule of law is the same thing as a system of regularly operating rules of law.

Second, Rawls equates a legal system with rules. A system of law, and a system of rules, are one and the same. "A legal system is a coercive order of public rules ..."[17]

Rawls' understanding of a legal system is similar to the view put forward by legal philosopher H. L. A. Hart. Rawls says that "the legal order is a system of public

---

[9] *TJ*, p. 237.   [10] *TJ*, p. 58.   [11] *TJ*, p. 237.   [12] *TJ*, p. 241.   [13] *TJ*, p. 240.   [14] *TJ*, p. 238.
[15] *TJ*, p. 235.   [16] *TJ*, p. 236.   [17] *TJ*, p. 235.

rules."[18] Hart says that rules have "a central place in the structure of a legal system."[19] According to Hart, the main constituents of law are formal – nonmoral – rules. Existence of the rules of a legal system is knowable by factual inquiry, not moral inquiry. For Hart, legal argument appealing to formal rules is the most important kind of legal reasoning.

Rawls acknowledges the affinity between his understanding of law and Hart's view. Rawls tells his reader to turn to Hart for "discussion of when rules and legal systems may be said to exist."[20]

A System of Rules

Early in the present chapter, we noted that fully law-like law manifests certain basic features. Law-like legal argument invokes precepts of standing law as grounds of consistent decision. John Rawls shows that formal rules of law, in the service of the rule of law, display the requisite features. Formal rules are standing laws, and so are grounds of legal entitlement. Rules support consistent decision, and so serve to sustain legal justice.

Also, we noted that fully law-like argument engages in a certain – distinctive – activity. It seeks law's coherence. Coherence-seeking is more or less the defining trait of law-like legal argument. Coherence-seeking argument works to organize related laws, so that separate laws fit together and work together.

On the matter of coherence, Rawls has only a little to say. He speaks of "consistency" and "system," rather than coherence. He says that argument in service of the rule of law seeks consistency of "all rules," and he speaks of a "system of rules." The idea of a system of thoroughly consistent rules seems to imply law's coherence, but Rawls doesn't go into this.

On the topic of coherence-seeking, Rawls' idea of a system of rules is a bare beginning. A lot more needs to be said in order to define the characteristic way in which formal legal argument, formed within practice of liberal law, constructs coherence among law's rules and doctrines. On this topic, our guide will be Max Weber, analyst of formalization of law. As we will see, later in the present chapter, Weber spells out the conditions of law that together constitute a system of interconnected rules. He identifies the argumentative operations needed in order to construct formal coherence. Where Rawls is suggestive, Weber is very emphatic. Weber says that quest of coherence is a fundamental project of formal legal argument.

6.2 A CONTRARY VIEW

What does coherent formal law look like? This question is on the table. We will turn to the answer given by Max Weber, an answer in line with analysis of this book,

---

[18] *TJ*, p. 236. [19] Hart (1961), p. 133. [20] *TJ*, p. 55 n. 1.

shortly. But before we look at Weber's picture of formal law, a brief digression is in order. First, we will come at the matter of formal coherence from a different angle.

Instead of asking what formal coherence looks like, let us first ask the contrary question: what would formal law without coherence look like? What would formality look like if formalizing argument were unable to bring about coherent inter-relation of legal rules? We may throw a lot of light on coherence-building formal argument by first imagining what formal law would look like in its absence.

Ronald Dworkin's view of formal law shows what formality without coherence looks like. According to Dworkin, law as a whole is coherent, but formal argument by itself does not supply law's coherence. Law's unity comes from another source. Coherence is the product of ideal – not formal – argument. In other words, the rules of an area of law are, for Dworkin, a collection of separate items, not a coherent whole – when the rules are understood and developed by themselves, apart from ideal argument.

Like all other legal theorists discussed in this book, Dworkin offers a theory of law in two parts. One part addresses formal law; the other part addresses law's ideals. Dworkin's view of law's ideals will be discussed at length in the following chapter; that view is well in line with analysis of the present study. Right now, what's of interest is Dworkin's other view, the part about formality.

Following immediately below is a summary of Dworkin's picture of law's formality. It says that formal law, on its own, lacks coherence. Dworkin's view of law's formality is sharply opposed to that of Max Weber, to be examined shortly – and it is contrary to analysis of this book. We will digress briefly to consider Dworkin's contrary view.

Dworkin's Contrasts

In various writings, Dworkin presents a series of comparisons between formal law and law's ideals. His contrasts show lack of coherence of formal law by itself. Throughout, Dworkin says that law's coherence comes from nonformal – ideal – argument. By themselves, rules display consistency, but not coherence.

Following are two notable contrasts between formal law and law's ideals posited by Dworkin. The two contrasts distinguish, by Dworkin's lights, between different kinds of reasoning leading to judgment by law, and different kinds of connection linking laws with one another.

First, Dworkin distinguishes two kinds of reasoning looking to decision of cases.[21] The first kind is deductive argument which invokes rules one by one. This simple kind of reasoning views laws as separate precepts. The second kind makes use of a unifying theory. It views related laws as a whole.

---

[21] Earlier in the book, we saw that Dworkin says the second kind of argument – coherence-seeking – is prescribed by governing canons of our legal practice. See Chapter 2, pp. 23–25.

In the first form of legal reasoning, argument develops particular entailments of the laws. The first kind of argument is formal. According to Dworkin, formal reasoning focuses on particular rules taken one by one. A formal proposition of law is "derived from settled law . . . simply by deduction."[22] Here "settled law" refers to given rules.

In simple formal reasoning, the given rules are seen to exist in a "mechanical state." The rules are "just there." They lack "any greater significance."[23]

By contrast, in the second form of reasoning, argument has a wider focus. This kind of argument is ideal. An ideal proposition – a principle or policy – is used as the ground of judgment. This proposition is established by "the theory of law that best justifies settled law."[24] A justifying theory of law shows how particular rules fit together – that is, how they cohere. By light of their best justification, the several rules are seen to speak "with one voice."[25]

Second, Dworkin contrasts two basic kinds of legal precepts, used in the two kinds of reasoning. The different kinds of precepts are grounds of two kinds of connection among laws. Rules – the first sort – are grounds of consistent resolution. Practical moral principles – the second sort – are grounds of coherence.

By Dworkin's definition, a legal rule is "applicable in an all-or-nothing fashion." Rules contain exceptions. "[I]t is . . . incomplete to state the rule . . . without enumerating the exceptions." Since each rule applies when its exceptions do not apply, all completely stated rules are strictly consistent. But bare consistency is not the same thing as coherence.[26]

According to Dworkin, ideal principles organize law. Principles state the general aims of groups of related rules. Ideal argument works to find a "coherent set of principles." This is "a scheme of . . . principles that provides a coherent justification" of formal rules and rulings.[27]

Dworkin says that practical moral principles are grounds of "articulate consistency."[28] Here is the definition of coherence. Coherence is not just consistency. Coherence is consistency plus a unifying ground: consistency shown to exist by an organizing precept. For Dworkin, ideally organized law – not formal law – displays coherence.

A Mistaken View

Dworkin affirms liberal law's duality. He recognizes the existence of two kinds of law, formal and ideal. But, as understood by Dworkin, law's duality is superficial, not deep. One kind of law – idealized law – is fully law-like. The other kind of law is

---

[22] Dworkin (1977), p. 288.   [23] The three quoted phrases are from Dworkin (1986), pp. 49, 47, 49.

[24] Dworkin (1977), p. 283.   [25] Dworkin, *Law's Empire* (1986), p. 273.

[26] Quotes here are from Dworkin, "The Model of Rules" (1967), p. 25.

[27] The two quotes in this paragraph are from Dworkin, "Hard Cases" (1975), pp. 1098, 1094.

[28] Dworkin (1975), p. 1064.

rudimentary. Formal law is a disunified collection of separate items. Formal reasoning focuses narrowly on one rule at a time. The formal mode of connection among laws is minimal.

Dworkin's belittling view of formal law as it operates by itself, apart from ideal guidance, is a mistake. Dworkin's portrait displays unorganized simplicity. This is a false picture of formality formed within the practice of liberal legality. It is a mistake to think that formal law, left to its own devices, is unable to achieve the level of order and generality realized by nonformal striving.

First, it is a mistake to think that formal reasoning is limited to simple deduction based on separate, unorganized rules. Formal argument builds structure. It organizes related rules, and uses the structures it builds as frames for decision. Pursuit of structure arises for a fundamental reason. An imperative of coherence operates powerfully in liberal law. Commitment to achieve legality impels argument to build and show rational connection of laws. In formal law, argumentative operations work to connect related rules and to develop organizing generalizations. Persistent processes of interconnection and generalization combine to construct pervasive formal structure.

Second, it is a mistake to think that formal law, by itself, displays consistency but not coherence. According to Dworkin, the force of coherence operates within one kind of law, and not within the other. But why should that be? Why should we suppose that one mode of argument in liberal law aims at mere consistency, while the other seeks full coherence? The fundamental imperative of rational connection addresses any sort of argument looking to judgment in liberal law. Therefore, for precisely the same reason that ideal argument seeks coherence, so does formal argument, on its own.

At the outset of the present section, we undertook to address the main question then on the table in a roundabout way. The question, still up for discussion, is: what does formal coherence look like? Instead of consulting an author who gives an affirmative answer to the question, we have looked at a naysaying view: Ronald Dworkin's denial of formal coherence. Now it is time to get back on the direct path.

In the following section, we will look at length at the affirmative understanding of legal formality put forward by Max Weber. According to Weber, formal legal argument by nature is coherence-seeking. According to analysis of this book, Weber's view of formal law is the antidote to Dworkin's mistakes. On the matter of formality's coherence, Dworkin is wrong; Weber gets things right.

6.3 LAW-LIKE FORMALITY: WEBER

Max Weber, student of formalization of law, presents a systematic view of the features and processes that constitute law's formality.[29] He identifies the connective

---

[29] See Max Weber, *Economy and Society*, vol. 2 (1925). Hereafter, in this chapter, *Economy and Society*, vol. 2, is cited as ES2.

operations that build structure throughout formal law. He explains how formal argument moves beyond consistency to coherence. Weber shows what fully law-like formal law looks like.

Max Weber, legal sociologist, viewed modern law as a distinct type.[30] It is both "formal," that is, nonmoral, and – as he put it – it evinces "logical rationality." This is one type among several within Weber's typology of historical legal orders. Weber speaks of "the peculiarly professional, legalistic, and abstract approach to law in the modern sense."[31] Still, the modern type has a long history. Its mode of formal rationality "developed out of Roman law."[32]

When Weber, who died in 1920, characterizes qualities of modern formal law, he has in mind a signal achievement of the law of his day: development of the German Civil Code. The exemplar of modern law, for Weber, is the Civil Code, promulgated in 1896. He is "especially interested" in the Code's subject, private law.[33] The Code offers a systematic statement of the law of contracts, torts, property, the family, and inheritance.

Weber's portrait of modern formal law shows two ways in which formal law and argument are law-like. First, formal law possesses law-like qualities. It is law-like in expression and in operation. Second, formal argument undertakes to make laws cohere. It engages in coherence-seeking. Together law-like qualities and quest of coherence constitute fully law-like formality.

Law-Like Argument

Nomological argument, as defined by the present study, invokes general legal precepts as grounds of particular judgments. Laws are formulated as generally applicable prescription able to support consistent judgment. Law-like argument states the meaning of standing general law and proceeds, by impersonal reasoning, to connect general premises to adjudged results. It works to establish a pattern of consistent decision by rational resolution of concrete cases.

The kind of rationality exemplified by formal law, as described by Weber, is pretty much the same thing as nomological rationality, as defined by this book. For Weber, rationality refers to reasoning based on generalized grounds. It lies in the logical connection between an abstract category and its concrete instances. In formalized law, "legal decision [is] the 'application' of an abstract legal proposition to a concrete 'fact situation.'" Decision is derived "from abstract legal propositions by means of legal logic." Formal judgment pays attention to those particularities of cases which are instances of law's classes, and ignores the rest. "[T]he facts of life are juridically 'construed' in order to make them fit the abstract propositions of law."[34]

---

[30] Quotes in the second sentence of this paragraph come from *ES2*, p. 657.   [31] *ES2*, p. 657.
[32] *ES2*, p. 656.   [33] *ES2*, p. 655.
[34] The three quotes in this paragraph come, in sequence, from *ES2*, pp. 657, 657, 885.

The opposite of formally rational decision is judgment based on practical moral assessment of all the circumstances of a particular situation. Practical moral assessment and formal decision are opposites in two ways. In Weber's terminology, moral decision is "substantive," not formal, in content. And, because concrete assessment of circumstance doesn't proceed from general premise to particular conclusion, it is, for Weber, not "rational" in argumentative logic.[35]

First, practical moral assessment comes to decision "on the basis of . . . ethical, or political considerations."[36] Decisive grounds of moral assessment figure in ethical and political debate outside law; they are not specifically legal. By contrast, formal law and argument are quintessentially legal. For Weber, formal means not moral, as it does in the lexicon of this book. Formal reasoning in legal discourse is differentiated – cut off – from moral and political argument.

Second, moral assessment of a particular situation "is influenced by concrete factors of the particular case . . . rather than by general norms."[37] Decision is dependent on unique features of a situation to be judged. Therefore, judgment of the case is ungeneralizable. By contrast, formal judgment of a state of affairs is controlled by abstract grounds, not concrete context. Abstract law is applied to concrete circumstance. Formal grounds are logically general.

Formal assessment of a state of affairs sees the general in the particular, the abstract in the concrete. "[O]nly . . . general characteristics of the facts of the case are taken into account." In formal law, plenary assessment of circumstance is blocked. "[W]hatever cannot be 'construed' rationally in legal terms is also legally irrelevant." Thus formal judgment treats all concrete situations within the same generalized classification the same.[38]

Rational Coherence

According to our analysis, argument in nomological practice is directed by the imperative of coherence. The imperative of coherence says that related rules of law should be read in association with one another so that they fit together. Coherence-seeking argument works to fit rules together in patterns demonstrable through general propositions.

Max Weber contrasts two kinds of formal law. Primitive formal law – "a youthful law"[39] – is a mass of separately stated rules. Modern formal law is a mass of rules structured by organizing ideas. The first type displays consistency. The second type seeks coherence.

Primitive formal law displays consistency, an absence of flat contradiction among laws, but not coherence. In primitive formality, laws are separate commands. All of law is an aggregation of concrete rules, and nothing more, without organizing

---

[35] The two quotes of the paragraph are from *ES2*, p. 656.   [36] *ES2*, p. 813.   [37] *ES2*, p. 656.
[38] The two quotes of the paragraph, in sequence, are from *ES2*, pp. 656–657 and 657.
[39] *ES2*, p. 656.

structure. Weber speaks of "the rigidity of concrete formalism." Legal results depend on technicalities like "the execution of a signature." The laws are laid out in "a merely paratactic association" – that is, side by side, one after the other, but not in an ordered relation. Absent unifying structure, legal argument "exhausts itself in casuistry."[40]

Modern formal law, by contrast, displays rational coherence. In modern formality, law's formal rules are generalized and unified. Development of doctrine proceeds by what Weber calls "logical interpretation of meaning." This is a mental process whereby formal rules and rulings are restated in order to produce "integration."[41]

Legal argument starts with specific rulings stated in terms of the facts of cases. "[T]he legally relevant characteristics of the facts are disclosed through the logical analysis of meaning." By analysis of particular rulings, general rules are framed. "[D]efinitely fixed legal concepts in the form of highly abstract rules are formulated ..." Particular formal rules and categories are associated with one another as parts of a whole. "[T]he several rules recognized as legally valid" are brought together "into an internally consistent complex of abstract legal propositions." The result is a "system of rules" – formal structure.[42]

Formal Structuring

According to analysis of this book, formal argument, driven by the imperative of coherence, builds formal structure. Structuring argument brings about two kinds of order among laws. The two kinds of order are the earmarks of demonstrable coherence in law.

First, coherence lies in harmonious fit of legal ground with legal ground. Coherence-seeking draws legal elements together, in order to bring about ordered association of laws. Related rules are read together, each in light of the others, so that they fit together.

Second, coherence is displayed by propositions that say how, in general, laws fit together. Coherence-seeking develops organizing ideas. General propositions articulate the pattern according to which the rules of an area of law cohere.

According to Max Weber, two processes of active structuring are undertaken in the formalization of law. Weber's two processes work to establish the two aspects of coherence – harmonious fit, organizing ideas – just noted. Weber's first process is, in his description, "the construction of legal relationships." The second process is "the analytical derivation of legal propositions." Together these two activities, conducted within the various domains of modern formal law, build and show structured relations among laws.[43]

---

[40] The four quotes, in sequence, are from ES2, pp. 657, 657, 655, 657.
[41] Quotes in sequence are from ES2, pp. 657, 656.
[42] Quotes in sequence are from ES2, pp. 657, 657, 657, 656.
[43] The two quotes in this paragraph are from ES2, p. 656.

The first process identified by Weber is "synthesis."[44] Synthesizing argument addresses collateral rules, separate rules sitting side by side in an area of law but not in ordered relation. It brings the separate rules together. Synthesis is coordination.

Weber equates synthesis and "construction." "[S]ynthetic work" constructs "legal relations" and "legal institutions." Among legal relations are contract and inheritance; legal institutions include property and marriage. The process of synthesis starts with separate rules that say "which aspects of a typical kind of social or consensual action are to be regarded as legally relevant." A number of rules combine to constitute an action such as assertion of ownership, or a consensual relation such as an employment contract.[45]

"[C]onstructional" reasoning defines relations among the various categories of mutually qualifying rules. It establishes "in which logically consistent way these relevant components are to be regarded as legally coordinated." Coordination of separate concepts and precepts states unifying definitions and distinctions. It formulates general rules in association with particular qualifications, rules and exceptions. The result is rationalization of "the several rules ... into an internally consistent complex ..."[46]

The second process identified by Weber is "generalization."[47] Generalizing argument addresses a group – a complex – of related formal rules. Its product, an encompassing precept, says what, in general, the rules of the complex, taken as a whole, prescribe.

Weber calls generalization a "process of reduction." It starts with specific rules and rulings, and generates widely applicable prescriptions that encompass the specifics. "[T]he reasons relevant in the decision of concrete individual cases [are reduced] to one or more 'principles,' i.e., legal propositions." The method of generalizing argument is "logical analysis of ... meaning."[48]

Analysis of meaning formulates more highly general legal expressions that fit less highly general items. Analysis leads to "the development of legal propositions of high logical sublimation." Such propositions articulate in abstract terms the definitions and distinctions that serve to organize interrelated rules. Generalization of meaning is complementary to synthesis. The extraction of general teachings from particular items aids, and is aided by, the putting together of collateral elements. Weber says that "the analytical derivation of 'legal propositions' ... goes hand in hand with the synthetic work ..."[49]

---

[44] ES2, p. 656. In fact, in his brilliant exposition of formalization in the brief section of ES2 entitled "The Categories of Legal Thought," Weber deals with generalization first, and goes on to describe synthesis.

[45] The five quoted words and phrases in this paragraph come from ES2, pp. 655 (emphasis in original omitted) and 656.

[46] The three quotes in this paragraph come, in sequence, from ES2, pp. 656, 655 (emphasis omitted), and 657.

[47] ES2, p. 655.   [48] Quotes in this paragraph come, in sequence, from ES2, pp. 655, 655, 656.

[49] The two quotes here are from ES2, p. 655.

Synthesis and generalization, conducted together, work to achieve "integration" of the rules and categories within a domain of law.[50] The product is formal structure.

A formal structure is a complex of rules standing in defined relations within a scheme of distinctions. A structure contains generalities and specifics. Together the generalities provide a framework which contains, and orders, particular rules.

Within a developed formal structure, rules are coordinated, so that their prescriptions are aligned. The structure organizes rules pointing in different directions. It identifies rules that apply generally, and rules that apply exceptionally. Categories used by particular rules are linked. A situation may fall within one category and be handled one way, or may fall within another category and be handled another way. Generalizations about the complex of rules as a whole help to order the mutually qualifying rules in relation to one another.

Structuring in Domains

Weber's inventory of the constituents of formal structure is in line with analysis of this book. A formal structure is made up of linked rules, displaying a set of distinctions, plus associated generality. According to our analysis, the imperative of coherence, at the heart of law-like law, impels coherence-seeking – structuring – throughout law. This view is substantially the same as Weber's, in a different vocabulary – with one qualification.

When he describes formal structuring, Weber has in mind, as an example, the organizing project of the Civil Code. It is possible to think of a civil code as a vast effort of coordination whereby separate legal subjects are, despite their apparent diversity, unified within a single set of generalized concepts and organizing propositions. Structuring brings laws together. It might be thought that there is no logical stopping point for coherence-seeking in law short of bringing the whole of law together within one immense structure.

The analysis of this book is much more modest. There is no implication that structuring on a very large scale is the most important – much less the only – sort of coherence-seeking regularly undertaken within formal law. Yes, structuring is constantly conducted everywhere in law-like law. But demarcation – the separation of one legal subject from another legal subject – is a form of structuring. Separately statable structures are formed in particular areas of legal doctrine. Structuring goes on in the domains of law – plural. Structuring argument builds structures – plural.

A domain of related laws may be large or small. Large domains encompass small ones. The same features that constitute structure in a large domain – linked rules, a set of distinctions, associated generalization – may be found within small domains. For example, the features of formal structure can be seen within fairly technical doctrine concerning admissibility of evidence about change in a product's design,

[50] ES2, p. 656.

which is one component of doctrine concerning design defect, which is a part of doctrine of products liability, within tort law, within private law.

What is vital in Weber's view of formality is his recognition that the processes of structuring – synthesis and generalization – are fundamental activities of formalizing argument in modern legal practice. While argument in diverse domains develops a diversity of structures, the activities of linking up related rules and developing organizing generalities are ubiquitous. The structures developed are different, in the many domains of law; the logic of structuring is the same.

6.4 HALF-RIGHT VIEWS

In the present chapter, we have studied the views of two notable commentators on law, political philosopher John Rawls and legal sociologist Max Weber, who alike affirm the law-like character of liberal law's formality. Rawls says that formal law possesses the qualities necessary in order to realize the rule of law in society. Weber says that formal legal reasoning is sufficient to establish coherent interrelation of rules and categories throughout law. Their views about the law-like nature of formality are in line with analysis of this book.

But both of our tutelary commentators, while they are valuable guides to the understanding of law-like formality, are only half-right. As we have seen, each develops a line of argument focusing on one half of deeply dual liberal law – but not on the other half.

There are two modes of prescription and argument in law, formal and ideal. Formed within practice of liberal law, both modes develop to become fully law-like – that is the thesis of this book. But John Rawls in *A Theory of Justice*, which states Rawls' first view of law, and Max Weber in all his writings, are partisans of formality exclusively. Neither recognizes the equal status of the other half of law's duality. On account of their failure to affirm the fully law-like character of nonformal – ideal – argument in liberal law, their one-sided views are half-wrong.

Rawls' Mistake

As we may recall, in *A Theory of Justice* John Rawls identifies the rule of law with formal law exclusively. Rawls says that the idea of formal justice is the same thing as the rule of law. Formal justice is "the regular and impartial administration of public rules." "[T]he conception of formal justice . . . becomes the rule of law when applied to the legal system."[51]

Rawls' identification of the rule of law with formal law exclusively is a mistake. It is a mistake to think that what we are calling liberal legality, which includes the rule of law in the world, is realized only by formal rules and rule-governed argument. Yes,

---

[51] Quotes in this paragraph are from *TJ*, p. 235.

judgment based on rules is one method of securing the governance of law in the world. But judgment based on nonformal – practical moral – grounds is another. Formal law is one way of realizing the rule of law; development of law in line with law's ideals is another way.

The idea of a regime of law at work securing entitlement and justice is larger than the idea of formalized law: it is twice as large. Since liberal – or law-like – legality might be realized in either of two ways, therefore commitment to achieve legality gives rise to an impulse to develop two kinds of law and argument, formalized law and also idealized law, law-like legal rules and also law-like legal ideals.

Earlier in this book we saw that the mistake now under discussion – mistaken identification of the rule of law with formality exclusively – is an error propagated within a particular tradition of legal thought.[52] We called this line of thought Weberian. Max Weber, in his influential sociology of law, emphasized the vital importance of formality in modern law. Within the Weberian tradition, nonformal – practical moral – argument is disparaged. It is understood that legal argument governed by practical moral aims cannot sustain the rule of law. We called this error the Weberian mistake.

Weber's Mistake

For all his brilliance in identifying processes that combine to construct coherence in formal law, Weber is, in all his views about modern law, only half-right. He is right about the law-like, structure-producing character of formal argument in law. He is wrong about ideal argument.

As we saw in detail earlier in the book, Weber claimed that, while formal law is law-like, nonformal law – law governed by ideal aims – is not.[53] The great strength of Weber's analysis of law is its affirmative understanding of formality. The great weakness of Weber's analysis is the other side of the coin, his disparagement of nonformal argument in law.

Weber takes the position that use of practical moral grounds in law defeats specifically legal rationality. Argument based on practical moral aims – ideal argument – is, in Weber's lexicon, substantive, as opposed to formal. Weber defines legal rationality in such a way that it is upheld fully – indeed, it is upheld more or less by definition – by modern formal law. But, he finds, it is not upheld by pursuit of substantive justice. According to Weber, substantive reasoning does not support rules in regular – consistent, generalizable – operation. Formal law on the one hand, and ideal argument on the other hand, are necessarily opposed.

---

[52] See Chapter 4, pp. 44–45. [53] See Chapter 4, pp. 45–46.

This is a mistake. Analysis of the present study shows that legal rationality is not the monopoly of formal law. Two modes of law, formal and ideal, are alike ways of realizing specifically legal – nomological – rationality. Formal pursuit and ideal pursuit alike seek coherence. Both develop tectonic processes that bring multiple legal elements together in systematic union. The idea of structure controls fully developed ideal argumentation, the same as it does fully developed formal argument, in law-like legal practice.

What Dworkin Gets Right

In order to see how legal ideals are formed within what we may call, following Weber, modern practice of law, meaning law today, we need to turn to a legal theorist who, unlike Weber, does not understand law's ideals to be implacably at war with law's rules. In the following chapter, we will look at ideas of legal theorist Ronald Dworkin, who believes that ideal aims embodied in formal rules are vitally important constituents of law. Dworkin does for ideal argument what Weber does for formal argument: each shows what fully law-like legal argument looks like.

Earlier in the present chapter, we saw that Ronald Dworkin's understanding of formal law is inadequate. He considers formal law to be a disorganized collection of separate items. This is a bad portrait of formality formed within practice of liberal legality. So, within these pages, where we have yet to examine the law-like nature of law's ideals, Dworkin starts out half-wrong.

But on the matter of ideal argument in law, the topic of the following chapter, Dworkin gets things right. Therefore, Dworkin's view of law as a whole is, like Weber's, half-right and half-wrong. Indeed, it is the exact reverse of Weber's. Dworkin is wrong about the character of formality, where Weber is right; he is right about the character of law's ideals, where Weber is wrong.

As we shall see, Dworkin's explication of the law-like nature of law's ideals runs pretty much in parallel to Weber's portrait of law's formality. And that congruence, according to analysis of this book, which says that two modes of law-like law, on a par, take shape in practice of legality, is as it should be.

7

Deep Duality: Law's Ideals

In our search for a comprehensive picture of deep duality of liberal law, we are halfway to our goal. Complete, such a picture will display the two branches of law-like law and legal argument in full flower: first, fully law-like formality; second, fully law-like legal ideals. In the prior chapter, we looked at one half of this composition, as presented by Max Weber. There we saw the features of formalization of law as it develops within modern liberal practice. In the present chapter, we will focus on idealization of law – the other half of deeply dual liberal law. Here we will study the picture of law's ideals drawn by Ronald Dworkin.

General analysis of the present study tells us that law must possess certain qualities in order to be in accord with nomological commitment – that is, in order to be able to sustain legal entitlement and legal justice. In a nutshell, law-like law, whether formal or ideal, necessarily displays three defining features. First, it is standing law. Second, it supports consistent decision. Third, it seeks coherence. According to Dworkin, ideals in liberal law – law's principles and policies – manifest each of these three traits.

First, in order to sustain legal entitlement, a ground of judgment must be part of standing law. To be entitled by law is to depend on law's meaning. Preexisting law upholds the entitlement.

According to Dworkin, legal ideals are a vital part of the meaning of extant law. Ideal principles and policies are anchored in law's rules. They are practical moral aims embodied in law that exists.

Second, in order to sustain legal justice, a precept of law must support consistent decision. A law-like law confers evenhanded treatment. Its prescription is the same for all members of a class.

According to Dworkin, law's principles and policies are generally applicable directives. They state the rationales of law's rules. Like the rules, they prescribe consistent disposition.

Third, law-like legal argument, by nature, seeks coherence. Through coherence-seeking argument, laws are fit together. General propositions of law state the pattern of their association.

Dworkin shows that ideal argument works to bring about demonstrable coherence. Law's ideal aims are organizing premises. Ideals in law are structured in relation to one another and used to structure law's rules.

7.1 A CONTRARY VIEW

The outline of features of law-like ideals just presented will be fleshed out shortly. The main business of the present chapter is to examine Ronald Dworkin's understanding of law-like ideals. We are on our way to close study of Dworkin's view of ideal aims formed in liberal law. But before we get there, a brief digression is in order. Again, as in the prior chapter, we will employ – briefly – a method of looking at contrasts.

In the prior chapter, where our topic was law-like formality, we followed a method of developing an understanding of law-like law by thinking about its opposite. There, before examining Max Weber's view of law-like formality in detail, we took a moment to look at a contrary understanding. As we saw, qualities of law-like law are thrown into relief by first looking at law without those qualities.

Now our topic is law-like idealization of law. We may throw light on the nature of law-like ideals by considering what ideal argument without law-like qualities would look like. A picture of legal ideals without law-like qualities is the opposite of Dworkin's view. Such a picture is presented by legal philosopher H. L. A. Hart.

The central point of Hart's legal philosophy is that law is an affair of rules. For Hart, formal rules, knowable without moral inquiry, are the chief constituents of law. Hart shows that formal legal rules – unlike ideals – possess law-like features. As we have seen, John Rawls, in A *Theory of Justice*, says that Hart's view of law as rules describes the kind of law needed in order to carry out the rule of law.[1] Hart's showing that rules in liberal law possess law-like qualities is in line with analysis of this book.

But presently the focus of our interest is not Hart's affirmative understanding of law's formality, but rather Hart's contrasting – negative – view of law's ideals. Hart says that ideal argument in law is not law-like in nature. Hart's portrayal of ideals in law is sharply opposed to that of Ronald Dworkin – and it is contrary to analysis of this book. Following immediately below is a summary of Hart's contrary view.

Hart's Contrasts

H. L. A. Hart's legal theory postulates a fundamental difference between law's rules on the one hand, and ideal aims used in law on the other hand.[2] Law's rules are law-like. Rules are mutually compatible grounds of decision under law. By contrast, ideals lack law-like qualities. Ideals are rival grounds of discretionary judgment.

---

[1] See Chapter 6, pp. 92–93.
[2] See Hart, "Positivism and the Separation of Law and Morals" (1958); Hart, *The Concept of Law* (1961). Hereafter, in this chapter, Hart's 1958 article is cited as "Positivism"; *The Concept of Law* is cited as CL.

According to Hart, law that exists is made up of rules. Rules are at the center of "the structure of a legal system." Decision by law is decision under rules. Legal argument undertakes "rule-governed operations." A number of related legal rules, associated as rules and exceptions, constitute "the framework" used in decision of cases. Rules are grounds of regular resolution.[3]

Hart's portrait of ideals in law displays two main contrasts between legal ideals and law's rules. First, while rules are precepts of standing law, ideal considerations are not. Ideal argument leads to legislative judgment.[4] Standing law is formal. Second, while rules in law are consistent grounds, ideals are not. Ideals are conflicting aims, at odds with one another. Law's consistency is formal.

First, according to Hart, ideals are grounds of lawmaking. Ideal argument in law invokes practical purposes and policies as the basis of decision. Judgment based on this sort of argument is "legislative activity," "judicial law-making."[5]

Ideal argument by a court, leading to a legal conclusion, is "exercise of discretion." Decision is reached "by reference to some conception of what law ought to be." The court's decision is not the application of existing law. It is "choice between moral values." The resulting ruling of the court is new law. It arises from assertion of "law-creating power." "Judges . . . legislate and so exercise a creative choice between alternatives." Ideal decision is the opposite of rational resolution under law.[6]

Second, ideals in law are disorganized, according to Hart. In ideal argument, multiple "aims, purposes, and policies" address the same legal matter. They are incompatible considerations, contrary "social values," "conflicting interests."[7]

The pertinent aims say "what from many different points of view ought to be." Divergent practical aims point in different directions. Choice among opposing ideals requires "striking a balance . . . between competing interests." Prior to legislative choice, the opposition of rival ideals is unresolved. The ideals are not grounds of consistent disposition. Rather they are the basis of "fresh judgment from case to case."[8]

A Mistaken View

Like other legal theorists discussed in this book, H. L. A. Hart affirms law's duality. Hart recognizes the existence of two kinds of legal argument, formal and ideal. But, for Hart, law's duality is superficial. One kind of argument – reasoning based on

---

[3] Quotes in this paragraph come, in order, from CL, pp. 133, 150, 133.

[4] The text here speaks of "standing law" in the sense used to define legal entitlement as dependence on standing law only. This sense has nothing to do with so-called "soft positivism," defined in Hart's "Postscript" to CL, p. 250.

[5] The two quotes in this paragraph are from CL, pp. 131, 150.

[6] Of the five quotes in this paragraph, the second and last are from "Positivism," p. 612. The other three, in order, are from CL, pp. 132, 200, 141.

[7] The first two quotes of the paragraph are from "Positivism," pp. 614, 610. The third quote is from CL, p. 128.

[8] The first quote of the paragraph is from "Positivism," p. 613. The other two are from CL, p. 132.

rules – is law-like, but the other kind is not. Ideal considerations invoked in law are not standing law, nor the basis of consistent decision.

Hart's disparaging view of law's ideals is a mistake. Hart's portrait displays multiple aims detached from law in constant collision. This is a false picture of ideals formed within liberal legal practice. Hart ignores the regimen that controls ideal argument in liberal legality. When it comes to law's ideals, he pays no attention to the discipline of nomological commitment.

First, it is a mistake to think that ideals used in legal argument are free-floating values or purposes detached from law.

Ideal propositions formed in liberal practice are the opposite of free-floating. They are grounded in law, anchored in law's formality. Legal ideals are practical moral aims seen to be embodied in existing rules of law. An aim embodied in a rule is the rule's rationale. The ideal fits the rule, and justifies it. Aims that fit and justify law's rules are, like the rules, prescriptions of existing law. Ideals embodied in law are constituents of law.

Second, it is a mistake to think that ideals put to use in law are, by nature, disorganized, in constant opposition, unable to yield consistent decision.

Legal ideals are formed to fit and justify general rules. The rules prescribe the same treatment for all members of the classes they define. Ideals that fit the rules likewise prescribe like treatment. Moreover, law's ideals are developed, within liberal law, in line with the imperative of coherence. This imperative instructs legal argument to bring multiple ideal aims into structured relation. Accordingly, law's ideals, formed to fit general rules within coherence-seeking liberal law, are, by nature, law-like.

As noted at the outset of the present section, our consideration of ideas of H. L. A. Hart about legal ideals serves an introductory purpose. The point of our brief look at Hart's inadequate view is to highlight, by contrast, the main features of Ronald Dworkin's essentially opposite view. On the matter of the law-like nature of legal ideals in liberal law, Hart is wrong; Dworkin gets things right.

Unlike Hart, Dworkin pays attention to the specific character of idealizing argument conducted within liberal – nomological – practice. According to Dworkin, ideals put to use in practice of law-like law exhibit the three salient features of law-like law. Legal ideals, first, are grounded in standing law; second, are formed to support consistent decision; and third, serve in argument as the basis of law's coherence.

7.2 LAW-LIKE IDEALS: DWORKIN

Ronald Dworkin says that principles and policies of law are the most important legal grounds.[9] Law's principles and policies are practical moral aims. They say what formal law ought ideally to bring about. They are used to guide and shape formal rules.

---

[9] See generally Dworkin, "Hard Cases" (1975). Hereafter, in this chapter, "Hard Cases" is cited as "HC."

Because ideals are practical moral grounds, ideal argument makes a break with law's formality. Formal rules are nonmoral. In order to find out that a rule exists as law and what it says, an arguer must conduct a factual – not a moral – inquiry. In contrast, in order to identify law's principles and policies, it is necessary to conduct a kind of moral inquiry – a justificatory inquiry.

A single phrase defines the fundamental relation between ideals in law and law's formal rules. Legal ideals fit and justify. They fit and justify law's rules. An ideal aim fits a rule when its prescription is in line with that of the rule. The ideal is a practical moral reason; when it fits, it provides a good reason for the rule. It is the rule's rationale, the spirit behind the letter. When a principle or policy fits, it justifies.

According to Dworkin, policies and principles are two different types of practical aims. As defined by Dworkin, a policy is a directive "that sets out a goal to be reached, generally an improvement in some economic, political, or social feature of the community . . ." For example, the desirable objective that "automobile accidents are to be decreased" is a policy. A principle is a precept "that is to be observed, not because it will advance or secure [a] situation deemed desirable, but because it is a requirement of justice or fairness or some other dimension of morality." The imperative that "no man may profit by his own wrong" is a principle.[10]

As we have noted, argument based on policies and principles is, in a way, discontinuous with formal law. While formal means nonmoral, ideal objectives and imperatives are grounds that justify as a matter of practical morality. But legal ideals fit as well as justify rules. First they must fit. The requirement of fit ensures a significant degree of continuity between formal law and ideal reasoning.

The Requirement of Fit

The key to the legality of law's ideals is the requirement of fit. Legal ideals are aims which are shown to fit and justify law's formal rules, and then are used to guide and shape the rules. An ideal that fits a formal rule is in prescriptive accord with the rule. What the ideal prescribes, and what the rule prescribes, are in accord. Given fit with law's rules, the policies and principles of law are specifically legal grounds.

According to Dworkin, the process of formulating the ideal objective served by a given rule, or group of related rules, is a demanding undertaking. Upon an initial look, alternative formulations might each seem plausible. Careful assessment is needed to find the alternative that fits best.

Dworkin gives an example designed to show the care required in order to find the policy that fits underlying formal law.[11] His example has to do with a statute enacted by the United States Congress making it a federal crime to cross state lines, say from Pennsylvania to Ohio, in furtherance of conduct that is illegal under state law, say

---

[10] The quoted phrases in this paragraph are from Dworkin, "The Model of Rules" (1967), p. 23.
[11] "HC," pp. 1085–1086.

law of Pennsylvania. Stated in broad terms, the practical aim that justifies the statute's definition of a federal crime is a policy of effective law enforcement, specifically, a policy in favor of federal enforcement. But, according to Dworkin, policy argument should be more precise than that.

Good policy argument, according to Dworkin, is as follows. A policy in favor of federal enforcement must be limited to situations where state enforcement is significantly hampered. Otherwise, the policy would not fit law of federalism, which gives the state primary responsibility in matters of criminal law. The penalties provided by the statute in question are large. A policy that fits the penalties is one that focuses on major crime. In sum, the aim that fits the statute, its penalties, and surrounding law of federalism, is this: a policy in favor of federal enforcement, when state enforcement is hampered, in cases of serious crime.

The policy that fits, since it is a practical moral aim, also justifies. Effective enforcement is a desirable objective. It is, as Dworkin says, a "justification of the statute."[12] It is a good reason for the rule established by the statute. Rooted in law, it is law's own morality.

Law's morality is made up of principles as well as policies. Principled argument, like policy argument, is controlled by the requirement of fit. Dworkin gives an example of carefully conducted argument to establish a principle of law. This time the example, an argument made in the nineteenth century, is, as he says, "famous."[13]

In 1890, Samuel Warren and Louis Brandeis, in a well-known article, argue that the law of their day supports the principle of privacy – "the right to be let alone."[14] Warren and Brandeis point to doctrines having to do with the common-law right to intellectual and artistic property. Decisions in this area hold unpermitted publication of someone's diary or letters to be wrongful. After exacting analysis to determine the principle that fits these doctrines in detail, Warren and Brandeis find that, while the decisions may speak of intellectual property, their aim is to protect personal privacy. They conclude: "The principle which protects ... personal productions ... against publication ... is in reality not the principle of private property, but that of an inviolate personality."

Together, Dworkin's examples of the policy of effective enforcement underlying the federal statute, and the principle of privacy embodied in the common-law doctrines, demonstrate three things. First, law's policies and principles are aims that fit formality; second, finding out what fits is a rigorous inquiry; third, what fits is law's own practical morality.

Standing Law

Law's morality is, for Dworkin, fully part of law. Policies and principles that fit the rules of law are, along with the rules, constituents of law that exists. Developing ideal

---

[12] "HC," p. 1086.   [13] "HC," p. 1097.
[14] See Warren and Brandeis, "The Right to Privacy" (1890). Quotes in this paragraph are from the article at pp. 193, 205.

grounds of legal argument is a way of apprehending the meaning of the standing law. The meaning of standing law is the basis of legal entitlement.

As defined by analysis of the present study, the idea of legal entitlement breaks down into three components. First, legal entitlements are valued positions of persons in social life. Second, entitlement by law depends on the meaning of the standing law. Third, entitlement does not depend on the will of the authorities.

Dworkin, in his own vocabulary, says that legal argument based on principles and policies exemplifies all three components of legal entitlement.

First, for Dworkin, valued positions of persons in social life are defined by "legal rights." Argument invoking principles and policies of law establishes people's rights under law. "[P]arties have rights in hard cases as well as in easy ones ..."[15]

Second, for Dworkin, meaning of standing law includes law's morality. Law's principles and policies, taken together, constitute "morality presupposed by the laws." Judgment based on law's morality secures "institutional rights," rights upheld by the institutional processes of existing law.[16]

Third, for Dworkin, judgment based on the will of someone in authority is the opposite of impersonal judgment based on law's morality. A judge's reliance on personal moral conviction is "offensive." By contrast, judgment based on morality rooted in law is both "how judges actually decide cases" and also what judges "must" do in order to determine people's rights. Ground rules defining good argument and proper judging in our legal system call for decision according to the theory of law that "best justifies settled law."[17]

Consistent Decision

According to analysis herein, legal ideals, formed within liberal practice of law, are law-like grounds. Ideals are formulated as general precepts able to support consistent decision. A law-like ideal is a general directive that yields the same prescription for all members of a class. Ideal argument based on law-like grounds works to sustain legal justice.

According to Dworkin, law's principles and policies are grounds of evenhanded disposition. They secure consistent decision "from one case to the next." A principle or policy used in law is an "individuated" aim. That is, it applies to all individuals similarly situated. Thus it sustains "the fairness of treating like cases alike."[18]

---

[15] Quotes in this paragraph are from "HC," pp. 1104, 1108.
[16] Quotes in this paragraph are, in sequence, from "HC," pp. 1105, 1078.
[17] The first three quotes in this paragraph come in sequence from "HC," pp. 1102, 1066, 1066. The fourth quote is from Ronald Dworkin, *Taking Rights Seriously* (1977b), p. 283.
[18] Quotes in this paragraph are, in sequence, from "HC," pp. 1064, 1068, 1090. Dworkin says that "the general justification of the practice of precedent ... is fairness." "HC," p. 1093.

In contrast to law's principles and policies, Dworkin points to a well-known practical moral aim which is "nonindividuated." This is the aim of bringing about, as a consequence of action, "overall general welfare or utility." Decision in line with this aim chooses the alternative course of action which will, in the circumstances, maximize good consequences. The aim of "overall benefit for the community as a whole" is nonindividuated because it doesn't "call for any particular opportunity or resource or liberty for particular individuals."[19]

Dworkin gives the following example of nonindividuated judgment. A judge rules in one case that a certain liberty should be protected, for the sake of overall welfare, but declines to protect the same liberty in the next case, because "the first decision gave the community just the amount of ... liberty it needed, so that no more is required at the time of the second."[20]

Dworkin says that a type of practical moral argument which, because it is non-individuated, is unable to support consistent judgment, is disallowed in our legal system. He is right about that. While radically particularistic – ad hoc, anomic – moral reasoning may be appropriate in contexts outside law, it is barred from law, ruled out by fundamental commitment to legal justice.

This is not to say that ideal argument in law cannot appeal to such goals as welfare or economic efficiency. It can, according to Dworkin, so long as argument proceeds in the manner of "the ethical theory called rule utilitarianism."[21] A rule-utilitarian says that, when a general rule is justified because it serves overall utility, the rule ought to be followed each time its terms apply to a particular case. Since the rule itself supports consistent decision, so, in operation, does the utilitarian aim that supports the rule.

Here is the reason why policy goals formed and used in law are by nature law-like. Rules of law are law-like; they support consistent decision. Law's policies fit and justify legal rules in regular operation; therefore, they are themselves law-like.[22]

---

[19]   Quotes in this paragraph are, in sequence, from "HC," pp. 1068, 1073, 1068, 1068.
[20]   "HC," p. 1065.   [21]   "HC," p. 1072.
[22]   In his essay on "Hard Cases," Dworkin draws a distinction between "principle" and "policy." He says a principle secures "an individual right," while a policy promotes "a collective goal." Then he states a preference for principles over policies. He accepts that policy-based reasoning is perfectly appropriate in constitutional law and in statutory interpretation. But he suggests that interpretation of the common law should be based on "arguments of principle rather than arguments of policy." See "HC," pp. 1067, 1085, 1086, 1093.

Dworkin's preference for principles in interpreting the common law is beyond the scope of the present book. What is important for purposes of discussion herein is that Dworkin does not say that policy argument should be barred from law altogether because it suffers from some sort of fundamental defect. He grants that policy argument in law supports consistent decision. After all, he thinks that policies are perfectly proper grounds of judgment in constitutional law, the most important kind of law. In short, he believes that policies, like principles, when formed and used in law, are law-like.

Coherence-Seeking

In his jurisprudential writings, Dworkin imagines how an exemplary judge would argue and decide. He calls his exemplary judge "Hercules." Hercules, the figure of myth, takes on big jobs; Hercules, the imagined judge, does the same. Dworkin's Hercules engages in coherence-seeking argument based on principles and policies of law. Such argument surveys a group of given legal elements and works to make the several elements fit together. Making a lot of things cohere is a big job.

In the prior chapter[23] we saw that, according to Dworkin, law's practical moral aims are grounds of "articulate consistency."[24] Articulate consistency is another name for coherence. Coherence exists among a group of legal items when two things are true. First, the items are consistent in their particular prescriptions. Second, the items fit together in a pattern articulable by general propositions.

Coherence-seeking argument develops organizing principles and policies. An organizing principle or policy provides a general justification of a body of law. The general justification is the articulate ground according to which the related laws cohere.

Dworkin gives an example of organizing argument working to establish coherence within a whole field of law. The field is "law of negligence and accidents." As Dworkin describes it, this domain of law contains doctrines and decisions having to do with such diverse topics as defective products, incompetent accountants, waiver of liability, industrial accident, and airplane crashes. Organizing argument seeks to find "a coherent justification" for law of the field as a whole. Coherent justification, according to Dworkin, affirms the "right of each person to the reasonable care of others." Reasonable care is an aspect of the "respect due a fellow human being." The overall justification integrates the law of the domain. By its light, particular doctrines and decisions fit together.[25]

Dworkin shows how the general justification of a group of specific decisions may lead to the resolution of an undecided case. The case presents a big issue. In his example, the undecided case presents the question whether a woman has a constitutional right, under the due process clause, to have an abortion. The pathway to decision, says Dworkin, might proceed as follows. "Suppose the earlier due process cases can be justified only by supposing some important right to human dignity." Then women may be found to have a right to an abortion "as an aspect of their . . . right to dignity." Thus, the general justificatory idea of "dignity" both organizes a group of past decisions and generates a new one.[26]

According to Dworkin, coherence-seeking argument builds justifying theories. A justifying theory of law addresses a domain of formal doctrine. It states the general ideal conception that organizes law of the domain. In light of its governing

---

[23]   See Chapter 6, p. 95.   [24]   "HC," p. 1064.
[25]   Quotes of the paragraph are from "HC" in sequence at pp. 1097, 1098, 1097, 1075–1076.
[26]   The quotes in this paragraph are from "HC," pp. 1105, 1106.

conception, the theory orders particular principles and policies of the area of the law with respect to one another and with respect to underlying formal material. An ideal theory of a body of law provides a framework for use in argument interpreting that law.

In constitutional interpretation, Dworkin's exemplary judge, Hercules, develops "a theory of the constitution." This is "a complex set of principles and policies that justify" law of the constitution. "It must be a scheme that fits the particular rules of this constitution, of course." In interpreting a statute, Hercules asks: "Which arguments of principle and policy might properly have persuaded the legislature to enact just that statute?" In common law, Hercules asks, "What set of principles best justifies the precedents?"[27]

Though Hercules, who personifies quest of coherence throughout law, develops large theories, Dworkin emphasizes that, in workaday legal argument, Hercules focuses on the specific body of law involved in a case up for judgment. He follows a "doctrine of local priority." If Hercules finds that a particular justifying principle makes a good fit with a particular body of law, he is prepared to use that justification in interpretation of that law, even if the principle is not so well sustained by law outside the "local" department. Thus, Hercules accepts the "compartmentalization of law." Drawing lines demarcating distinct domains is a way coherence may be achieved.[28]

7.3 HALVES OF A WHOLE

Our search for a comprehensive picture of law's duality, conducted in the prior chapter and the present one, is almost at an end. The main object of these two chapters, announced at the outset, is to examine in succession two separate pictures of liberal law, constructed by two tutelary legal theorists, which together constitute a comprehensive portrait of deeply dual liberal law. In other words, we set out to build a composite portrait of law by putting together two separately constructed parts, one showing law-like formal law, the other showing law-like ideals.

The separate parts, fully crafted, are supplied by two different accounts of law. The two accounts are the handiwork, respectively, of Max Weber and Ronald Dworkin. We have studied each in some detail. First, in the prior chapter, we considered Max Weber's findings about formal law. Weber describes fully law-like formality. Then, in the previous section of the current chapter, just concluded, we examined Ronald Dworkin's ideas about ideal argument in law. Dworkin defines fully law-like legal ideals.

Following is a short review of what we have learned in our study of these complementary pictures of law: Weber plus Dworkin.

---

[27] Quotes in this paragraph are in sequence from "HC," pp. 1085, 1085, 1084, 1086, 1093.
[28] The two quotes in this paragraph are from Ronald Dworkin, *Law's Empire* (1986), in sequence at pp. 252, 251.

Weber plus Dworkin

Two separate accounts combine to display fully law-like law. One picture, by Max Weber, shows that law is made up of law-like rules – logically rational formality. The other picture shows ideals in law to be likewise law-like – practical aims in individuated operation. The two pictures proffered by our tutelary theorists focus on different kinds of legal striving, formal and ideal, but their compositions develop in much the same way. Both show legal argument going beyond consistency to coherence. Both describe a process whereby unity arises out of law's multiplicity: for Weber, by formal synthesis and generalization; for Dworkin, by use of organizing principle and policy.

Together the two depictions combine to portray the dual impulse of law-like law in full development. In practice of liberal legality, two modes of law and argument arise and evolve in parallel. Instructed by the imperative of coherence, argument draws elements of law together, squares one item with another item, lines things up – makes things fit.

Formalization builds formal structure. A formal structure is a scheme of related rules unified by organizing generalization. In achieved formal structure, law's rules work together.

Idealization builds ideal theories that structure law's doctrines. An ideal theory of law is a body of argumentation working out a governing ideal conception. Argument of the theory states the ideally prescribed order of a complex of legal stuff.

But while Weber and Dworkin each show one of the types of legal argument to be fully law-like, each shows the other type to be far from a fully developed specimen of law-like law. Weber underscores law's formality, and disparages ideals. For Weber, practical moral aims in law – considerations of substantive justice – are at war with formal rules. Dworkin affirms law's ideals, and deprecates formality. For Dworkin, formal argument, operating by itself, is plodding, disorganized, a bare beginning.

Each theorist is shortsighted. Therefore, we need to construct a synoptic view of law-like law as a whole ourselves. In order to produce a comprehensive portrait of deeply dual liberal law, our method is to put two partial views together. Two one-sided understandings, jointly affirmed, display law's duality.

Weber is right about development of formality, wrong about ideals. So is Dworkin half-right, but in reverse. Dworkin's picture of law is one-sided; Weber's picture of law is one-sided in reverse. Neither author is right twice. Each fails to capture law's deep duality. But together the lop-sided depictions balance out. Two half-right views are the halves of a whole.

Rawls plus Rawls

The same method of putting one-sided views together is needed in order to construct a whole out of ideas of John Rawls about the kind of law needed in order to realize the rule of law. On account of his focus on the requisites of the rule of law in a free society, Rawls is a leading light of this book, along with Weber and Dworkin. Rawls is our third tutelary theorist. In separate writings spanning twenty years, Rawls put forward two separate views of liberal law. Rawls never synthesized the two contrasting views. Still, if the two are jointly affirmed, they can be seen to make a whole. Once again, we need to put together a pair of separately constructed views in order to produce the unified portrait of liberal law we seek.

So far we have considered, in the prior chapter, Rawls' first view of law, presented in *A Theory of Justice*. There, Rawls says that formal law is a means of realizing the rule of law in the world. This is correct. But Rawls goes further to suggest that the rule of law is secured only by means of formal rules and rule-based reasoning. This identification of the governance of law with formality exclusively is a mistake.

In the following section, which concludes our quest for a unified portrait of law-like law, we will look closely at Rawls' second view of law. As we will see, John Rawls changed his mind about the kind of legal prescription needed in order to realize the protections of the rule of law. Rawls himself, in later writing, undoes his own earlier mistake made in *A Theory of Justice*. The understanding that idealizing argument is a fundamental project of law in quest of the rule of law is an insight which, eventually, became Rawls' own. Thus Rawls' cumulative understanding of law, stated in successive writings, and the understanding of the present study, in the end agree.

Rawls doesn't acknowledge the evident contrast – much less any inconsistency – between his two views of law. This feature of Rawls' writing – his vacillating understanding of the kind of law needed in order to carry out the rule of law – is not his finest hour. Each of Rawls' two views of liberal law is one-sided, and so only the half of a whole. But Rawls, unlike Weber or Dworkin, is the author of both halves. Half-right twice, Rawls is right in the end.

7.4 RAWLS' SECOND VIEW OF LAW

Among the tutelary theorists discussed in this book, John Rawls stands out in two ways. Our group of instructive theorists consists of political philosopher Rawls, sociologist Max Weber, and legal theorist Ronald Dworkin. Rawls is unique in what he doesn't do, and in what he achieves. First, Rawls doesn't try to do something that the other two both accomplish. Second, he accomplishes something the other two are unable to achieve.

First, unlike Max Weber and Ronald Dworkin, Rawls does not attempt to give a detailed account of how law works. He is interested in the general nature of liberal law, not in law's full development. Rawls sets out to answer a basic question of liberal political theory. The question has to do with the rule of law. Rawls says that commitment to equal liberty in the polity requires the rule of law. The question is, what kind of law is needed in order to realize the rule of law? What kind of legal argument is sufficient to sustain legality? Rawls' two views of law provide answers.

Second, unlike Weber and Dworkin, Rawls, in all his writings taken together, affirms both modes of liberal law, formal and ideal, equally. Rawls alone offers a view of formal law, and a view of idealized law, which show the two legal modes to be able to do the same thing. As we noted in the prior section, Weber constructs a one-sided view of law; so does Dworkin. Rawls, in the end, does not. By contrast, Rawls constructs a cumulative picture of law in which law's two modes are on a par.

Rawls' two views of liberal law, presented in successive major writings spanning two decades, are, in a nutshell, as follows.

In 1971, in *A Theory of Justice*, Rawls showed that formal – rule-governed – legal argument arises as a basic entailment of commitment to liberty. His first principle of justice requires equal liberty; equal liberty requires the rule of law; and the rule of law is secured by a law of formal rules. This is Rawls' first view of law.

In 1993, in *Political Liberalism*, Rawls continued to investigate the conditions and requirements of free institutions of a democratic society. There he showed that ideal – nonformal – legal reasoning is essential in the courts of liberal democracy. Fundamental arrangements of a liberal society are secured by argument of judges invoking law's practical moral aims. This is Rawls' second view of law.

Moral Disagreement

In the opening pages of *Political Liberalism*,[29] Rawls says that a main purpose of this book is to take fully into account a point that was not emphasized in his earlier work, *A Theory of Justice*. The point Rawls wants to underscore is that deep moral disagreement is an inevitable feature of a liberal society. Thus the later book, which ends up praising practical moral argument in law, starts by calling attention to intractable moral disagreement outside law.

As we will see later on, after this chapter concludes, it is a general assumption of liberal law itself that, in the world outside law, moral disagreement persists. Seen from the standpoint of nomological practice, society beyond law is divided by the differences of practical moral discord. People in society embrace rival creeds, and advance conflicting programs.

According to Rawls, modern democratic society is the arena of continuing debate among incompatible "comprehensive doctrines."[30] Rawls uses the term "comprehensive" to indicate systems of belief – religious, philosophical, ideological – that address a wide range of prescriptive matters. In a modern democratic society, free and equal citizens are "profoundly divided."[31] Rawls asks: "How is it possible that deeply opposed ... doctrines may live together ...?"[32]

---

[29] Rawls, *Political Liberalism* (1993), pp. xv–xviii. Hereafter, in this chapter, *Political Liberalism* is cited as *PL*.
[30] *PL*, p. xvi. See also Chapter 9 note 2.   [31] *PL*, p. xviii.   [32] *PL*, p. xviii.

Rawls imagines that, within a well-ordered society, a kind of restrained political discourse addresses important matters of common concern. The citizens are divided by moral disagreement, but, Rawls supposes, they share commitment to the institutions and values of political democracy. Within a well-ordered society, the citizens, in conducting public discussion on political questions, employ a commonly acceptable vocabulary of practical moral justification. They appeal to "values that the others can reasonably be expected to endorse"[33] consistently with "their freedom and equality."[34] In relying on values which all might accept, citizens display what Rawls calls "public reason."[35] Public reason is a process of reasoning on the basis of commonly held values of political democracy which might bridge the differences of deep disagreement on other matters.

The Task of the Judges

Rawls says that courts in a democratic society ought to turn to public values in justifying their decisions. The most important job of the judiciary is to interpret and apply constitutional law. According to Rawls, interpretation of "constitutional essentials" is controlled by the political values of public reason.[36]

> ... [I]t is the task of the justices to try to develop ... the best interpretation of the constitution they can ... Here the best interpretation is the one that best fits the relevant body of those constitutional materials, and justifies it in terms of the public conception of justice ...
>
> The justices cannot, of course, invoke their own personal morality ... Rather, they must appeal to the political values ... of justice and public reason. These are values that they believe ... all citizens as reasonable and rational might reasonably be expected to endorse.[37]

The legal argument put forward by the judges in Rawls' regime of political liberalism is not formal ratiocination. They appeal to "values," not to formal – nonmoral – rules as decisive grounds. Liberal legal argument, as portrayed by Rawls, invokes law's ideal aims, the principles and policies of law. Rawls says that the best legal interpretation both "fits" and "justifies" existing legal materials. Law's ideals are practical moral aims that "fit" existing rules, and also "justify" them. Finding grounds that fit and justify formal rules is idealization of the law.

---

[33] *PL*, p. 226.
[34] "[K]nowing that they affirm a diversity of reasonable religious and philosophical doctrines, they should be ready to explain the basis of their actions to one another in terms each could reasonably expect the others might endorse as consistent with their freedom and equality." *PL*, p. 218.
[35] Rawls says that citizens should keep to the vocabulary of public reason in discussion of "fundamental" matters. "The point of the ideal of public reason is that citizens are to conduct their fundamental discussions within the framework of what each regards as ... values that the others can reasonably be expected to endorse ..." *PL*, p. 226.
[36] *PL*, p. 214.   [37] *PL*, p. 236.

Rawls' account of legal interpretation based on political values is similar to the view put forward by legal philosopher Ronald Dworkin. According to Dworkin, argument appealing to practical moral aims that fit and justify existing legal materials is the most important kind of legal reasoning.[38] Rawls acknowledges the affinity between his account of legal interpretation and Dworkin's view. He writes: "This account of what the justices are to do seems to be the same as Ronald Dworkin's ..."[39]

As we saw at length earlier in this chapter, Dworkin says that ideal argumentation in law is law-like. According to Dworkin, law's ideals are general prescriptions, rooted in standing law, which are able to support evenhanded judgment. Plainly Rawls agrees. Ideal argument, for Rawls, is suitable for use in developing and applying the most important type of law, constitutional law. In the constitution of a well-ordered society, according to Rawls, "the protections of the rule of law" are specifically guaranteed.[40] The kind of argument used in order to realize protections of the rule of law must, of course, itself comport with the requirements of the rule of law.

Two Kinds of Law

And so it is that, in all his writings addressing law taken together, Rawls demonstrates that allegiance to the rule of law gives rise to law's duality. Within a legal system working to maintain the protections of the rule of law, two modes of legal argument go forward in the courts. In *A Theory of Justice*, Rawls shows that commitment to the rule of law leads to legal reasoning controlled by formal rules: it impels formalization of law. In *Political Liberalism*, Rawls shows that the same commitment gives rise to reasoning appealing to practical moral aims that fit and justify the rules – idealization of law.

The first book affirms one mode of law-like law, but not the other. The second book affirms the other, while ignoring the one. Each affirmation is too narrow, but the two, conjoined, come out right in the end.

In his separate studies of liberal law, Rawls affirms each of two modes of legal argument, formal argument and ideal argument, the preferred modes of H. L. A. Hart and of Ronald Dworkin respectively, alike in the service of legality. The two studies, taken together, constitute a composite portrait of law which, as a whole, displays the dual impulse that lies at the heart of liberal law.

---

[38] See Dworkin, *Taking Rights Seriously* (1977b). [39] *PL*, p. 236 n. 23. [40] *PL*, p. 227.

8

Two Perils for Law

So far, we have seen how nomological commitment gives rise to a dual impulse. Now I want to show how fear of failed legality gives rise to a parallel double aversion.

Just as the highly general aspiration to secure law-like legality yields two specific argumentative impulses, projects proceeding along alternative paths, so too does abstract fear of legality's failure – fear of arbitrary judgment – generate two concrete apprehensions, awareness of danger in different directions. This symmetrical double fear is the main topic of the remainder of this book.

In the present chapter, I will touch briefly on some preliminary matters having to do with fear of legality's failure. I will note some contrasting ways in which peril for law has been viewed in legal thought. After the introductory comments of the present chapter, step-by-step analysis of liberal law's two fears will commence. The analysis will show how a double fear, parallel to dual impulse, develops within the practice of law-like law. When we have worked out the content of binary fear, we will have before us the full complement of particular motivations, positive and negative, that drive liberal legal practice.

Both the aspiration to realize legality, and the fear of legality's defeat, focus on the conduct of legal argument leading to legal judgment. What's sought is the success of law-like legal reasoning, a situation in which legal argument is able to sustain entitlement and justice. What's feared is failure of argument, issuing in arbitrary decision.

Aspiration to secure legality yields a dual impulse to formalize and to idealize law, as we have seen. It impels pursuit of specific modes of argument and decision, in line with alternative understandings of law-like law. Formative aspiration is a generic commitment encompassing two positive projects. Formal argument and ideal argument are alternative ways of operating on given legal stuff for the sake of legality.

The two kinds of nomological endeavor fail, if they do, in different ways. Corresponding to the alternative ways of understanding law-like legality are two different understandings of how legality might be undone. Associated with each mode of argument is a mode of failure, a distinctive kind of peril, a bad condition of law and decision which, if it should happen, would amount to defeat of legality.

When the fear of failed legality is stated in terms of the two argumentative undertakings of liberal law, the result is a double fear. Abstract fear of failure becomes concrete when it is formulated with reference to the distinct perils that threaten each of legality's projects. In this way, generic fear of arbitrariness comes to encompass quite particular apprehensions, which serve to direct legal striving negatively, away from specified dangers.

In other words, when the two specific conceptions of law-like law come to instruct positive pursuit in liberal practice, two parallel conceptions of failure tell practical striving what to avoid. Thus, generic fear, worked out in terms of dual impulse, becomes a double aversion.

8.1 LIBERAL LAW'S FEARS

Following below is an introductory statement of the two fears that take shape in practice of law-like legality. I will first summarize the fear associated with formality: fear of open form. Then I will sketch the fear having to do with idealization: fear of free ideals.

First is fear of open form. Formalization fails if formal categories and rules are irremediably open-ended. Fear of open form is the fear that formal argument in law may be afflicted with the openness that is a pervasive feature of common language outside law.

Formalizing argument seeks to hammer out extant laws as rules, and to build structures of rules, so that the specifically legal meaning of any one rule jibes with that of the others. Everything turns on whether formal law's own concepts and precepts are able to achieve the regular classification and judgment of particulars arising in the world. If formality's categories, in particular cases, are subject to the same infirmities that characterize ordinary linguistic resource, so formal laws become ambiguous in purport and vague in application, then formalization cannot sustain legality. Then formal meaning in law will be undecidable in detail, and formality will come to impasse. Formal argument fails when law's concepts, like common concepts, are equally open to alternative resolutions.

Second is fear of free ideals. Idealization fails if the ideal grounds that guide and shape legal norms are freely chosen. Fear of free ideals is the fear that ideal argument in law may become embroiled in moral disagreement that goes on outside law.

Idealizing argument seeks to develop principles, policies, and purposes grounded in the standing laws, legal ideals that fit and justify extant rules and together constitute law's own practical morality. Everything turns on whether ideal resolutions within law are sufficiently constrained by law's distinctive argumentative processes. If idealizing operations in law are free of specifically legal restraint, so that law's ideals are formed by the same sort of deliberation that yields moral preachment outside law, then idealization cannot sustain nomological legality. Then legal argument will be exposed to moral disagreement, and ideal conflict will break out within law. Ideal argument fails if its judgments are referable to moral convictions ungoverned by law.

The fear of open form, and the fear of free ideals, are persistent within practice of liberal legality. These concrete worries arise from the standpoint of the practice as a whole, which dreads failure of legality. Argument in practice is continuously directed by awareness of twofold peril. Like dual impulse, double aversion is deep, vigorous, ever operative.

Underlying practice's two fears are premises about the condition of morality and language apart from law. What practice of legality fears is that something untoward, which happens beyond the realm of law, may come to happen inside it. From the standpoint of liberal practice, a legal discourse that is indistinct from common linguistic activity outside law, and from free moral debate outside law, cannot sustain law-like legality. If law's language works no better than common language, then formal legality, in case after case, fails. And if law's morality turns out to be the same thing as extralegal morals, then ideal legality fails.

In each case the fear is that law's own processes of argumentation may break down, causing the bounds of the specifically legal realm to rupture, leaving legal argument exposed to the disorder of an unsettled intellectual world beyond law. Fear takes shape in light of practice's awareness of disordered conditions outside itself. Awareness of pervasive linguistic infirmity underlies fear of open form. Awareness of incessant moral disagreement underlies fear of free ideals. Argument in nomological practice proceeds on the assumption that meanings and morals developed outside the practice are insufficient to sustain legality.

8.2 OVERCOMING PERIL

What I have said so far about law's fears is meant to be no more than a quick overview. We are going to go a lot deeper into the matter of peril for law. Awareness of law's peril owing to disorder outside it is a fundamental feature of liberal law. Disorder outside law locates – indeed, it forms – the project of liberal legality.

As a preliminary matter, before we undertake our step-by-step analysis of the specific perils facing law, it may be well to come at the question of peril from another angle. One way to get a handle on liberal law's conception of peril outside itself is to consider how, generally speaking, danger might conceivably be overcome.

The opposite of peril is rational resolution. Law's peril is overcome when legal argument achieves rational resolution by law. Peril for law is the danger that law's own processes of reasoning may break down, exposing law to disorder outside. Peril arising from disorder outside law can be overcome only if law is able to differentiate itself – only if legal argument, formal or ideal, diverges from similar discourse outside law in the direction of greater rational constraint.

Following below, by way of further introduction, is brief discussion of how law might differentiate itself and so avert peril. Two quick sketches below show how the modes of liberal law might, generally speaking, achieve rational resolution, and so, for the most part, steer clear of linguistic vagueness and moral disagreement.

It is important to keep in mind that the perils posited by liberal law to exist outside itself might – possibly – be overcome. To be sure, awareness of peril of exposure to disorder outside law is constant. There never comes a time when it is safe for law to merge with discourse outside itself. Still, so far as liberal practice's assumptions about extramural disorder are concerned, it is continuously possible for law – most of the time, if not always – to succeed. Legality's two projects, formalization and idealization, go forward on the assumption that peril can be overcome.

We may see what it would mean to overcome peril by considering, briefly, the views of two legal philosophers, H. L. A. Hart and Ronald Dworkin, each of whom says that a mode of legal argument – formal argument for Hart, ideal argument for Dworkin – is able, for the most part, to avoid the disorder that afflicts similar discourse outside law and so is able, generally speaking, to achieve rational resolution by law. Each theorist thinks that the mode of argument affirmed by the other often doesn't succeed – but never mind that. Each thinks that law as a whole does, by and large, succeed.

Hart says that formal argument can, for the most part, avoid the peril of linguistic vagueness. Dworkin says that ideal argument can, for the most part, avoid the peril of moral disagreement.

Hart and Vagueness

According to H. L. A. Hart, the main thing about law is law's formality.[1] As portrayed by Hart, formal reasoning in law largely avoids the peril of crippling vagueness. That is, argument based on formal rules largely succeeds in sustaining rational resolution in particular cases – not always, but most of the time. Thus, the peril that formal argument in law might be widely disabled by the vagueness that afflicts language outside law is overcome.

Hart believes that vagueness is "a general feature of human language." It afflicts common language used in communication outside law. Openness of general classifying terms is "inherent in the nature of language." When uncertainties owing to vagueness "break out" in particular cases inside law, legal argument is unable to come to rational resolution. Instead judges exercise lawmaking discretion. "[A] choice between open alternatives must be made."[2]

It would be a big problem for law if vagueness inside law should build up. Legal argument works to bring interrelated legal items into alignment. If each item by itself is vague – each concept of each legal precept – in the same way that language used in general communication is vague, then the ensemble, made up of many vague

---

[1] See Hart, *The Concept of Law* (1961). Hereafter, in this chapter, *The Concept of* Law is cited as *CL*.

[2] The four quotations in this paragraph, in sequence, are from *CL*, pp. 125, 123, 123, 124.

constituents, might be readable quite a number of different ways. The vagueness of one law might compound the vagueness of another. Vagueness that afflicts each of interacting laws might add up to the point that rational resolution by law is widely undermined.

On the other hand, law's own processes might reduce – not eliminate, but reduce – the leeways of law's concepts.

Argument seeking coherence in law may construct law's concepts and meanings by stipulating definitions of legal categories and distinctions among them, and by specifying how precepts using the categories interconnect, so that in the end law's working language is substantially different from common language. Formed within law, the character of law's concepts changes. Law's concepts are different from categories used in general communication conducted apart from specialized practices. They are the terms of a distinctive discursive activity – law's own language.

Hart acknowledges that law's concepts are different from categories used in language outside law, even when the term used in law and outside law is the same. For example, Hart considers a legal rule that prohibits bringing a "vehicle" into the public park. He lists some conveyances that may or may not be classified as vehicles. Outside law, the question for a user of language is straightforward: are these conveyances, properly speaking, vehicles? Inside law, the question, according to Hart, is subtly different: "Are these, as we say, to be called 'vehicles' for the purpose of the rule ...?"[3]

Speaking of uncertainties in the classifying of particulars under general legal categories, Hart says: "Canons of 'interpretation' cannot eliminate, though they can diminish, these uncertainties."[4] Since law's own processes construct legal language different from common language, and put it to use differently, it is possible that law's rules may, for the most part, avoid the pitfall of vagueness and, by and large, achieve rational resolution.

Hart concludes that law's rules are not disabled by vagueness. Despite occasional uncertainties, law's formal rules work smoothly "over the great mass of ordinary cases." Courts undertake "unquestionably rule-governed operations over the vast, central areas of the law."[5]

Dworkin and Disagreement

Ronald Dworkin says that the main thing about law is the control of law's formality by law's ideals.[6] According to Dworkin, ideal reasoning within legal argument largely avoids the peril of moral disagreement. That is, argument based on ideal principles and policies of law by and large succeeds in sustaining rational resolution by law. Thus, the peril that ideal argument in law may

---

[3]   Hart, "Positivism and the Separation of Law and Morals" (1958), p. 607.   [4]   *CL*, p. 123.
[5]   The two quotes in this paragraph are from *CL*, pp. 124, 150.
[6]   See Dworkin, "Hard Cases," (1975). Hereafter, in this chapter, "Hard Cases" is cited as "HC."

become embroiled in the sort of interminable moral disagreement that goes on outside law is largely overcome.

Dworkin distinguishes between moral argument inside law and morality outside law. Inside law, lawyers and judges invoke practical moral aims that fit and justify law's formal rules as grounds of decision. Outside law, people engage in moral debate about what's right and good and just in the ordering of social life.

Inside law, legal arguers appeal to principles, policies, and purposes grounded in existing formal rules. They develop justifications of the rules that show how the rules cohere. In Dworkin's terminology, principles and policies of law constitute "institutional morality." This is law's own morality – "the political morality presupposed by the laws." In appealing to law's morality, judges are not relying on their "own political convictions" developed apart from law.[7] Rather they are sticking to law.[8]

Outside law, people discuss issues of practical morality. In matters of moral conviction, people hold contrary views. Dworkin calls moral prescription affirmed outside law "background morality." It is part of the background of the instituted legal system of society. Legal rights, for Dworkin, are "institutional rather than background rights." "[N]o one may claim an institutional right by direct appeal to general morality."[9]

It would be a big problem for law if decisions arising from ideal argument in law amount to imposition of "background convictions." Background convictions are a judge's own moral views. When decision rests on a judge's "independent judgment of political morality," the decider relies on "the fact that he himself has a particular political preference." Deciding on the basis of one's own moral preferences is "unfair, contrary to democracy, and offensive to the rule of law."[10]

Dworkin imagines a judge who is called upon to decide whether, under the constitution, a woman has a right to choose to have an abortion.[11] This is the case of *Roe* v. *Wade*.[12] The imagined judge finds that earlier constitutional decisions "can be justified only by supposing some important right to human dignity." But Dworkin's judge, as a matter of personal conviction, believes that the idea of "dignity" is an unimportant part of morality. Nonetheless, according to Dworkin, the imagined judge is able to construct an understanding of the law's concept "dignity," by seeing how it figures in the justification of decided cases, and may

---

[7] The three quotations of this paragraph are from "HC," pp. 1107, 1105, 1104.

[8] Dworkin acknowledges that, in hard cases in law, judgments of political morality "might be made differently by different judges." "HC," p. 1101. "[R]easonable lawyers [may] disagree whether a litigant in a hard case has a right to win, even after all the facts ... are agreed ..." (Dworkin 1977b, p. 280). However, the existence of legal controversy does not preclude the availability, in principle, of right decision under law. According to Dworkin, conscientious judges who come to different conclusions about what law's principles and policies require commonly assume that right legal resolution is possible. See Dworkin (1977b), pp. 281–284.

[9] The three quotes in this paragraph are from "HC," pp. 1106, 1078, 1078.

[10] The four quotes in this paragraph come from "HC," pp. 1079, 1104, 1102, 1102.

[11] Quotes in this paragraph are from "HC," p. 1105.   [12] 410 US 113 (1973).

well come to the conclusion that "that concept, properly understood, embraces the case of abortion."

Dworkin's example of the judge who disparages dignity but nonetheless enforces it is designed to show that a legal arguer may invoke a moral conception rooted in law "to reach a decision that, as a matter of background morality, he would reject." The key is to maintain the "distinction between background and institutional morality" – between moral conviction formed apart from law and morality grounded within law.[13]

8.3 DEEPER DANGER

The perils for law addressed by Hart and Dworkin are conditions of disorder that exist beyond law. Language outside law is pervasively vague. Morality outside law is divided by disagreement. The peril for law is that disabling disorder seen to exist outside law may break out within law. If law is unable to overcome pervasive vagueness, then law is disabled. If law is persistently open to moral disagreement, then rational resolution by law is defeated.

Vagueness affecting common language, and disagreement happening in moral discussion, are general – indeed, ubiquitous – phenomena outside law. Yet, by nature, these particular disabilities of discourse beyond law might – possibly – be avoided in law. Hart may be right that, despite vagueness in ordinary language, formal argument in law largely achieves rational resolution; he may be wrong. Dworkin may be right that, despite moral conflict beyond law, ideal argument in law is able to secure law-like resolution; he may be wrong. But each is right in thinking that a particular discursive disability – vagueness for Hart, disagreement for Dworkin – is one that by its nature might possibly be overcome.

There are deeper dangers that law might be thought to confront. It is not difficult to imagine perils for law, having to do with disorder in language and morality in general, that law might not be able to overcome. The deeper dangers are conditions underscored by philosophical skepticism about reason and truth in discursive exchange.

Linguistic skepticism identifies ways in which reason fails in communication of meaning by language. Moral skepticism displays failure of rational possibility in discussion of moral matters. If deeply skeptical premises about meanings and morals are taken to be true, and if they apply to meanings and morals inside law, it follows that legal argument will fail to achieve rational resolution – and fail irremediably.

In discussion following immediately below, we will look briefly at some tenets of deep skepticism about language and morality. These tenets, when applied to law, disable it. The purpose of this discussion is to indicate, by quick example, kinds of failure of rationality which are far more threatening to liberal law than the perils that

---

[13] The two quotes in this paragraph are from "HC," pp. 1106, 1107.

liberal law itself imagines to exist. Thus we may throw into relief the more modest challenge – avoiding vagueness of language and disagreement in morals for the most part – that liberal law sets for itself.

Our sources for skeptical ideas are two works of legal theory which alike criticize liberal law: Roberto Unger's *Knowledge and Politics* and Duncan Kennedy's *A Critique of Adjudication*.[14] The first, from 1975, inaugurates a tendency of critical legal thought whose lines of development are summed up by the second, in 1997.

Moral and Linguistic Skepticism

Roberto Unger affirms two highly general skeptical premises. The two premises are skeptical about rational possibility in making of moral judgments and in communicating by means of language. They are, respectively, postulates of deep moral skepticism and deep linguistic skepticism. They assert much deeper failure of rationality than the tenets of moral disagreement and linguistic vagueness which we have been considering.

In a nutshell, Unger's two premises posit that values are subjective and that concepts are conventional. First, moral values have no basis other than subjective choice. Second, concepts and meanings of language are arbitrary conventions.

Unger says that the premises of subjective values and conventional concepts are assumptions embraced by modern liberal thought. Liberal thought is a body of ideas that prizes individual liberty in society and prescribes that liberty should be secured by rational law. However, according to Unger, the liberal credo is incoherent.[15] Liberalism's two skeptical assumptions, about morality and language in general, combine to defeat the possibility of rational law.

First, let us consider Unger's premise of subjective values. This is the proposition that "all values are individual and subjective." Moral judgments are not controlled by reason. They are not grounded in objective understanding of what's morally good. It is impossible to establish "objective value." Assessments of moral worth depend on standards which have no foundation other than their acceptance. "Values are subjective in the sense that they are determined by choice." There are no objective and impersonal standards of "right and wrong, good and bad."[16]

According to Unger, moral subjectivity disables ideal argument in law. Ideal reasoning in law invokes practical moral aims, purposes and policies, as decisive grounds. Such reasoning requires "some independent mechanism for the combination and weighing of policies" in order to determine which aim is "controlling." However, since moral judgments are subjective and personal, "no such method ... exists." The policy that controls decision is freely chosen by the judge. "[T]he judge will inescapably impose his own subjective preferences ... on the litigants." Thus

---

[14] Hereafter, in this chapter, Unger's *Knowledge and Politics* (1975) is cited as *KP*; Kennedy's *A Critique of Adjudication* (1997) is cited as *CA*.

[15] See *KP*, pp. 6, 7, 18, 21, 35.   [16] Quotations in this paragraph come from *KP*, pp. 76, 77, 79.

legal argument based on principles, policies, and purposes cannot achieve rational resolution.[17]

Second is the premise of conventional concepts. This is the proposition that the concepts and meanings of language rest on arbitrary "conventions of naming." There are no "essential qualities" that distinguish facts and situations from one another. Categories of language have no foundation in "nature." "For the conventionalist, there are an infinite number of possible ways of dividing the world up . . ." Different ways of classifying states of affairs serve varying purposes. "Classification must always be justified by some interest or purpose it serves."[18]

According to Unger, the arbitrariness of classifications of language disables formal argument in law. Formal argument classifies situations in the world under the categories of law's rules. However, since there are no essential qualities that separate one situation from another, "there are no . . . clear standards by which to classify the particular instances under rules." "The only standard is whether the classification serves the particular purpose we had in mind when we made it." Therefore, in order to apply law's rules, "it is necessary to engage in a discussion of purpose." But when decision depends on discussion of purpose, formal argument "has been abandoned." What ensues is purposive reasoning, that is, ideal argument – which, according to Unger, fails in its turn because values are subjective.[19]

Omnibus Skepticism

The skeptical tenets given voice by Unger, premises of subjective values and conventional concepts, are instances of a larger skeptical outlook identified by legal theorist Duncan Kennedy, who like Unger engages in critique of liberal law. Kennedy draws together a package of skepticisms advanced in criticism of law's rationality. He finds that diverse lines of disbelief in rational capability converge to constitute a common project of critique. He calls the common project "mpm."

Kennedy's term "mpm" refers to the outlook of "modernism/postmodernism." The way of thinking of mpm has been at home in the realm of art since the nineteenth century. It celebrates escape from constraint by shattering of forms and fixities. The goal of modernist and postmodernist artistic expression – visual, literary, performative – is to achieve "transcendent . . . experiences at the margins of or in the interstices of a disrupted rational grid."[20]

In legal thought, mpm criticizes "discourse of legal correctness and rights." It rejects "normative objectivity." It is "hostile to rightness in all its forms," that is, to "'[b]eing right' in the rationalist sense." It aims at "liberation from . . . experiences of constraint by reason." "The mpm counter to rights and the rule of law

---

[17] Quotes in this paragraph are from *KP*, p. 95.   [18] Quotes in this paragraph are from *KP*, pp. 80, 93.
[19] Quotes in this paragraph are from *KP*, pp. 32, 80, 93.
[20] Quotes in this paragraph are from Kennedy's *CA*, p. 7.

[undertakes] critique to loosen the sense of closure or necessity that legal and rights analyses try to generate."[21]

In particular, the project of mpm stands ready to demonstrate the "plasticity" of any legal text by the method of "deconstruction." Deconstructive method, used by philosopher Jacques Derrida to deflate claims of reason outside law, posits, as Kennedy says, "the omnipresence of ... 'dangerous supplements.'" These are elements of a text which, given rein, disrupt the purported structure of the text. Brought to bear on legal materials, deconstruction works to defeat "all claims of determinacy in law."

In short, Kennedy's mpm, applied to law, thoroughly undermines it. The failures of rationality proclaimed by mpm, assigned to law in particular, are way too much for law in quest of nomological legality to hope to overcome.[22]

8.4 WHAT FOLLOWS

The aim of the present study as a whole is to find out what happens when the aspiration to achieve law-like legality is entrenched in legal practice. Given liberal commitment, what persistent pursuits arise in the practice of argument? What cautionary assumptions about peril for law arise?

We have seen what pursuits take shape: formalization and idealization. My claim is that certain assumptions about peril threatening law arise – and not others.

In the discussion of law's fears that follows after the present introductory chapter, we will do three things. First, our main objective is to spell out the ideas about peril for law that law embraces. Second, we will identify skeptical claims that liberal law does not embrace. Third, we will consider why liberal practice embraces the assumptions it does embrace, and why it rejects the others.

First, we need to conduct a close examination of the fears that direct argumentative striving in liberal legal practice, which are very specific, and especially the premises behind the fears, lest these be confused with similar sounding assumptions that liberal practice does not accept. In the discussion that follows I will articulate, one after the other, the two aversions that motivate argument negatively within practice of liberal legality. I will discuss legality's fears in the following order: first fear of free ideals, then fear of open form.

Presentation of the two fears will lay out the premises about morality and language in general – assumptions about disagreement and vagueness – that are the basis of liberal law's apprehensions. The premises underlying the fears are assumptions embraced within the practice of legality. They are views about conditions outside law which are taken as true in the doing of law-like law.

Second, we will see that liberal law does not embrace deeply skeptical assumptions about morality and language. Liberal practice, while keenly aware of forms of

---

[21] Quotes in this paragraph are from CA, pp. 11, 340, 342, 347, 357.
[22] Quotes in this paragraph are from CA, pp. 7, 8, 348. On Derrida, see also Chapter 10 notes 9 and 10.

disorder outside law, does not accept Unger's postulates about subjective morals and conventional concepts. It rejects the global skepticisms brought together within Kennedy's jamboree of disbelief, mpm. Each one of these deeply skeptical views might or might not be found to be worthy of adherence when investigated from the standpoint of philosophical inquiry conducted apart from legal practice. But none is accepted as true by liberal legal practice. Deeply disbelieving assumptions are not premises of liberal legality.

Third, we will see why liberal practice embraces the premises it does embrace, and does not embrace the others. In a nutshell, the reason is this: legality's premises about morality and language – the ones it does embrace – arise from the self-understanding of nomological enterprise. On the one hand, liberal practice understands that, in order for law to succeed, legal argument must do better than discourse outside it. Practice posits the existence of perils outside that must be struggled against. On the other hand, it posits perils that can be overcome.

Our glance at Hart and Dworkin earlier was for the purpose of seeing how – possibly – peril might be overcome. It is not part of the project of this book to find out whether Hart's claim, that formal law mostly avoids the peril of openness owing to vague language, is correct, nor to determine whether Dworkin is right in his contention that appeal to principles and policies in law for the most part avoids getting embroiled in moral disagreement. Such assessments are beyond the scope of the book.

Rather, the aim of ensuing analysis is to show that, according to assumption in control of liberal law, certain specific perils – vagueness and disagreement – must be faced and must, one way or another, be overcome, lest liberal law fail. This understanding of the challenge for law is part of the definition of liberal legal striving. Posited disorder beyond law defines liberal law's struggle. The assumption that pervasive vagueness and unending disagreement happen beyond law is a consequence of liberal aspiration itself. How legal argument in liberal practice views language and morality apart from law depends on practice's self-conception, and that depends on law's aspiration.

Some time ago, during our investigation of the characteristic features of instituted discourse of law, we saw that practice of law-like law has a particular self-conception. That self-conception, which arises when liberal aspiration is entrenched in legal practice, is, as we shall see, at the root of law's assumptions about morality and language which, in turn, form the basis of legality's fears. Liberal practice's view of morals and meanings outside law is a consequence of practice's view of itself. Liberal law defines itself in opposition to unreconstructed – but legally constructable – morality and language.

9

Fear of Free Ideals

Let us conduct a little review of legal idealization, and then turn to what legality fears with respect to it.

Legal ideals, as we know, are fashioned to fit and justify society's standing laws, and are used to guide and shape those laws. They have the same subject matter as the laws they steer. Idealizing argument formulates practical precepts and goals that speak to all the many areas of life touched on by law.

Ideal legal argument is wide-ranging in its subject matter, but it is a fettered, not a free, argumentative activity. Legal ideals are not freely developed. There are, as we know, important elements of constraint.

Legal idealization takes place in legal practice, so it is controlled by the regimen that defines instituted discourse of law. Instituted legal discourse is a restricted mode of discussion. Argument within bounded practice of law is directed by imperative tests of good legal reasoning. The discourse of practice is anchored in an established institution whose inner circle is made up of officials specially empowered to judge.

More particularly, legal idealization takes place in nomological practice, so it is constrained by requirements of nomological legality. To sustain law-like legality, legal ideals must be specifically legal. Idealizing argument must take as given society's stock of standing laws, and project ideals that fit and justify the formal stuff of law. The imperative of fit between ideals and legal rules is a basic require-ment. It ensures that the content of law's ideals – what they prescribe – is in accord with what law's rules prescribe. Ideal aims in prescriptive accord with formal rules constitute law's practical morality. Ideals that satisfy the material test of fit are law's own moral precepts and goals. So, idealization of law works to develop the pre-scriptive content of a specific, socially extant morality, one that is embodied in extant law.

Fear of free ideals is fear that law's own processes of argumentation may fail, leaving ideal argument in law the same as moral debate going on outside. The freedom that is feared, from the standpoint of law, is the absence of specifically legal constraint. Fear of free ideals is fear of the plenum of moral possibility.

Free ideals are the prescriptions that arise in a moral discussion not governed by law's own argumentative discipline. Put another way, free ideals are moral prescriptions developed in a free – unconstrained – moral inquiry. When law's ideals are free, ideal argument in law is indistinct from moral debate outside law, and ideal resolutions in law are referable to moral convictions formed apart from law. It is understood, in the practice of law-like law, that free ideals cannot sustain nomological legality. When ideal argument in law is the same as moral debate beyond law, legality fails.

9.1 WARRING CREEDS

The premise of legality's fear of free ideals is the assumption that a battle of warring creeds and programs exists in free moral inquiry. From the standpoint of liberal practice, moral discussion apart from law is locked in deep and unending disagreement. So, if legal ideals are not distinct from morality outside law, deep ideal conflict will develop within law. Then law would become just another forum for interminable moral debate. Legal argument fears exposure to the battle of moral convictions, something it sees to exist outside itself, because such exposure would lead to arbitrary judging based, not on law, but on personal moral choice ungoverned by law.

Our procedure for examining fear of free ideals, in the present chapter, will be to start with the premise at the base of the fear. The premise of legality's fear says that a battle of warring creeds exists in free moral inquiry – in other words, disagreement exists in moral debate beyond law. After we investigate this underlying premise, we will turn to the fear proper, the apprehension that what occurs in moral debate outside law might come to occur within law, and we will see just why liberal legal argument fears free ideals.

The premise of disagreement in free inquiry states liberal legality's characteristic view of morality in general, outside law. Legality's view may be broken down into two constitutive tenets. According to the first tenet, deep disagreement persists in moral colloquy. According to the second, disagreement occurs in free moral inquiry ungoverned by practices. Notice that these propositions are about moral discourse outside, not inside, law. The combination of the two tenets is a unified assumption embraced by all legal argument within practice of law-like law. It is a vital fact about liberal legal practice that it proceeds on the basis of a formative premise concerning the condition of moral discourse outside itself. Practice of legality has a distinctive view of morality outside law.

The ideas that make up legality's view of extramural morality are not especially hard to grasp. The basic idea of moral disagreement, persisting in fact, is pretty straightforward. And the idea of a free moral inquiry is just the notion of inquiry free from the constraints of instituted discourse, which have already been discussed in detail. So it may seem the presentation of these ideas needn't delay us long. But, I think, there is good reason to go a bit slowly – carefully – over this ground.

The premise of moral disagreement is of great practical importance in the conduct of legal argument. We need to be quite clear, not just about what the premise affirmatively says, but also about what it does not say.

There is a real danger that legality's premise of moral disagreement might be confused with full-blown moral skepticism. There are, indeed, some similarities between legality's view of morality and a deeply skeptical view of morality. But these resemblances are superficial. The assumption that disagreement persists in free moral inquiry is not the same as the assumption that moral argument is by nature nonrational. Legality's view is not the same as radical skepticism about moral truth, but rather is compatible with belief in moral reason and moral truth. We need to establish the limit of legality's assumption.

We begin by considering the two tenets that make up legality's view of morality, which underlies fear of free ideals. Remember that this is the view from a particular standpoint, that of practice of law-like law. It is how morality is viewed from inside law, looking out. The exposition below is not at all meant to be a statement of free-standing philosophical truths, but rather is an explication of tenets about morality accepted as true in the doing of liberal law.

Moral Disagreement

First, deep and intractable disagreement is an abiding feature of moral discussion carried on independently of law. This is the first of legality's two tenets about morality. Simply put, it says that moral disagreement exists.

A large debate, prescriptive in nature, goes on outside legal practice. In this debate, arguers justify and criticize social arrangements by appealing to practical reasons that I call moral, using the term in a capacious sense. Reasons adduced could also be called ethical, or axiological, or political, or ideological. Moral debate beyond law addresses the full range of matters also addressed within law, but it is not governed by the regimen of legal practice. So the prescriptive grounds put forward in extramural debate are not legal ideals, but simply ideals – free ideals. As observed from the standpoint of liberal legal practice, the moral debate outside law encompasses a rich array of conflicting positions, conceptions, judgments. Practical moral discourse beyond law is understood to be deeply divided. Disagreement is seen to be a fact of moral life.

In discussion about what ought morally to be in social life, people disagree.[1] They disagree about what's politically right, economically desirable, and socially just – about what's due, valuable, equitable, and what's wrong, bad, unfair – and about

---

[1] For legal commentator Owen Fiss, "[P]rofound and pervasive disagreement ... often characterizes moral life .... [P]eople disagree about what is right and good, as, for example, whether the separate-but-equal doctrine is consistent with equality or whether the state should be allowed to interfere with the freedom of a woman to decide to have an abortion. The existence of this disagreement cannot be denied ..." (Fiss, "Objectivity and Interpretation," 1982, p. 751).

what's prudent, efficacious, not unworkable. Different people hold different views about how to carry on society: how social relations ought to be conducted; how political and economic affairs should be organized and regulated; how common institutions ought to operate, and be directed. This is legality's assumption.

Different people make arguments based on different schemes of moral understanding. Moral arguers embrace conflicting creeds. They hold different fundamental conceptions and assumptions to be true and essential.[2] And arguers advocate conflicting programs. They translate moral premises – freedom, democracy, equality, community – into sets of concrete prescriptions in incompatible ways. Within moral colloquy, basic convictions diverge, and programmatic commitments working out convictions diverge.

Moral disagreement, along these and other lines of schism, is seen to be unarbitrable in fact. Disagreement in moral debate is irresolvable in the factual sense that it doesn't ever get resolved. Moral conflict is interminable, in the same sense: as a matter of fact, it doesn't quit, but is incessant. So far, the moral debate has gone on without end, and on the assumption the moral future will be like the past, it will keep going on without end.

Free Moral Inquiry

Second, moral disagreement happens in free inquiry ungoverned by practices. This is the second of legality's two tenets about morality. The second tenet identifies a location, a realm of discourse, where moral argument is free and where moral disagreement incessantly occurs.

Consider the elements of constraint – the fetters – that characterize idealizing argument in legal practice. Make a mental list. Such argument is bounded discourse; it is anchored in a judging institution; it is controlled by special tests; it must fit and justify given legal stuff; it develops a specific morality, law's morality; and so on. Now imagine a moral discussion in which none of these qualifications obtains. The result, imagined by systematic negation of constraint, is a free moral inquiry. Free moral inquiry is ungoverned deliberation about matters of morality. From the

---

[2] According to John Rawls, people in society hold "deeply opposed" moral views. Society, though well-ordered, is "profoundly divided" by persistent moral disagreement (Rawls, *Political Liberalism*, 1993, p. xviii).

"A modern democratic society is characterized ... by a pluralism of comprehensive religious, philosophical, and moral doctrines ... No one of these doctrines is affirmed by citizens generally. Nor should one expect that in the foreseeable future one of them ... will ever be affirmed by all, or nearly all, citizens. Political liberalism assumes that ... a plurality of reasonable yet incompatible comprehensive doctrines is the normal result of the exercise of human reason within the framework of the free institutions of a constitutional democratic regime" (Rawls 1993, p. xvi).

Rawls distinguishes "reasonable" comprehensive doctrines, which support the essentials of a democratic regime, from "unreasonable" doctrines, which do not. The "reasonable" doctrines, among themselves, are "deeply opposed"; opposition between reasonable and unreasonable doctrines is deeper still (Rawls 1993, pp. xvi–xviii).

standpoint of the practice of liberal law, incessant conflict of convictions occurs when moral deliberation is not controlled by the regimen of an argumentative practice.

Unregimented moral deliberation is, by definition, an open activity. Anyone can engage in it. Free deliberation about a moral question happens when someone steps outside the constraints of special roles and tasks, and assumes a generally accessible position, that of a moral questioner trying to get at the truth of the matter.

In putting forward claims and arguments from the standpoint of free deliberation, an arguer enters the discursive activity of free moral debate. Free moral debate is a self-governing discussion, open to participation by all moral agents. It is argumentative exchange among different people who occupy the same standpoint and have identical status. Arguers – one and all one's interlocutors – have equal standing in a free discourse of morals.

In free inquiry, the questioner is not bound to affirm the precepts of any socially established morality. The inquirer is not bound by moral views that others in society happen to avow, nor by moral imperatives that happen to be entrenched within some form of common life, nor by moral conceptions that happen to make sense of present social arrangements, nor by any other shared or embodied morality. Free inquiry is an independent activity. It stands apart from all established prescriptions.

Free moral deliberation is governed just by its aim of discovering the truth of the matter. The matter under investigation is what morality truly requires. Put another way, the question is what true morality prescribes. In unregimented moral discourse, among free inquirers, about true morality, many incompatible answers contend for adherence. Rival truths struggle for mastery of moral understanding.

The conception of free moral investigation, ungoverned by practices, links readily with the idea of moral disagreement, incessantly happening. It is easy to see how the two tenets we have elaborated join together to form a single assumption about the condition of morality outside law.

The first tenet says moral disagreement is persistent. The second says it persists in free moral inquiry. The two, conjoined, yield a unified premise, the premise of warring creeds in free morals, which is embraced as true within liberal practice of legality. Legality's premise of moral disagreement in free inquiry underlies legality's fear of free ideals.

It is less easy to see, by direct inspection, that this premise is not a denial of the possibility of rational moral discussion. Yet it is crucial to be clear, not only about what the premise says, but also about what it does not say.

9.2 MORAL SKEPTICISM

If we are not careful, talk about interminable moral debate, deep moral division, absence of regimen, free prescription, and the like, might be confused with fundamental philosophical doubt about rational possibility in morals, or deep moral skepticism. But this would be a big misunderstanding of what liberal legality presumes.

To forestall this mistake, I want to take a moment to indicate what deep skepticism about morality would look like. I think the best way of underscoring the quite specific and limited content of legality's assumption about morality is through an indirect method of exhibiting contrasts. I want to show what deep moral skepticism would assert in order to make plain the sort of thing legality's premise does not assert – and, by contrast, what it does say.

In a nutshell, deep skepticism about moral rationality asserts, as a matter of their logic, the radical precariousness of moral prescriptions, conceptions, and credos. It rejects the idea that general moral truths might be established by a common faculty of moral cognition. It teaches that morality is inevitably anarchic. It sees moral assertion to be, in principle, nonrational: arbitrary, vacant, contradictory.

Below, I will briefly state three deeply skeptical contentions about morality. Each view is a picture of failed moral rationality: of morality, by its nature, forever in a pickle. The point of presenting these claims in the present context is to display large dissimilarities between their radical views and legality's own modest assumption about morals.

Three Skeptical Claims

The radical claims represent three kinds of moral disbelief. They focus on different aspects of morality, and put forward different reasons for disbelief in rational possibility. The first view focuses on moral judgment: it says moral judgments are groundless because they depend on frameworks that are arbitrary. The second focuses on moral principle: it claims that abstract moral principles are vacuous, one-sided and manipulable. And the third addresses the moral credo of liberalism: it says that liberal commitment in particular is incoherent and self-defeating.

First is deep skepticism about moral judgments. Here the line of thought is that moral judgments are groundless because they make use of prescriptive frameworks without rational foundation.[3] Many incompatible frames are embraced by moral

---

[3] For ethical philosopher Alasdair MacIntyre, "The most striking feature of contemporary moral utterance is that so much of it is used to express disagreements . . ." "[T]here are rival conceptions of justice formed by and informing the life of rival groups." "[O]ur pluralist culture possesses no method of weighing, no rational criterion for deciding between [the rival claims]" (MacIntyre, *After Virtue*, 1981, pp. 6, 229, 235). "It is precisely because there is in our society no established way of deciding between these claims that moral argument appears to be necessarily interminable. From our rival conclusions we can argue back to our rival premises; but when we do arrive at our premises argument ceases and the invocation of one premise against another becomes a matter of pure assertion and counter-assertion" (MacIntyre 1981, p. 8).

arguers, and none is uniquely commended by moral reason, and so moral disagree-ment is unarbitrable.[4]

Second is deep skepticism about moral principles.[5] Here the main idea is that moral principles are vacuous because they make use of abstract conceptions that are one-sided,[6] blind to the many-faceted substance of moral life.[7] Detached from concrete substance, abstract principles are manipulable, and produce conflicting prescriptions.

Third is deep skepticism about liberalism in particular. Here, the main claim is that the liberal credo, which seeks to support liberty, when taken as a whole, is an incoherent allegiance.[8] The central categories of liberal commitment,

---

[4]   Modernism, according to Roberto Unger, says that "our mental and social life" is shaped by "the contexts of our ideas and actions." "There is no unconditional context – no set of frameworks that can do justice to all our opportunities of insight and association . . ." "Nor . . . can any activity go forward without selecting from the indefinitely large range of possible frameworks the one that it will tentatively take for granted" (Unger, *Passion: An Essay on Personality*, 1984, pp. 7–8).

[5]   Moral psychologist Carol Gilligan describes a "conception of morality" associated with women, rather than men, which emphasizes care and responsibility rather than abstract moral rules and rights. "In this conception, the moral problem . . . requires for its resolution a mode of thinking that is contextual and narrative rather than formal and abstract. This conception of morality as concerned with the activity of care centers moral development around the understanding of responsibility and relationships . . ." (Gilligan 1982, p. 19). The morality of responsibility, with its "contextual mode of judgment," connects moral decision to a "network of relationships," and "focuses . . . on the limitations of any particular resolution" of a moral dilemma, "removing the possibility of a clear or simple solution" (Gilligan 1982, pp. 22, 147).

[6]   According to Karl Marx, "[A]n *equal* right . . . is . . . *a right of inequality, in its content, like every right*" (Marx, "Critique of the Gotha Program," 1875, p. 24; emphasis in original). "Right by its very nature can consist only in the application of an equal standard; but unequal individuals (and they would not be different individuals if they were not unequal) are measurable only by an equal standard in so far as they are . . . taken from one *definite* side only, . . . and nothing more is seen in them, everything else being ignored" (Marx 1875; emphasis original).

[7]   Legal sociologist Max Weber says that there is an "insoluble conflict between the formal and the substantive principles of justice." This is conflict between "desire to realize substantive goals" on the one hand, and "abstract formalism of legal certainty" on the other (Weber, *Economy and Society*, vol. 2, 1925, pp. 811, 893).

Substantive justice, for Weber, is concrete, contextual, controlled by commitment to bring about desired consequences. It aims to realize "expediential and ethical goals." Its precepts are "ethical demands" and "moral exhortations." Proponents of substantive justice "refuse to be bound by formal rules." ". . . [D]ecisions are reached on the basis of concrete, ethical, or political considerations or of feelings oriented toward social justice" (Weber 1925, pp. 810, 811, 813).

Formal justice, by contrast, makes use of nomological prescription, abstract norms that judge all concrete situations within the same generalized classification the same. Formal reasoning is "self-contained" and "strictly professional." By definition, it does not seek substantive justice. Formal judgment necessarily will "produce consequences which are contrary to . . . substantive postulates." "[J]ustice and administration [can] serve to equalize . . . economic and social life-opportunities . . . only if they assume a character that is informal because 'ethical' with respect to substantive content . . ." (Weber 1925, pp. 810, 812, 885, 980).

[8]   For "total criticism" of liberal belief as a whole, see Roberto M. Unger, *Knowledge and Politics* (1975), pp. 1–7. "[Liberal] principles of psychology lead to an antinomy in our conception of the relation between reason and desire in the moral life . . . Liberal psychology justifies . . . conceptions of the self and of morals that are inconsistent [and] cannot be reconciled on the basis of the premises from which

relating to the opposition between private freedom and public order, collide in mutual defeat.[9]

The three large claims just noted are all deeply skeptical in that each presents a picture of failed moral reason. All three affirm not just the observed fact but also the inevitability of moral conflict.

Each says, about a sort of moral argumentation, that it cannot conceivably amount to a rational morality. Each sees, beneath the surface of moral debate, a deep and ineluctable logic that precludes the possibility of rationally terminable moral discussion. The three claims – about groundless judgments, vacuous principles, and incoherent liberalism – assert, respectively, the unavoidable frame-dependence, one-sidedness, and self-defeat of moral talk. In different ways, the three positions claim that moral discourse in itself is necessarily anarchic: subjective, foundationless, hollow, manipulable, self-subversive.

Disagreement and Rationality

Legality's premise, by contrast, says that moral conflict is a stubborn matter of fact, not that it is inevitable as a matter of intrinsic logic. It asserts the noticeable existence of moral discord, not the impossibility of rational agreement. No deeply skeptical conclusion, about the logic of moral discourse, is entailed by the modest observation that moral disagreement keeps happening when inquiry is free.

None of the large skeptical claims surveyed above is embraced by liberal practice; no such view is part of nomological commitment. These views of hopelessly precarious morality are what liberal legality does not assume.

To assert legality's premise – that disagreement exists in free moral inquiry – is not to disavow moral rationality. Recognition of actual conflict within moral discussion, from the standpoint of legal practice, is a far cry from denial of the possibility of right moral resolution. Awareness that moral disagreement occurs in fact is quite compatible with belief that moral truth may be accessible to reason in principle, and that true morality may be nomologically realizable, both general in form and as a whole noncontradictory. In short, fear of free ideals in law has nothing to do with whether moral inquiry is ultimately a rational affair. It rests on a limited basis, the assumption that deep disagreement persists in moral debate.

---

they are derived . . ." (Unger 1975, p. 6). "[L]iberal political theory . . . generates an antinomy in the conception of the relation between public rules and private ends. This antinomy in the liberal doctrine is fatal to its hope of solving the problems of freedom and public order . . . and it leads to conflicting, irreconcilable . . . theories of society" (Unger 1975, p. 7).

[9] Critical legal scholar Clare Dalton says that "The critique [of liberalism] seeks to demonstrate . . . our inability to decide . . . how we should understand and police the boundary between self and other. Liberalism's obsession with, and inability to resolve, the tension between self and other suggests that our stories about politics, policy, and law will be organized along dualities reflecting this basic tension" (Dalton 1985, p. 1006). Chief among the liberal dualities of self and other is the opposition of "private" and "public" (Dalton 1985, p. 1001).

The condition of moral disagreement, assumed by liberal law to exist, is hardly fatal for free moral inquiry itself, beyond law. Outside the legal realm, free moral debate continues, spurred – not halted – by the clash of convictions. An awareness of dissension does not preclude one's affirmation of rational discovery. In the conduct of moral discussion, awareness that discussants disagree morally is not inconsistent with faith that there are true answers to moral questions, knowable by exercise of rational moral capacity common to humans. Indeed, common capacity to recognize the better moral argument may well be a presupposition, or regulative assumption, of the activity of moral exchange. To press one's moral point as true rather presumes truth's apprehensibility. Continued moral colloquy may make little sense absent a presumption that one's interlocutor, like oneself, is able to get at the truth of the matter. Moral debate takes place given present discord and may well presuppose its possible dissolution.

9.3 WHAT'S FEARED

But still, exposure to moral disagreement is a bad condition for liberal law. If the ideals that guide and shape law are formed in a free moral inquiry, then idealizing argument within law will be embroiled in moral debate that goes on outside law.

Exposure to the incessant disagreement of moral debate is a fatal affliction for legal idealization. Free idealizing argument in law could not come to conclusion until some one of the prescriptions contending in free debate happened to be affirmed by a particular legal decider. Legal decision would be hostage to moral choice uncontrolled by law. So free moral decision, inside law, defeats legality even if morality itself should be thought to be, in principle, thoroughly rational. When moral disagreement exists in fact, law's ideals cannot be free and at the same time secure rational nomological resolution.

I should think it is pretty obvious, prior to any close investigation, that free moral decision of particular cases, when done by society's judges, amounts to failure of legality. But it is not so obvious, at a fleeting glance, just how – in what manner – legality fails. We need to take a close look in order to identify the specific character of legality's failure in a situation of free moral judging.

I believe a good way to proceed is to imagine a judging institution that affirmatively authorizes free moral judgment of cases, and to ask what happens when decision ensues. Again, it is obvious at the outset that an authorized activity of this sort is, from legality's standpoint, a nightmare. But why? What specific suite of evils attends judging based on ideals formed in free moral deliberation?

In order to make plain just why liberal legality fears free ideals, and also the depth of the aversion, let us carry out a thought experiment. Let us imagine an instituted activity of moral decision, or moral judging. This is an activity of argument and decision in which judging officials resolve cases based on ideal grounds that come direct from unregimented moral inquiry. Our aim is to assess the imagined activity by light of the nomological conception of legality. We must assume throughout, since nomological legality does, that deep disagreement exists in free moral discourse.

At the center of the imagined enterprise are society's judges, particular people empowered to hear and resolve controversies arising in social life. Their decisions are backed by the force of the collectivity. But the designated deciders are not bound by any distinctively legal argumentative regimen. Rather, we suppose, each judge is authorized – indeed, instructed – to decide each case on the basis of the moral truth of the matter. So the enterprise is a differentiated institution, but not a differentiated discourse. The judges as judges engage in the same moral colloquy which they and everybody else may enter just as moral beings. Judgment is free of any discipline except the test of practical moral truth.

In the decision of a case, we assume, the deciding officer conducts an unfettered moral inquiry to find out what is right, good, just, prudent in the area of social life in question. The ground of decision is whatever prescription the judge in the case determines to be morally appropriate. Each judge decides according to that judge's own moral insight. In the imagined activity, each resolution is a free moral decision. Judges judge by direct appeal to true morality.

To pretend this instituted activity of judging really is a legal practice, and that the decisions it comes up with are legal decisions, would be, from the standpoint of nomological conception, a kind of fraud. What's missing from the activity is impersonal law. What happens within it is exercise of will, ungoverned by law.

What's absent in an instituted activity of moral judging is the regimen of legality. Plainly such an activity cannot guarantee legal entitlement. Legal entitlement is secured when valued positions of persons depend on commonly knowable laws, not the say-so of the authorities. Entitlement requires law-governed argument, which takes extant legal materials as given, and yields resolution under law. But in the activity we imagine, argument is not required to find a starting point in standing law. Nothing must be taken as given prior to moral inquiry. By definition, free moral deliberation is not governed by specifically legal criteria.

In a case to be judged, any of a large number of precepts might be affirmed as the proper ground of free moral decision. The judgment given depends on the moral views of the judge. Since, by hypothesis, there is deep disagreement about morality, the moral deliberations of multiple deciders will affirm divergent prescriptive grounds. Judges with different views will decide differently.[10] The whole mass of decisions over time will be irregular in total effect.

---

[10]   According to legal philosopher John Austin, "[M]oral obligation is anything which we choose to call so, for the precepts of positive morality are infinitely varying, and the will of God, whether indicated by utility or by a moral sense, is equally matter of dispute. [A procedure] which assumes that the judge is to enforce morality, enables the judge to enforce just whatever he pleases" (John Austin, *The Province of Jurisprudence Determined*, 1832, p. 526).

What happens in moral judging is decision based on personal choice. The moral belief that turns out to be decisive in a case is one among many rival views within moral inquiry, a contested position in an unresolved debate. And the judge who decides is one among very many moral inquirers, all able to participate in free debate outside the legal realm on an equal footing. The decisive view prevails simply because it happens to be embraced as morally correct by someone who happens to have power of coercive decision over others. To be sure, from the standpoint of the judging official, decision may seem compelled by reasoning grounded in true morality. But from the standpoint of commitment to nomological legality, the morality that controls is personal – that judge's view. It is a chosen morality – what that judge chooses to affirm. The root of decision is the self-assertion of a particular decider.

According to legality's equation, absence of law-governed resolution is the presence of resolution by will, volition, choice. Uncontrolled by law, moral decision is an exertion of sway. Imposition based just on a particular judge's own conviction of moral correctness, not on law, is a form of domination, or subjugation of one by another. Being subjected to someone else's moral code, which governs by virtue of that other's say-so, is subjection to personality. Moral resolution is accountable to fiat, ungovernable affirmation, an event of positing. Free moral judging issues in nomothetic arbitrariness.

10

Fear of Open Form

Now we should turn to liberal legality's second fear, the fear of open form. This is the second of the two specific apprehensions that spring from generic fear of failed legality.

As we have just seen, legality's first fear – fear of free ideals – dreads the prospect of law's getting swept away, caught up in a battle, on a field where everything is in play. It imagines a swirling superabundance of moral possibilities, from which law must seek shelter.

As we shall see, the sensibility of legality's second fear is rather different. Fear of open form abhors the prospect of law's winding down, coming to a standstill, at a place of impassable deadlock; it imagines exhaustion of meaning, the running out of language, in the vexed silence of a vacuum law must escape. But still the two fears – of the plenum and the void, battle and impasse – actually have a lot in common.

Fear of free ideals, and fear of open form, constitute the double aversion of liberal law. Both motives steer argument negatively within liberal practice. Each of these fears directs attention to a peril of disorder that argument in nomological practice must strive to avoid. The two fears, implications of generic fear, are of common origin, and are homologous, the same in structure.

The basic shape of the second fear – its morphology – is the same as that of the first: each aversion rests on a premise, made up of two tenets, about a disordered condition outside law. Also, the nature of the premise underlying the second fear is basically the same as that of the first: neither's view of disorder is equivalent to deep skepticism, though in either case the disorder imagined would be a bad condition for liberal law.

So our discussion of fear of open form will run in parallel to the exploration already conducted of its twin, the cognate fear of free ideals. But of course, the content of the second fear is different. Fear of free ideals formulates an idea of how idealizing argument in law might fail, while fear of open form contains a conception of how formal argument might fail. The first imagines disordered morality, and the second disordered language, outside law.

Formalizing argument, in order to sustain entitlement and justice, seeks to render the established laws as law-like rules, and to structure law's rules in relation to one another, and then it works to subsume examined cases under the general categories of pertinent rules. In formally structured law, the meaning of any one legal rule, or category of a rule, is gathered by reading related rules and categories together, each in light of the others, so that the ensemble coheres. Formalization tries to develop interrelated concepts and distinctions and definitions – a specifically legal language – able to accomplish the law-like classification of situations arising in the social world. When formalizing processes succeed, law's own terminology stands ready to classify the world, legally.

Fear of open form is the apprehension that law's distinctive processes of construction may fail, leaving formal law as open-ended as common language outside law. It is fear of the void of meaning that yawns when law's concepts, like common concepts, are unsure.

Open form in law is legal formality afflicted with linguistic openness. Formal argument fails if law's classifications are open-ended. Open concepts are uncertain in reach, their application unconstrained by definite limits; in operation such concepts are inconclusive, irresolute. If formal law's own constructive endeavors do not succeed in building specifically legal concepts and meanings, then law's language would be no different from language outside law, and could work no better. Then, formal law would be afflicted with the same openness that afflicts common language, and formal argument could not secure legality.

10.1 UNSURE CONCEPTS

Underlying fear of open form in law is a premise about the condition of language outside law. Legality's premise is that concepts and meanings of language used in general communication beyond law are infirm, indecisive, unsure in their grasp of the world. Open-endedness is seen to be a pervasive characteristic of ordinary linguistic resource.

From the standpoint of legal practice, concepts and meanings of common language are irremediably vague. That is, the openness of common concepts is accountable to their vagueness. So, if law's categorical apparatus cannot do better than common language, but rather turns out to be subject to the same infirmity that affects the generally usable linguistic stock, then law's concepts in operation will likewise be terminally vague. Formal reasoning in law, when made to work with vague categories, will come to a point of impasse, where meaning has run out, and argument freezes, unable to decide.

Our procedure for examining fear of open form will be the same as the approach taken in investigating legality's first fear. Here we will start, not with the feared condition of open form inside law, but with the premise at the root of the fear, the assumption that concepts of common language are unsure. This premise states legality's view of language in general, outside law.

The bulk of the present chapter will be devoted to an exposition of legality's view of common language, first by direct statement, and then by a method of contrasts. At the end of the chapter, we will return to the fear proper, the apprehension that what happens in use of language beyond law might come to happen within law, and see just why liberal practice fears open form.

The reason for devoting so much time to a discussion of legality's premise about language is not that this view, by itself, is particularly abstruse, or hard to grasp. The reason is that, unless we are careful, the premise of unsure concepts might be confused with something liberal legality does not entertain: radical doubt about rational possibility in the use of language. It is vital to establish that, despite superficial similarities, legality's view of language is not the same thing as deep linguistic skepticism. To this end, after legality's view has been laid out, we will juxtapose and distinguish three deeply skeptical views about language. Our aim is to make quite explicit, not only what legality's premise affirmatively says, but also what it emphatically does not say.

Legality's view of common language – the premise of unsure concepts in general communication – may be broken down into two constitutive tenets.

The first tenet is that openness, owing to vagueness, is a pervasive feature of common concepts and meanings. The second tenet is that linguistic openness happens in general communication outside practices. Notice that these propositions are about the use of language beyond, not within, law. In the conduct of legal practice, the vagueness of common language beyond law is taken to be a stubborn, evident fact. The conjunction of the two tenets is a guiding premise embraced by liberal legal practice as a whole.

In what follows, I will give voice to the two tenets that make up legality's view of language, which underlies fear of open form. Remember that this is the view from a particular viewpoint, the perspective of practice of law-like law. The presentation below is not at all a report of discoveries about language made from the standpoint of independent philosophical study. Rather, it is a statement of tenets about language entertained as general truths in the doing of nomological law.

Linguistic Openness

First, common language is unsure, on account of its vagueness. This is the first of legality's two tenets about language. Less tersely put, the tenet says that general terms of common language, employed outside law, are unsure in application to states of affairs in the world.[1]

---

[1] According to H. L. A. Hart, uncertainty in application is an unavoidable feature of language. "[U]ncertainty at the borderline is the price to be paid for the use of general classifying terms in any form of

The many varieties of communicative activity, going on outside nomological practice, using generally available linguistic resources, are not regimented by the special discipline that defines a nomological discourse. The medium of general discussion, beyond law, is not a specifically law-like language, but common language. As observed from the standpoint of legal argument, concepts and meanings of the language used outside law are unsure: infirm, unsteady, liable to break down. Common concepts are open-ended. Their areas of correct use are not well bounded.

Linguistic openness is manifest as persistent vagueness. Viewed from the perspective of law, concepts of common language are open-ended because in operation they are vague. The terms of language outside law, and concepts they express, are thought to be vague not in some profound philosophical sense, but in the ordinary sense that sometimes they are quite indefinite in application. Afflicted with vagueness, common language persistently runs into concrete situations at the margins of its concepts where meaning is quite irresolvable.

According to legality's assumption, ordinary vagueness is a property of common linguistic terms that are applied to states of affairs.[2] All such terms and their concepts – common concepts – exhibit vagueness at the margin, not just certain words that seem to be intrinsically or especially uncertain in denotation. On the other hand, ordinary vagueness is an affliction, not all the time, in every application, but sometimes, in some connections. Sometimes the categories of common language, in particular applications, are just vague.

In short, vagueness is a pervasive sometime property of common linguistic terms that are susceptible of many applications to many unclassified states of affairs. Ordinary vagueness afflicts classificatory activity. It is a feature of the meaning of concepts that are used to take hold of things, objects and events in the world.

Vagueness of a concept is shown by instances of doubtful application. These are the times when it is impossible to be sure whether the concept does or does not apply to a specified state of affairs. In an unsure instance, the case for applying the concept is no better, and no worse, than the case for withholding it. On one rational rendering of the concept's meaning, the category pertains to the situation at hand, and not to apply it is to restrict it by fiat. But on another understanding, the concept must be withheld: to apply it is to expand it by fiat. It is not clear what a situation in the area of vagueness should be called. There

---

communication concerning matters of fact. Natural languages like English are when so used irreducibly open textured" (Hart, *The Concept of Law*, 1961, p. 125). "In all fields of experience ... there is a limit, inherent in the nature of language, to the guidance which general language can provide. There will indeed be plain cases ... to which general expressions are clearly applicable ... but there will also be cases where it is not clear whether they apply or not" (Hart 1961, p. 123). For more on Hart's view of vagueness, see Chapter 8, pp. 123–124.

2   According to Joseph Raz, "The truth is that all, and not only some, nouns, verbs, adverbs, and adjectives of a natural language are vague" (Raz, *The Authority of Law*, 1979, p. 73).

is no definite answer to the question whether the mooted category covers the situation. The contrary possible renderings of the concept annul one another, leaving a void of meaning.

For any common concept, there are always unsure instances where meaning is an open question. Each concept arrives at a point where application is uncertain, and conceptual understanding has no way to decide. Here categorizing activity, poised between incompatible alternatives, can go no further. This is the point of linguistic impasse, the impasse of unsure concepts and meanings, seen to develop beyond law.

General Communication

Second, linguistic openness happens in general communication outside practices. This is the second of legality's two tenets about language. The second tenet identifies a general sphere of discussion, the locus of a communicative activity in which everyone participates, and within which linguistic openness persistently occurs.

General communication is any verbal exchange that takes place outside special discursive realms. Special realms of discourse, like law itself, are restricted spheres, set apart from the common run of talk, in which uses of language are controlled by uncommon canons, special methods serving special purposes. Imagine a totality of all linguistic activity going on in society; subtract communication that takes place inside special realms; what's left, a vast residuum, is general communication, outside practices.

General communication, in common language, is colloquy between anybody and anybody else that is not governed by the specific constraints that form specially differentiated circles of discussion. In its lack of specific regimentation, general communication is the opposite of law-like legal argument. From the perspective of nomological practice of law, pervasive infirmity of meaning develops when linguistic exchange is not controlled by the regimen of an argumentative practice.

General communication is verbal activity invoking concepts and meanings of common language. This is the language people use to discuss the wide world of human concern. In general discourse participants – speakers and listeners, writers and readers – engage in the giving and taking of meaning by use of common linguistic resource. A common language is the medium of expressive intercourse shared by people who live together in a society, who talk with one another using vocabulary and grammar learned from their forebears, and whose meanings may be grasped in turn by succeeding generations, who do the same.

The domain of discussion in common language is the most extensive discursive sphere within society. This largest sphere encompasses an illimitable range of conversational contexts, indeed all the generally communicable situations of personal striving and social relation. In the community of all and sundry speakers of a common language, who are at odds in many ways, the only necessarily shared project is communication. Common language is the language we share despite our other disagreements.

In general discourse – general communication – outside restricted circles, language is not specially constructed. There linguistic endeavor proceeds as best it can apart from specialized canons, drawing on the common store of meanings. Within the sphere of general discourse, communication by common language is seen, from the standpoint of law, to be afflicted with linguistic openness. Ordinary vagueness is an observed feature of generally usable language. In the most extensive sphere of verbal interchange, concepts and meanings are unsure.

The conception of general communication, outside practices, links readily with the idea of linguistic openness, constantly developing. It is easy to see how the two tenets we have considered join together to form a single assumption about the disordered condition of language outside law.

The first tenet says that vagueness of language is persistent. The second says it persists in general discourse. The two, together, amount to a unified premise, the premise of unsure concepts in general communication, which is embraced as true within liberal practice of legality. The premise of language's openness underlies legality's fear of open form.

It is less obvious, perhaps, that this premise does not undercut the possibility of linguistic rationality in a common discourse. Yet it is important to have well in mind not only what legality's premise says, but also what it does not say.

10.2 LINGUISTIC SKEPTICISM

If we are not careful, talk about irremediable openness of concepts, the void of meaning, unregimented language, and the like, might be confused with fundamental philosophical doubt about rationality in the use of language, or deep linguistic skepticism. But this would be a major misunderstanding of what liberal legality presumes.

To forestall this misconception, I want to take a little time to show what deep skepticism about language would look like. I believe the best way of highlighting the quite restricted reach of legality's assumption is an indirect approach of exhibiting contrasts. I want to show what deep linguistic skepticism would assert in order to demonstrate the sort of claim legality's premise does not avow – and, by contrast, what it does say.

In a nutshell, deep linguistic skepticism asserts the radical precariousness of language and the stuff of language: concepts, distinctions, terms of discourse. It teaches that language by nature is anarchic. It denies that interpretation of meanings, or grasp of abstractions, or communication through texts, may be rationally secured. It contests the possibility of rationally founded conceptual endeavor, or achieved rational discourse.

Below I will briefly present three deeply skeptical views about language. Each is a picture of communication by language in profound deadlock. I will quickly line up this trio of disbelieving positions so that, by comparison, the moderate nature of legality's own view of openness of language will be apparent.

Three Skeptical Claims

The radical views represent three kinds of linguistic skepticism. They focus on different aspects of linguistic endeavor, and put forward different reasons for disbelief in rational capability. The first view focuses on assignments of meaning: it says interpretive disagreements are unarbitrable because meanings depend on frameworks that are arbitrary. The second focuses on use of abstractions: it claims that abstract categories for human realities are one-sided, false to connectedness of life, and mutually contradictory. And the third addresses the structured discourse of texts: it says that texts are self-subverting structures, undone by their own constituents.

First is deep skepticism about meaning. Here the central idea is that interpretation of meaning is arbitrary because it depends on an interpretive framework without foundation other than its acceptance.[3] Many conflicting frameworks are available to intellect;[4] rival meanings arise from rival frames;[5] and choice among them is nonrational.

Second is deep skepticism about abstraction. Here, the line of thought is that abstract classifications for human realities are one-sided,[6] and ultimately

---

[3] According to Stanley Fish, "it is interpretive communities ... that produce meanings" (Fish 1980, p. 14). "An interpretive community is not objective because as a bundle of interests, of particular purposes and goals, its perspective is interested rather than neutral ..." "[P]erspectival perception is all there is, and the question is from which of a number of equally interested perspectives will the text be constituted." "[N]o one can claim privilege for the point of view he holds ..." (Fish 1980, pp. 14, 365–366, 368).

[4] Critical theorist Roberto Unger says that, in modern understanding of language, concepts are conventions. "[T]here are no natural distinctions among things ... This is the modern or conventionalist idea of nature and science. For the conventionalist, there are an infinite number of possible ways of dividing the world up and of classifying particular things under general words." "The conventions of naming rather than any perceived quality of 'tableness' will determine whether an object is to count as a table. In the same way, convention rather than nature will dictate whether a particular bargain is to be treated as a contract" (Unger, *Knowledge and Politics*, 1975, pp. 80, 93). For more on conventional concepts, see Chapter 8, p. 128.

[5] For Stanley Fish, conflict among frames is unending. "[M]embers of the same community will necessarily agree because they will see ... everything in relation to that community's assumed purposes and goals; and ... members of different communities will disagree because from each of their respective positions the other 'simply' cannot see what is obviously and inescapably there ..." (Fish 1980, p. 15).

[6] Critical scholar Peter Gabel sees one-sided classifications to be deadening. "[H]uman relationships within contemporary capitalism are characterized by a traumatic absence of connectedness ... [E]ach actor is passivized within a role that denies him recognition as a connected, active, potentiated, and intersubjective *person*. One is never, or almost never, a person; instead, one is successively a 'husband,' 'bus passenger,' 'small businessman,' 'consumer,' and so on" (Gabel 1980, p. 28; emphasis in original).

empty,[7] since it is impossible to separate their concrete spheres. Abstract categories do violence to human relatedness, interpenetrate one another, and lead to contradiction.[8]

Third is deep skepticism about texts. Here the main claims are that a structure of ideas within a text is subject to inversion,[9] so texts overturn themselves, and that self-subversion of the text never comes to an end. Ideas inscribed at the margin of the text disrupt the center, and textual structure dissolves in unstructured play.[10]

The three large claims just noted are all deeply skeptical in that each presents a picture of failed discursive reason. Each says words fail. In its own way, each affirms the existence of a profound, sweeping, and corrosive logic of linguistic failure.

According to all three positions, there is an implacable logic of linguistic incapacity, lying deep beneath the surface of familiar uses of language; this disabling logic operates, not some of the time, but all of the time; and it thwarts the possibility of rationally terminable discursive exchange. The three claims – about arbitrary meanings, empty abstractions, and self-subverting texts – assert, respectively, the unavoidable frame-dependence, one-sidedness, and self-defeat of linguistic device.

---

7 According to Peter Gabel, "when we 'reify,' we draw an abstraction from a concrete milieu and then mistake the abstraction for the concrete" (Gabel 1980, p. 26). "The activity of thinking up political theory ... consists in ... drawing abstractions from the movement of concrete social actors [and] reifying these abstractions ..." "[T]he motive force behind this thought-process is the concealment of 'a traumatic absence of connectedness ...'" (Gabel 1980, pp. 42, 44).

8 Critical scholars Clare Dalton and Gerald Frug see abstract dichotomy to be self-cancelling. "[T]he terms of our polarities are empty ... [T]he only way we can define form, for example, is by reference to substance, even as substance can be defined only by its compliance with form" (Dalton 1985, p. 1002).

"All the stories of bureaucratic legitimation ... attempt to define, distinguish, and render mutually compatible the subjective and objective aspects of life ... [But] no line between subjectivity and objectivity can ever be drawn. Instead, as each model of bureaucratic legitimation has developed, it has included subjectivity on the objective side of the boundary and objectivity on the subjective side" (Frug 1984, p. 1287).

9 "[T]he 'deconstructive' textual strategies developed by Jacques Derrida" are, according to Clare Dalton, "singularly apt for the analysis of a legal order that has, like the philosophy he critiques, founded its authority on objectivity ..." (Dalton 1985, pp. 1007–1008). "Derrida affirms the role of conceptual duality ... [He] observes that all discourse tends to favor one pole of any duality over the other, creating a hierarchical relationship between the poles. The disfavored pole he calls the dangerous supplement, 'dangerous' because of its undermining potential ..." (Dalton 1985, p. 1007).

10 According to Jacques Derrida, "[I]n a classical philosophical opposition we are not dealing with the peaceful coexistence of a *vis-a-vis*, but rather with a violent hierarchy. One of the two terms governs the other (axiologically, logically, etc.), or has the upper hand. To deconstruct the opposition ... is to overturn the hierarchy at a given moment ... The necessity of [overturning] is structural; it is the necessity of an interminable analysis: the hierarchy of dual oppositions always reestablishes itself" (Derrida 1981, pp. 41–42).

See also Irigaray (1985), p. 79 ("every dichotomizing ... break ... has to be disrupted. Nothing is ever to be posited that is not also reversed"); Culler (1982), pp. 86, 133 ("to deconstruct a discourse is to show how it undermines ... the hierarchical oppositions on which it relies"; "An opposition that is deconstructed is not destroyed or abandoned but reinscribed").

Vagueness and Communication

Legality's premise, by contrast, says that common concepts are ordinarily vague. Vagueness is nothing fancy, right on the surface; it is a sometime disability, not operative in every instance; it does not seal the doom of rational interchange. To claim that vagueness is a pervasive property of concepts in general communication is not to deny that language can work, that meaning can be conveyed, that one can succeed in understanding another.

None of the large skeptical claims just reviewed is embraced by liberal legal practice. No such view is part of nomological commitment. These views of unraveled discursive rationality are what liberal legality does not assume.

Legality's assumption about the openness of general terms of language involves a modest notion of conceptual infirmity. Concepts are seen to be open, not in any deeply skeptical sense, but in the ordinary, garden variety sense that they are sometimes unsure in particular applications. Awareness of unsure concepts and meanings, from the standpoint of legal practice, is not equivalent to radical doubt about discursive capability outside law. In general discourse, as observed from the viewpoint of legal argument, joint understanding is possible, and common categories are serviceable, and texts are knowable – all up to the point that vagueness breaks out.

The condition of ordinary vagueness is a relatively minor failing on the part of common language, and in some respects not a failing at all. In linguistic exchange using common concepts, discussion is subject to further discussion. Failure of communication owing to opacity of meaning may be sidestepped by subsequent paraphrase. Any given concept will come to a halt, sometimes, but then, other concepts may take over. Meaning may be secured by new communication. Moreover, open linguistic resource serves inquiries that are open. Vagueness of common language, an ever-present feature, is a hedge against an always unfamiliar future. Applications of an open concept are not fixed in advance, but rather make an open series, to be continued by finding of unexpected instances. Open terms are projectable from one context to another, able to be extended along with stipulation of new connections. Closed terms would be mute in strange contexts, or could speak only as metaphors; a language of closed concepts would be freighted with coinages. Common concepts are malleable and so compliant to needs of surprising discovery and uncommon purpose.

10.3 WHAT'S FEARED

But still, affliction with vagueness is a bad condition for formal law. Indeed, openness unresolvable without invention is a fatal affliction for legal formality.

Subsuming of particulars under general terms is the heart of formal decision. A general formal law is meant for innumerable applications to particular situations. The whole body of formal law is meant for application across the whole range of human affairs. And law-like formality must be ready to speak to any of these situations, through provisions already extant, sufficiently to sustain legality, right now.

Formality's task is one of linguistic correlation. Formal argument must line up – correlate – established legal categories with other ways of describing situations, not in terms of the law's classifications. Correlative questioning asks whether a described state of affairs does, or does not, come within the meaning of a general formal category: is so-and-so an instance of such-and-such? This sort of legal questioning is in principle endless. The world that formality addresses has an indefinitely large number of statable features and combinations of features. General law is always as yet incompletely correlated with possible particular descriptions of the world. Always more questions may be asked, about the specific coverage of the general laws, than have already been answered.

If formal law's categories and prescriptions are subject to the same infirmity that affects language outside law, then formal law will be similarly unsure in application to the world. Ordinary vagueness disables subsumption of particulars. It would bring formally rational classification of particulars to a point of impasse, the impasse of unsure concepts and meanings. When unable to categorize the uncategorized, formal legal argument will fail to secure nomological legality.

In order to see in some detail just why liberal legality fears open form, let us conduct a thought experiment. Let us imagine an instituted activity of legal argument and judgment in which argument is kept strictly formal. This activity, like liberal legal practice, is one in which judges resolve cases through judgments backed by the force of the collectivity. But unlike liberal practice, our imagined enterprise is governed by a ground rule that disallows any sort of nonformal reasoning to justify decisions made. Only formal laws, we imagine, are available as the basis of legal resolution. The judges have at their disposal a body of standing formal rules, which are the sole permissible grounds for decision of concrete cases that come up.

Now suppose that a situation of irremediable vagueness arises within the posited activity. That is, a concrete case comes up for decision, but the extant categories of pertinent formal materials, in application to the particular facts of this case, are terminally vague. We assume that extant formal laws are afflicted with the same openness that is a feature of common language in general communication. For simplicity, let us say the outcome in the case depends on whether a particular legal rule is applicable or not, but the concrete case falls in the area of vagueness of the categories of this rule. So the answer to the question whether the rule applies is both yes and no: on one reading of the vague rule it applies, while on another reading of the rule it does not. Alternative ways of classifying the case legally are equally available. Since the only law-like material that may be invoked is formal stuff, and by assumption this fails, nomological resource is exhausted before resolution can be achieved.

Let us suppose that the judge nevertheless pushes on to decision. Judges sit to decide cases, so the judge in this case goes ahead and decides, one way or another. The deciding officer picks one of the possible ways of reading the vague rule with reference to the particular situation at hand, claims this is the right formal reading of the law, and then says that the decision dictated by the chosen reading is the right resolution of the case.

If formal argumentation continues in this way, past the point of formal failure, the resulting exercise is sophistry, manipulation of meaning. Appeal to the failed categories of exhausted rules, as the rationale of coercive decision, is a mere gesture at judging legally. To affirm that one concrete reading of the pertinent ground is dispositive, when a contrary reading is equally available and would decide the case differently, is judgment by artifice.

Worse, the deciding officer's pretense that a correct formal resolution has been achieved, when none is possible, is official deception. This kind of dishonesty violates the democratic responsibility of judging officials to be candid in their execution of public authority. Democratic accountability requires that custodians of collective agency not tell lies about its use. Judges in a democracy should frankly avow the nature and bases of their decisions.

The coercive decision that ensues despite formal failure is not an expression of law-like reason. From the standpoint of commitment to nomological legality, decision is rather an exercise of law-less power. The formal law is, by hypothesis, the only law-like resource that can be employed in the legal enterprise we are imagining. But formal law afflicted with vagueness is indecisive, agnostic, unable to conclude. So, law-like law runs out short of decision. Legal argument is unable to achieve nomological resolution.

Candid formal argument would simply generate the equally available alternatives, expose them to view, and then stop, frankly irresolute. The alternative readings of open formality are mutually exclusive, and they cancel each other out, leaving a void. Ensuing decision then takes place in a void of law-like law and argument. There is an unbridgeable gulf between nomological grounds and concrete resolution. According to the fundamental equation of legality, absence of law is presence of power. What enters the empty space is force: the sheer decisional power of the legal authorities, unmediated by law.

From the perspective of nomological commitment, whatever disposition ensues is an instance of the absence of legal justice. Decision proceeding in a void of law-like law is, perforce, without nomological basis. It is nude of justification by general law-like reasons able to sustain like treatment of like cases. So there is no basis for the nomological treatment of persons required by law-like legality. Open formality is unable to accomplish law-like assessment, for want of dispositive legal criteria of sameness. Open form instead yields irregular resolution, the opposite of consistent judgment. When law-like law quits, but decision proceeds, rational connection cannot occur, and any treatment accorded to the person adjudged is special treatment. In short, open form, in a purely formal judging activity, defeats law-like legality. Open formal judging issues in anomic arbitrariness.

11

Modern Liberal Practice

In the last two chapters, which address legality's fears, most of the space is taken up by discussion of ideas – assumptions, premises – that lie behind the fears.

In the chapter that just ended, my main object was to lay out the content of an idea about language. This is the idea of unsure concepts, the view that common language outside law is afflicted with vagueness.

And in the preceding chapter, the main object was to present the content of a similar idea about morality, the idea of warring creeds. This is the view that free morality outside law is afflicted with disagreement.

These ideas are views of disorder beyond law. Unsure concepts, within general communication, lead to terminal irresolution; warring creeds, within free moral inquiry, are in ceaseless conflict. The views of disorder are also views of incapacity. Neither open language, nor conflictual morality, is capable of sustaining legality.

By now, I think, we have before us all we need to know about the substance of the two ideas of disorder. What remains to be examined is their status. The issue that remains is this: why should we suppose that the beliefs I have described, about disordered language and morality, are embraced in the doing of nomological law?

In the present chapter, my object is to show just why and how the ideas of extramural disorder are legality's own. I will show that these ideas are the consequence of other constituents of nomological commitment, familiar to us, and so are bound up with the nomological conception of law. Also, at the end of this discussion, I will say something more about the ideas' implication for the conduct of legal practice: how they instruct legal argument, what they provoke argument to do.

My claim is that the two views of disorder in language and morality outside law have a fundamental status within modern liberal practice of law. I have, in fact, been asserting this claim for some time. Right along I have spoken of the idea of unsure concepts, and the idea of warring creeds, as legality's assumptions, law's premises, practice's awareness. They are, I have said, legality's view of language and legality's view of morality.

My claim about the fundamental status of the views of disorder within practice of law may be put a number of different ways. For a start, it is an assertion about perspective.

Law's awareness of disordered conditions beyond law is, I maintain, the outlook from a particular standpoint. Such awareness is not the upshot of independent investigation conducted without preconception by stepping outside law. Rather, it is the view from within law looking out. This means that law's assumptions about language and morality are internally generated. The views of extramural disorder are internal to law. They arise inside legal practice. To say they arise within law's sphere is to say that they are taken as true in practice of law. They are entertained not as idle observations but as active assumptions. Argument in liberal practice goes forward on the assumption that meanings and morals developed outside law are insufficient to sustain legality. The two assumptions, of linguistic infirmity and moral division, are embraced as premises of legal argument. The two premises are used to direct legal pursuit. Indeed, they are part of the definition of what it is to pursue law-like law. They are vital constituents of the complex commitment that drives legal practice of the modern liberal type.

All these points can, I think, be borne out by a single showing. This is a showing of how the ideas of unsure concepts and warring creeds get generated – how they originate – inside legal practice. The story of their genesis tells why and how the premises of disorder are embraced as legality's own. Their origin ensures fundamental status. For the root from which they spring lies very deep in liberal practice. Their seed is the idea of law-like law itself.

11.1 PRACTICE'S VIEW OF LAW

The root of legality's premises is the self-conception of nomological practice. In brief, the story of genesis is as follows.

Practice's self-conception is the view of law, and of legal activity, that is embraced in the doing of law. The self-understanding of law-like law arises when the aim of law-like legality is fully entrenched in argumentative practice. We may call this self-conception legality's view of law.

Now according to practice's self-conception, law-like law is the fashioned product of a specially formed endeavor. Legality can be brought about only by law's own processes within the realm of law. Other discursive processes, in realms beyond law, are incapable of sustaining legality. It follows that processes operating in the realms of general communication and free moral inquiry cannot secure legality. Thus, law's assumptions about the incapacity of meanings and morals outside law are the consequence of law's self-understanding. Legality's view of language, and legality's view of morality, are the consequence of legality's view of law.

At an earlier point in the present study, as we concluded our examination of the basic features of instituted discourse of law, we saw that nomological practice comes to acquire a self-conception.[1] Characteristic self-conception was shown to be an emergent feature of the instituted discourse of law-like law. We saw that

---

[1] See Chapter 3, pp. 39–43.

nomological practice gets its notion of itself from the nomological conception of legality, the model of law entrenched as law's formative aim.

I don't want to repeat everything said in the earlier pages about self-understanding. But some repetition is needed here in order for us to link law's self-definition and its views of extralegal language and morals.

Practice's self-conception breaks down into two closely related presuppositions. Legality's view of legal enterprise insists upon the singularity, and the contingency, of law-like law. Put another way, it asserts the distinctive, and the constructive, character of legal practice.

First, law-like law is the object of a specific pursuit. Practice of legality is formed by its own discursive canons, its own criteria of good argument and good judgment. The criteria of rationality that control other communicative and prescriptive activities, of whatever sort, are not equivalent to nomological stricture. In particular, discursive activity that is itself unregimented – not conducted within any special practice, so not subject to any specific, instituted regimen – necessarily lacks the rigor and discipline of nomological argument.

Second, law-like law is the product of law-like legal practice. It does not happen without an intent and continuous effort of purposeful contrivance. Legality is the product only of argumentation conducted within law's realm. Argumentative processes in all other realms of discourse, not governed by specifically nomological canons and admonitions, are not sufficient to produce it. In particular, discursive activity that is conducted not just outside legal practice, but outside all specific practices, necessarily fails to generate the sorts of concepts and precepts that are the materials of law-like legal argument.

It follows immediately from the foregoing propositions, which make up practice's self-conception, that common linguistic concepts and free moral precepts are insufficient to sustain legality.

Law's view of itself is relational and comparative. Liberal practice of legal argument defines itself in relation to extramural – extralegal – activities. Nomological practice requires itself to do better, toward its end of law-like ordering, than discursive undertakings outside law. Thus, law's awareness of disorder beyond the legal sphere arises as the fruit of law's interior understanding of itself.

The activities of general communication by language, and free inquiry about morals, take place in discursive realms that are not regulated by any specially instituted discipline, much less by the full formative regimen of law-like law. According to law's relational self-conception, what goes on in an unregimented realm cannot satisfy tests of legality. So, from the standpoint of legal argument, classifications developed in general communication, and prescriptions developed in free morality, are necessarily unable to perform as law-like law must. Undisciplined meanings and morals outside law are understood to be inadequate, unsafe, disordered.

11.2 TWO VIEWS OF DISORDER

Of course, the particular incapacities seen to afflict common language and free morality are not the same. Viewed from the standpoint of liberal law, discursive activity beyond law exhibits two different kinds of disorder, owing to different kinds of incapacity. By legality's lights, common language is deficient because of openness, while free morality is deficient because of disagreement.

These distinct deficiencies take shape when the teachings of self-conception are brought to bear particularly on language and on morality. In order to see this, we need to address language and morality separately.

Legality's View of Language

First, I shall focus on legality's view of language, and point out how this particular view takes shape. In this connection, I will say something about the modern character of nomological practice, for legality's view of language is a good indication of the modernity of law-like law.

Legality's assumption about language outside law – the idea that language outside arrives at an impasse of unsure concepts and meanings – follows from legality's idea of language inside law.

Inside practice, the process of formalization aims to construct a sufficiently law-like language. In order to sustain legality, law's language must be able to carry out the vital task of sure classification. Use of legal language must accomplish the regular subsumption of particulars under general categories of extant law. Law's concepts are crafted, and their meanings refined, in order to achieve nomological judgment of the unending stream of cases flowing out of a multifarious world. According to practice's self-conception, a sufficiently law-like language can be constructed only within a discursive practice governed by specifically nomological regimen. Law's terms and distinctions are understood to be the product of purposeful construction.

By contrast, common language outside law is not developed in line with a nomological regimen. Common linguistic device is not constructed in line with any specific regimen at all. By nature, general communication takes place apart from practices constituted by special canons. Common language is the coin of a residual realm. It is the medium of communication conducted outside all particular spheres of discourse defined by adherence to special intellectual methods or special practical imperatives. It follows, from all the above, by legality's lights, that language in general discourse is not sufficiently sturdy to support the constant burden of nomological resolution.

From the standpoint of legal practice, uncrafted language outside law is seen to lack the particular capacity that linguistic construction inside law aims to achieve. Common language is understood to be disabled with respect to the vital task of a law-like language, which is sure classification of situations in the world. It cannot perform as law's language must: it fails to execute the rational subsumption of particulars in case after case after case. Thus, in nomological practice, the generally usable linguistic stock is regarded as infirm, open, unsure. Concepts of common language are seen to be afflicted with pervasive infirmity of meaning in application. Unconstructed concepts and meanings are liable to dissolve in undecidable vagueness.

Modern Understanding

Legality's view of language is an indication of the modernity of law-like law. According to legality's view, law's language is constructed within a distinct discursive realm: sufficiently law-like concepts and meanings are crafted only within specifically legal practice. Now a modern understanding of legal activity is one that affirms the differentiation of the legal system within society, and the artefactuality of developed law: it sees law to be a product of human manufacture built within identifiably legal institutions. So, legality's view of language in law, because it emphasizes the differentiated and the artefactual character of legal language, is a modern understanding of how law develops.

Legality's view of language might be thought to be not just modern, but modernist. By modernism,[2] in the present context, I mean the very highly general supposition that meanings get secured within frames that happen to be maintained by shared acceptance in particular spheres of discourse. This is the idea of frame-dependence, which we have encountered in the form of deep skepticism. The idea that rational assertion in general is dependent on framework accepted within a discursive circle is a tenet characteristic of the outlook of modernism.

Now it does seem that legality's view of law's language has some affinity with the much broader modernist supposition. Both would say that law's rationality may be realized only within the realm of law. But the modernism of modern liberal legality, and its view of language, is a rather minimal sort.

Legality's view of language does not claim that meaning is radically frame-dependent: that is, dependent on nonrational embrace of some particular one among conflicting frameworks. And legality's view of language outside all special realms is not radical at all. Legality's view insists only on the ordinary vagueness of common general terms. Common language, though pervasively vague, may work well enough in general communication. Still, according to legality's view, legal meaning sufficiently sturdy for law's purposes is constructable only inside the legal realm.

---

[2] The first principle of "the modernist position," according to Roberto Unger, is "the principle of contextuality ... the belief that our mental and social life is ordinarily shaped by institutional or imaginative assumptions that it takes as given" (Unger 1984, p. 7). "[C]ontexts can be broken"; but "[c]ontext-breaking remains both exceptional and transitory." "Either it fails and leaves the pre-established context in place, or it generates another context ..." (Unger 1984, p. 9). On modernist frame-breaking, see Kennedy, *A Critique of Adjudication* (1997), pp. 5–12 (defining "modernism/postmodernism").

Legality's View of Morality

Now let us turn to legality's view of morality. In this connection, we will encounter the liberal aspect of nomological practice, for legality's view of morals is a good index of the liberality of law-like law.

Legality's assumption about morals outside law – the idea that moral inquiry outside gives rise to a battle of warring creeds and programs – follows from legality's view of practical morality inside law.

Inside practice, the process of idealization aims to formulate ideal aims, practical moral precepts and goals, that are specifically legal. In order to sustain legality, law's ideal aims must exhibit the quality of rational coherence. The multiple principles, policies, and purposes of law must fit together, cohere with one another, so they may organize and guide the given formal stuff of law. Law's ideal grounds and judgments are fashioned to satisfy the nomological imperative of harmony.

By contrast, free morality outside law is not formed in line with legality's strictures. Free moral debate is not constrained by any instituted regimen at all. By nature, free deliberation is regulated just by the test of moral truth. Quest of true morality is an open activity everyone can enter without submitting to a special discipline. Moral arguers are not bound by constraints of institutional roles, are not bound to accept the canons of any instituted discourse, and are not bound ahead of inquiry to affirm the rightness or goodness or justice or prudence of existing institutions. It follows, from all the above, by legality's lights, that reasoning processes of free moral inquiry are not disciplined enough to secure nomological-connective rationality.

From the standpoint of legal practice, morality developed outside law is seen to lack the particular discipline that law's law-like ideals must display. Free moral argument fails to supply a harmonious body of moral reasons, a totality of precepts and goals that fit together, one with another. Prescriptions affirmed in moral debate are seen to be at odds with one another, in discord, not concord. Free morality is unruly, schismatic, divided and disordered. Unfettered moral argument is locked in unceasing disagreement.

Liberal Assumption

Legality's view of morality is an indication of the liberality of law-like law. As we saw quite a while back, liberal political commitment requires that the nomological practice of law exist, because law-like law is the perfected legal form of flourishing liberty. As we just saw, the self-conception of such a practice gives rise to an assumption, embraced within the practice, that moral disagreement happens outside law. In this way liberal commitment on the one hand, and the premise of moral disagreement on the other hand, are connected. But now I have in mind another connection that is much closer – and, I should think, pretty obvious.

The same view of moral debate that arises within liberal legal practice also flows directly from liberal political commitment itself. The very idea of a liberal polity presumes that people disagree on important issues of collective morality. Commitment to flourishing liberty assumes the persistence of practical moral discord. By definition, modern liberal commitment prescribes that a system of personal and political liberties should be well instituted in common life, including freedoms that constitute democratic self-government. A recognition of division and dissension among free citizens underlies a number of notable liberties. Freedom of conscience or religion, and freedom of thought or speech, presume that people's convictions on vital moral matters are divergent. Recognition of disagreement is part and parcel of liberal prescriptions for self-government. Prescribed mechanisms of democratic representation and resolution presuppose programmatic conflict and continuing – usually loyal – opposition in political society. So, liberal legality's assumption that multiple creeds and programs contend is also a routine assumption of liberal polity.

11.3 IMPLICATIONS OF DISORDER

In the last few pages, we have seen that legality's assumptions about language and morality are generated internally, inside legal practice, and that they are modern and liberal in character. What remains to be surveyed is the implication of these assumptions for the conduct, and success, of legal argument.

It would not be amiss now to add – carefully – that legality's assumptions are skeptical understandings. They do express disbelief in the achieved rational perfection of common language and free morality. Legality's premises amount to a kind of internal skepticism – law's own skeptical outlook.

Legality's premise of linguistic openness is a form of linguistic skepticism. Legality's premise of moral disagreement is a form of moral skepticism. Together they report law's internal awareness of treacherous and inhospitable mental terrain outside law.

But legality's own skepticism is minimal, not deep. Liberal legality's premises do not purport to cancel rational possibility in any field. They are not to be confused with deep philosophical skepticism about meanings and morals.

Minimal Skepticism

As sketched in the two prior chapters of this book, deep skepticism asserts the radical frame-dependence, one-sidedness, and self-defeat of language and morality alike. It imagines meanings to be arbitrary and judgments groundless; it sees abstractions to be empty and principles vacuous; it conceives texts in general to be self-subverting and liberalism in particular to be incoherent.

But legality's skeptical views affirm not one of these things. The conditions asserted by legality's premises do not add up to a vast opaque turbulence of anarchic language and anarchic morality, a formless mental world wherein conceptions depend on foundationless frames, where abstract ideas overreach multiform reality, and texts and credos defeat themselves.

Legality's linguistic and moral skepticism, all told, is sharply limited, quite compatible with affirmation of reason and truth in communication and prescription. For all legality assumes, conceptual activities in their spheres may be based in reason, meaningful, and noncontradictory, though common concepts are vague. Likewise, moral truth may in principle be discoverable by reason, and in principle true imperatives might each be regularly applicable and all be coherent, though disagreement persists in fact. The view that prescriptive disagreement exists in moral life is a commonplace observation, a workaday assumption of liberal politics. The view that ordinary vagueness is a feature of common language, prompting further discussion, is a modest notion of linguistic infirmity, likewise familiar.

Legality's premises are minimally skeptical because they are, after all, legality's premises. They are compatible with nomological pursuit. Legality's skeptical views are ones that may be entertained within practice of law-like law, and indeed are entertained in order to steer – not paralyze – law-like legal argument. Law's premises do not compel any skeptical conclusion about law itself. They do not subvert liberal aspiration from the start.

By their terms, legality's assumptions posit extramural, not internal, disorder. Infirm meanings and divided morals are conditions which, from the standpoint of law, are seen to exist beyond law. It does not necessarily follow from premises about exogenous conditions that argument inside legal practice gets exposed to those conditions. What happens in language and morality beyond law does not automatically come to pass within the modes of law.

Peril for Law

At the same time, formal argument in law is a species of classificatory activity, and ideal argument in law is a species of moral inquiry. In the event that legality's specific processes of argumentation should fail, this would mean law is unable to do any better than discursive endeavor beyond the bounds of law. Then there is no effective barrier between law and the irresolute realms of common language and free morality, and the same unsettled conditions that happen outside will afflict discourse inside. Ordinary vagueness, and commonplace disagreement, are, as we know, bad conditions for law. When external conditions are also internal, then the modes of law-like law are disabled, and legality is defeated.

Fear of open form and fear of free ideals are abiding motives of argumentative pursuit within practice of legality. Practice goes forward in constant awareness of the existence of unsure concepts and warring creeds beyond law, and in constant awareness of the peril of cognate developments inside legal argument. Nomological pursuit strives mightily to avoid internal affliction, to avert what's feared. Practice of legality posits disordered conditions outside itself in order to struggle against them.

Nomological practice seeks to build specifically legal meanings and morals. Law-like argument labors self-consciously not to replicate the disabilities of other realms, to be distinct, to do better. Law's specificity is law's bulwark. Within practice of legality, processes of formalization and idealization develop in order to structure law's own language and morality.

When law's distinctive mechanisms of construction succeed, then what happens outside need not happen inside. Success is avoidance of peril through law-like law's own operations. The twin perils of open form and free ideals might each be avoided in two ways.

Peril of open form may be handled two ways. Failure of argument owing to open form in law might be avoided either by reason of the success of formalization's structuring processes, or by recourse to legal ideals. Formalization seeks to hammer out rules, and the law-like categories of rules, and to organize these elements within connected schemes, thus forging specifically legal classifications whose application is governed by formality's own technique. When complex formality is able to succeed, legal argument may avoid widespread affliction with the same infirmity of meaning that is a feature of general communication. If formal resources should fail, argument may turn to legal ideals underlying formal rules in order to guide and shape unsure concepts.

Peril of free ideals may be addressed two ways. Failure of argument owing to free ideals in law might be avoided either by reason of the success of idealization's structuring processes, or by return to the shelter of formality. Ideal argument seeks to formulate principles, policies, and purposes that fit extant formality and fit together, one with another, thus developing the ordered prescriptions of law's own morality by means of ideal technique specific to law. When complex idealization is able to succeed, then legal argument may avoid law's exposure to the conflict of creeds and programs that goes on in free moral inquiry. If idealizing methods should fail, legal argument may turn to formal ratiocination to find a haven from the moral debate.

But if formalization first fails, prompting resort to ideals, and then idealization itself fails, so that all law's defenses are breached, and law lies open to disorder outside, then legality fails.

12

Legality Recapitulated

We have now completed what we set out to do. Our study of the elements that together constitute the modern liberal practice of legal argument is complete. By way of conclusion, let us take a moment to review our findings. Let us stand back from the detail of our subject and consider the main outline of what we have seen.

In retrospect, and taken as a whole, the study now completed is an extended exposition showing how a commitment develops to direct an activity.

In prospect, at the outset, I noted that two jobs of exposition needed to be done, one having to do with process and the other with substance. For liberal legal enterprise is the marriage of a particular sort of procedure, an instituted arrangement that goes on and on, and a particular substantive commitment, the tending always toward a definite end.

The first, and lesser, job was to state the features that suffice to make up an instituted discourse of law. This is an activity of argument and decision taking place in a distinctive realm, at the center of which are society's judges. We saw how different types of argument put forward by magistrates, advocates, and others – primary, derivative, and affiliated argument – are controlled by common canons, anchored in an institution. In such an activity, discursive variety converges to unity.

The second, and greater, task was to work out the constituents and implications of nomological commitment – what it comprises, what it yields. The substantive ambition of liberal practice is to realize the nomological conception of law-like legality. We saw how the basic commitment comprises formative hope and trepidation, which yield operative pursuits and aversions. This commitment is a unity that develops to produce variety.

The combination of such an activity and this very commitment is the specifically liberal practice of legal argument. In our survey of its elements, we have been looking at liberal practice much as the practice views itself. We have specified liberal legal enterprise from the standpoint of the idea of legality that drives its argument. We see what practice looks like according to its blueprint.

In what follows, I will focus on nomological substance one more time. Our analysis of process may now recede into the implicit background of discussion. What's distinctive about liberal practice is the substance of nomological commitment. Below, in outline, are our main findings about the content of nomological devotion.

12.1 PATTERN IN COMPLEXITY

The nomological conception of law, which directs liberal legal argument, when fully expressed, is quite complex. The commitment to realize the conception starts simple and singular, and unfolds to encompass an elaborate plurality of elements. The idea of law-like law produces a multiplicity of practical directives, instructions and admonitions informed by entrenched assumptions.

But there is a pattern, a complicated symmetry, that underlies the developing complexity of substantive detail. In the next few pages, I will assemble points already presented, in order to display the overall pattern of the unfolding of nomological commitment.

What follows is a summary. I won't say anything new, and will be brief. Pattern is best seen when we pass quickly from point to point.

The monotonic starting point of nomological preachment is the slogan that law should be law-like. At its simplest, the nomological conception says that law should have law-like qualities. Laws should be general, accessible, and coherent, and applicable by reason. Here is the gist of the basic commitment that undergoes development.

The development of nomological allegiance is a process of ramification. The governing idea of liberal legal endeavor undergoes a branching evolution. It divides, and divides again. The tutelary conception ramifies to produce positive and negative components, equally impelling. Then each term of the division divides, and reappears as a pair.

Formative commitment, in development, displays properties of polarity and duality. Polarity is the manifestation of opposite tendencies, good and bad aspects. Duality is the revelation of doubleness, alternatives arising from a common source. In a nutshell, the development is this: something basic shows itself as a plus and a minus, and then each appearance is multiplied by two. A substrate reveals antipodal aspects, which complement each other, and each evolves further to become twofold in nature. This is the pattern of the unfolding of nomological commitment.

Polarity in Striving

First, nomological commitment exhibits polarity. It is a single resolve constantly manifest in opposed aspects. Argumentative striving within liberal practice is always oriented negatively as well as positively. Nomological argument directs itself with reference to polar conditions: good and bad, happy and unhappy, sought and feared.

The conception of law-like legality is itself negative as well as positive. The idea of legality is an imagining of two contrary conditions that exclude one another: a good state of affairs that pertains when law-like law succeeds, and an evil situation that develops when nomological endeavor fails. Presence of either condition is the absence of the other. The nomological conception is of something that attracts, and something that repels.

At the positive pole is the sought condition of realized legality. According to nomological conception, law's object is to ensure due status and treatment of people subject to collective power, a law-full situation that is necessary in order to realize equal liberty. Argumentative striving in liberal practice is ever attracted by the prospect of achieving and maintaining a regime of law-like law. Practice is governed by the broad instruction always to pursue the dispensation of legality.

The nomological conception of what law ought to bring about is an amalgam of the ideas of legal entitlement, legal justice, and legal rationality. Entitlement exists when valued positions of persons depend just on the meaning of standing laws. Justice exists when legal argument sustains like judging of like cases. The third idea – law-like rationality – is contained within the other two. Entitlement, or the law-like status of persons, depends on rational resolution. Justice, or law-like treatment, depends on rational connection. Legal endeavor is powerfully drawn toward these happy conditions at the positive pole.

At the negative pole is the feared condition of failed legality. Nomological legality is a sought situation definable with reference to an evil condition that exists in its absence. Viewed negatively, in terms of what it negates, law-like legality is the exclusion of unmediated power, ungoverned volition, arbitrary imposition. The prospect of arbitrariness absent law-like law exerts a repelling force. Argument in liberal practice is controlled by an admonition to guard against, and steer clear of, arbitrary judgment.

There are two broad types of arbitrariness. Anomic – law-less – arbitrariness proceeds in a void of law-like reasons. Nomothetic – law-giving – arbitrariness draws from the plenum of possibility. Nomological legality abhors a void, and dreads the plenum. These bad developments are the obverse of happy ones. Anomic decision is injustice, failed rational connection. Nomothetic decision is disentitlement, failure of rational resolution under law.

Thus, nomological commitment is both positive and negative. It yields affirmative and negative undertakings, animated by complementary but oppositely charged motivations, aspiration and fear. Positive and negative impulsion – hope and worry, avidity and aversion – spring from the same root. The commitment to quest for law-like legality is a commitment to work to avert legality's failure. Constant peril of evils that occur absent legality is the negative spur of positive pursuit. Argument within practice of legality is doubly driven.

Biform Aspiration and Fear

Second, both aspiration and fear are dual in character. Basic commitment branches into positive and negative motivation, and then branches again, its biformity doubled. Formative aspiration gives rise to positive impulse in two directions, and formative fear gives rise to a parallel pair of apprehensions. Polarity multiplied by duality equals binary attraction and binary repulsion.

The aspiration and the fear that animate nomological argument are generic. They are highly general, and they are generative. Each may be translated into concrete terms in line with a more specific understanding of what is to be sought or feared. Each is translatable in two ways. The abstract idea of legality's success, and the abstract idea of legality's failure, are both subject to practical interpretation according to alternative working understandings.

At the positive pole, generic aspiration yields dual impulse. The sought situation of law-like entitlement and justice is subject to interpretation in terms of two specific ways of doing law. There are two modes of law-like law and argument. Each would be sufficient, if carried out in practice, to sustain legality. A dual impulse arises within liberal practice to pursue each of the alternative kinds of law, so that movements toward the generic goal may be in different directions. Nomistic law is not monistic.

Practice's dual impulse is to formalize law and to idealize law. Formal argument seeks to work out law's precepts as rules. Ideal argument seeks to articulate practical moral principles, policies, and purposes that rules subserve. Each mode is governed by the imperative of coherence that lies at the heart of nomological-connective rationality. In complex development, each pursuit seeks structure – formal or ideal. Complex formality brings rules into defined relations, and complex idealization orders law's practical moral grounds.

Both impulses are directly generated by the formative aspiration of practice. They are of common origin, but they are rivals; two different ways of doing law. By definition, each is the negation of the other. Formal law is nonideal; ideal law is nonformal; nomological legal endeavor, in any particular instance, is the one or the other.

At the negative pole, generic fear gives rise to a double aversion. The abstract worry about failure of legality, when worked out concretely in relation to dual positive pursuit, becomes a double fear. Each concrete fear formulates a distinctive peril that threatens one of legality's two projects. In line with two specific understandings of how the modes of nomological argument might fail, a twofold apprehension arises within argumentative practice.

Practice's two apprehensions are fear of free ideals and fear of open form. The first is fear that law's ideal judgments may turn out to be the same thing as unfettered moral choice. Free idealizing argument in law leads to nomothetic decision, failure of entitlement. The second is fear that law's formal rules and categories may turn out to be irremediably open-ended. Open formal argument in law leads to anomic decision, failure of justice. These concrete apprehensions take shape by light of practice's awareness of disorder in morality and language outside law.

From the standpoint of modern liberal practice of law, free morality outside law is deeply riven, and common language is pervasively vague. A battle of warring creeds and programs is seen to exist in free moral inquiry. An impasse of unsure concepts and meanings is understood to come about in general communication. Premises of disagreement in morals, and openness of language, underlie practice's negative resolve to avoid the twin perils of free ideals and open form.

The two specific fears add impetus to the two concrete projects of legality. A particular fear envisions a peril associated with one of legality's two modes, and so that fear tends to induce pursuit of the alternative mode. Fear of free ideals prompts formalization of law. Fear of open form provokes law's idealization. In this way, each positive project is spurred by cognizance of the characteristic peril of the other.

12.2 THE BIG PATTERN

We should break off recapitulation here, lest the further interplay of elements obscure the overall design we are trying to descry. The point of the foregoing review is to trace the broad outline of nomological evolution, the big pattern of polarity and duality in liberal law. This pattern, all by itself, is amply complex.

The unfolding of nomological commitment is a development marked by parallels, counterparts, twinning implication. The whole evolution makes a design of complex complementarity. A singular commitment unfolds to comprise positive and negative complements, each of which branches in turn to yield twofold pursuit and twofold aversion. Here is a thumbnail statement:

> Nomological commitment – to law-like law – general,
> accessible, coherent, and rationally operative
>
> comprises
>
> aspiration to secure legality – legal entitlement and
> justice – through nomological-connective argument
>
> and
>
> fear of failed legality – of evils pertaining absent
> legality – anomic and nomothetic arbitrariness,
>
> which yield
>
> dual impulse – to seek formalization and idealization of
> law – through each mode's complex development
>
> plus
>
> double fear – of free ideals and of open form – in
> awareness of warring creeds and unsure concepts.

Liberal legal practice, then, is that practice of law and argument which is self-consciously governed by all these directive ideas – the whole panoply of

constituents of nomological commitment arrayed above. Liberal practice is directed, at once, by foundational commitment, generic aspiration, generic fear, dual
impulse, and double fear.

Within this array of aspects of nomological enterprise, three sorts of striving stand
out. Each of the three is a positive pursuit, a concrete argumentative quest. Each
pursuit, constantly impelled, is regularly manifest throughout law. The three notable pursuits are, first, formalization; second, idealization; and third, coherence-
seeking. These three activities are prominent undertakings of workaday practice of
law-like law. Together they constitute a three-fold quest.

First, formalization, throughout law, hammers out legal rules. Formal argument
develops nonmoral concepts and precepts of law, legal prescription knowable and
applicable without the conduct of a moral inquiry. Together, the categories and
distinctions of formalized law constitute law's classifying language, different from
common language used outside law.

Second, idealization, throughout law, attributes practical moral aims to rules and
uses the aims to guide and shape the rules. Ideal argument develops principles,
policies, and purposes – legal ideals – that fit and justify formal law. Together, ideal
aims anchored in law constitute law's morality, different from morality freely
affirmed in debate outside law.

Third, coherence-seeking operates within both modes of law-like law. The imperative of coherence, a fundamental requirement of law-like legality, tells legal argument
to seek rational connection of laws. Quest of harmonious interconnection – structure –
in law impels complex development of law's projects. Complex formal argument
builds structures of rules. Ideal structuring harmonizes law's ideal aims.

All three undertakings – formalization, idealization, coherence-seeking – arise in
the same way. Dual impulse to pursue two modes of law-like law is the consequence
of nomological commitment. The imperative to develop rational interconnection of
legal elements, within both modes, stems from the same root.

If you come upon a legal practice in which the three-fold quest is manifest – that
is, in which formalization, idealization, and coherence-seeking, together, are regularly observable – you can be pretty sure what you are looking at. You can expect to
find, underlying repeated intent argumentative performance in execution of the
three-fold quest, more highly general nomological devotion – foundational commitment to develop law-like law, generic aspiration to sustain entitlement and justice,
generic fear of arbitrariness. You're looking at liberal legal practice.

12.3 UNANSWERED QUESTIONS

With the foregoing review and summary of findings, our investigation comes to an
end. We have established the formative commitment of liberal practice. We have
specified the component features of the practice, arising in consequence of the
aspiration that controls it.

But, one might think, at the very point that study aiming to define liberal legality ends, some insistent questions arise. How – one might ask – does liberal legal striving, so defined, work out? What happens when liberal practice is set in motion? How do the projects of legality fare? How do they end up?

These questions about the ultimate outcome of liberal legal striving are beyond the scope of the present inquiry. Its findings do not answer them. The present study tells us how liberal practice is constituted and directed. It says how liberal law, in light of what it aspires to achieve, gets going and moves forward, but not how such law ends up.

On the other hand, while the present study does not purport to provide an answer to the question that inquires how liberal law comes out, it does say how the question should be asked. It does tell us how to find out the answer.

The way to find out how liberal practice of law develops is to keep in mind – take as given – all the basic features of the practice which are specified in the present study. We assume the existence of a practice of legal argument governed quite strictly by nomological aspiration. We imagine that practitioners of argument are heedful of the full set of instructions, admonitions, and assumptions that guide nomological endeavor. We look to see how argument adhering to all the directives that constitute nomological enterprise comes out.

How does legal practice controlled by nomological commitment, in constant pursuit of two coherence-seeking projects, formalization and idealization, conducted in awareness of disorder in morality and language outside law, work out?

That, in a nutshell, is the question – for another day.

* * *

Back at the beginning of the investigation of liberal legality now concluding, I said that our aim in this inquiry was to specify the assumptions and instructions – guidelines and guideposts – that constitute nomological practice, and I noted that our setting up of guidelines and guideposts for argumentative practice was like the activity of preparing for the presentation of a dramatic performance.

Now, we may suppose, the stage is set, on which the play of argument will take place. The performers – legal arguers – have been given complex direction. Governing motivations are well in mind. The main motifs of the drama to ensue have been established. Props are laid out – in our drama, these are the laws.

What will transpire when the curtain parts? What dramatic developments – problems, interactions, thematic implications – will ensue? Performance has been prefigured only up to a point. There is no detailed script, and no predetermined denouement. The actors in our drama must proceed, working in character, reflecting their points of view, anticipating what will come next, cuing one another, as best they can.

The play, as we imagine, is closely watched. At some point the observers, including the performers, having observed themselves, now stepping out of role, and trying to put together an overall view of what's going on, will have to supply the unplotted ending, and so the moral of the story.

References

Adams, John (1780). Part the First, Art. XXX in *Constitution of Massachusetts*.

Anonymous (1886). "The Basis of Individualism," *The Westminster Review*, vol. 126, 118, July 1886.

Austin, John (1832). "The Province of Jurisprudence Determined," in G. C. Christie, ed., *Jurisprudence: Text and Readings on the Philosophy of Law* (1973).

Bohannan, Paul (1973). "The Differing Realms of Law" (1965) in D. Black and M. Milesky, eds., *The Social Organization of Law*.

Coke, Edward (1607). "Prohibitions Del Roy" (November 10, 1607), in J. F. Fraser, ed., *The Reports of Sir Edward Coke*, vol. VI (1826).

Culler, Jonathan (1982). *On Deconstruction*.

Dalton, Clare (1985). "An Essay in the Deconstruction of Contract Doctrine," 94 *Yale Law Journal* 997.

Derrida, Jacques (1981). *Positions* (A. Bass, trans.).

Dworkin, Ronald (1967). "The Model of Rules," 35 *University of Chicago Law Review* 14.

Dworkin, Ronald (1975). "Hard Cases," 88 *Harvard Law Review* 1057.

Dworkin, Ronald (1977a). "No Right Answer?" in P. M. S. Hacker and J. Raz, eds., *Law, Morality, and Society*.

Dworkin, Ronald (1977b). *Taking Rights Seriously*.

Dworkin, Ronald (1978). "Is There Really No Right Answer in Hard Cases?" in Dworkin (1985), p. 136.

Dworkin, Ronald (1985). *A Matter of Principle*.

Dworkin, Ronald (1986). *Law's Empire*.

Fish, Stanley (1980). *Is There a Text in This Class?*

Fiss, Owen M. (1982). "Objectivity and Interpretation," 34 *Stanford Law Review* 739.

Fried, Charles (1981). *Contract as Promise: A Theory of Contractual Obligation*.

Frug, Gerald E. (1984). "The Ideology of Bureaucracy in American Law," 97 *Harvard Law Review* 1276.

Fuller, Lon (1958). "Positivism and Fidelity to Law – A Reply to Professor Hart," 71 *Harvard Law Review* 630.

Fuller, Lon (1968). *Anatomy of the Law*.

Gabel, Peter (1980). "Reification in Legal Reasoning," *Research in Law and Sociology*, vol. 3, 25 (S. Spitzer, ed.).

Gilligan, Carol (1982). *In a Different Voice: Psychological Theory and Women's Development*.

Habermas, Jürgen (1979). *Communication and the Evolution of Society* (T. McCarthy, trans.).

Hamilton, William (1861). "Lecture VII," in H. Mansel and J. Veitch, eds., *Lectures on Metaphysics*, vol. 1, 2nd edn.

Hart, Herbert Lionel Adolphus (1958). "Positivism and the Separation of Law and Morals," 71 *Harvard Law Review* 593.

Hart, Herbert Lionel Adolphus (1961). *The Concept of Law* (2nd edn., 1994).

Hart, Henry M. Jr. and Sacks, Albert M. (1958). *The Legal Process: Basic Problems in the Making and Application of Law* (tent. edn., 1958; W. Eskridge and P. Frickey, eds., 1994).

Hayek, Friedrich (1944). *The Road to Serfdom*.

Hayek, Friedrich (1960). *The Constitution of Liberty*.

Hempel, Carl Gustav (1962). "Deductive-Nomological vs. Statistical Explanation," in H. Feigl and G. Maxwell, eds., *Scientific Explanation, Space, and Time*.

Holmes, Oliver Wendell Jr. (1881). *The Common Law* (M. D. Howe, ed., 1963).

Irigaray, Luce (1985). *This Sex Which Is Not One* (C. Porter, trans.).

Kennedy, Duncan (1997). *A Critique of Adjudication*.

Locke, John (1689). *The Second Treatise of Government* (J. W. Gough, ed., 1956).

Luhmann, Niklas (1982). *The Differentiation of Society* (S. Holmes and C. Laramore, trans.).

MacIntyre, Alasdair (1981). *After Virtue*.

Marx, Karl (1875). "Critique of the Gotha Program," in K. Marx and F. Engels, eds., *Selected Works*, vol. II (Moscow: Foreign Languages Publishing House, 1962).

Mill, John Stuart (1865). *An Examination of Sir William Hamilton's Philosophy*, vol. 2 (Boston).

Montesquieu, Baron de La Brède et de (1748). *The Spirit of the Laws*, vol. 2 (T. Nugent trans., 1949).

Nagel, Ernest (1961). *The Structure of Science*.

Neumann, Franz (1944). *Behemoth: The Structure and Practice of National Socialism, 1933–1944* (1942; 2nd edn. with appendix, 1944).

Rawls, John (1971). *A Theory of Justice*.

Rawls, John (1993). *Political Liberalism*.

Raz, Joseph (1979). *The Authority of Law*.

Searle, John R. (1969). *Speech Acts*.

Unger, Roberto M. (1975). *Knowledge and Politics*.

Unger, Roberto M. (1976). *Law in Modern Society*.

Unger, Roberto M. (1983). "The Critical Legal Studies Movement," 96 *Harvard Law Review* 561.

Unger, Roberto M. (1984). *Passion: An Essay on Personality*.

Voltaire (1752). "Thoughts on the Public Administration," para. xx in *The Works of Voltaire*, vol. 37 (Fleming, trans., 1901).

Warren, Samuel D. and Brandeis, Louis D. (1890). "The Right to Privacy," 4 *Harvard Law Review* 193.

Weber, Max (1925). *Economy and Society*, vol. 2 (G. Roth and C. Wittich, eds., 1978).

Index

Lightning Source UK Ltd.
Milton Keynes UK
UKHW022047251019

352339UK00020B/414/P